Guatemalan Politics

Guatemalan Politics

The Popular Struggle for Democracy

Robert H. Trudeau

Lynne Rienner Publishers ■ Boulder & London

Published in the United States of America in 1993 by
Lynne Rienner Publishers, Inc.
1800 30th Street, Boulder, Colorado 80301

and in the United Kingdom by
Lynne Rienner Publishers, Inc.
3 Henrietta Street, Covent Garden, London WC2E 8LU

Library of Congress Cataloging-in-Publication Data
Trudeau, Robert H., 1940–
    Guatemalan politics : the popular struggle for democracy / Robert
    H. Trudeau.
    p.   cm.
    Includes bibliographical references and index.
    ISBN 1-55587-415-0 (alk. paper)
    1. Guatemala—Politics and government—1985– . 2. Guatemala—
Politics and government—1945–1985. 3. Political participation—
Guatemala. 4. Democracy—Guatemala. 5. Elections—Guatemala.
I. Title.
JL1496.T78   1993
323'.042'097281—dc20   93-15354
                                           CIP

British Cataloguing in Publication Data
A Cataloguing in Publication record for this book
is available from the British Library.

Printed and bound in the United States of America

 The paper used in this publication meets the requirements
of the American National Standard for Permanence of
Paper for Printed Library Materials Z39.48-1984.

Contents

Tables

Preface

Guatemala, From Where the Rainbow Takes Its Colors: Ancient, Historical, Colorful, Picturesque, Modern.
—Joaquin Muñoz

[Guatemala:] . . . one of the most cruel, corrupt, and evil places on earth.
—Edward Abbey

Can any single nation possibly be described by two statements as extreme and opposite as these? Guatemala is a nation blessed with extraordinary physical beauty and abundant natural resources, but cursed with a wretched social history. Extremism has been the norm, socially, economically, and certainly politically. Guatemala's highland climate—"eternal spring" in the tourist literature—is as pleasant as anywhere, the scenic vistas as spectacular, and the residents as fascinating, but the poverty and political violence are terrible. In a wonderful physical and cultural setting, the social consequences of political extremism are particularly dispiriting. The contrasts in Guatemala are compelling.

This book is an attempt to understand the nature of political life in a social setting of stark contrasts, gross inequality, and continuing violence. The events of May and June 1993 make this effort more important. On May 25, President Jorge Serrano dissolved Congress and the courts and suspended several articles of the Constitution, in effect proclaiming an auto–coup d'état. Scarcely a week later, in the face of international pressure and increasing opposition from Guatemala's business elite, the military first withdrew its support for Serrano and then forced him to resign. Although the institutional outcomes were confusing as of early June, four points consistent with the conclusions of this book seem clear: (1) the military remains the central power in the political process; (2) the military's actions indicate a carefully planned and at least initially successful attempt to portray itself as the defender of democracy; (3) the political parties, which publicly requested that the military intervene, continue to play an antidemocractic role in Guatemalan politics; and (4) the 1993 coup was an attempt to reduce the ability of the popular sectors to move Guatemala toward democracy.

Although my first impressions of Guatemala resulted from travel there in the mid-1960s, research for this book began during a Fulbright lectureship in 1980 and has continued since then. During this lengthy process, I have acquired many debts of gratitude.

In 1980 I learned to recognize the extraordinary courage of many Guatemalans who, less protected than a North American visitor, nevertheless continued to attempt to reform their political and social system. Over and over, I heard them speak of their love for their country, their sadness over its domination by thugs and murderers, and their determination to continue the struggle in spite of the dangers. Many of these individuals were very helpful to me during my stay that year; I want to acknowledge my debt to them, but it would still be risky, in 1993, to name them in a book that is ultimately critical of the Guatemalan elite. Since 1980, many other Guatemalans have been central to my work on this book. But again, the prevailing political climate in Guatemala makes it impossible to acknowledge this assistance publicly.

Fortunately, I can name many others who were helpful, especially once this book began to take shape. Enrique Baloyra and Lars Schoultz provided insightful comments on earlier versions of the manuscript, and Bill Hudson helped on an early version of material that appears in Chapter 1. I am grateful to several anonymous readers as well; their efforts made this a much better study. Moss Blachman, Ken Coleman, and Ken Mijeski were helpful at various times, coincidentally when I most needed help.

I am especially in debt for all the reasons above, and others, to Ken Sharpe. It is safe to say that without his help at many stages, this book probably would not have been finished.

Chris Krueger, Marilyn Moors, Brinton Lykes, Elizabeth Kuznesof, Milton Jamail, Carol Smith, Margarita Melville, James Loucky, Susanne Jonas, Charles Brockett, Beatriz Manz, Gary Elbow, Chris Lutz, Sally Lutz, David Dent, and many other members of the Guatemala Scholars Network shared insights, information, connections, and data with me over the past ten years. Similarly, Frank LaRue, of the Guatemalan United Opposition, was consistently helpful, in spite of his busy schedule. Bonnie Tenneriello and others at the Washington Office on Latin America were always willing to share their insights.

I also wish to acknowledge Providence College's Committee to Aid Faculty Research, which supported research trips to Guatemala in the late 1980s. James McGovern has been supportive of this effort for many years, including loaning me the Laptop at critical moments. I am grateful for his support.

Thanks also to Chris Lutz and the Plumsock Mesoamerica Foundation for access to their Vermont archives and for regularly providing me documents and publications not otherwise easily available. I also wish to thank my student assistants, Tricia O'Hare and Matt Carlos, for help in preparing the manuscript.

Thanks also to Michelle Welsh of Lynne Rienner Publishers and Sarah Whalen, copy editor, for their editorial assistance.

All of these individuals, and others whom I am unintentionally neglecting to mention, helped make this book possible, and I thank them.

My wife, Patricia Trudeau, deserves much credit for tolerating this project for so long and for being so supportive, despite being left alone many times during both the research and the writing stages. Thanks, Pat.

Finally, I dedicate this book to my parents, Claire and Ted Trudeau, with love and in grateful acknowledgment of their constant support for the half century or so we've known each other.

Robert H. Trudeau

Acronyms & Abbreviations

AEU   Association of University Students (Asociación de Estudiantes Universitarios)

ANACAFE   National Association of Coffee Producers (Asociación Nacional de Caficultores)

ANC   National Campesino Association (Pro-Land Movement) (Asociación Nacional Campesina)

CACIF   Council of Commercial, Industrial, and Financial Associations (Cámara de Asociaciones Comerciales, Industriales, y Financieras)

CAN   National Authentic Center (Central Auténtico Nacional)

CCL   Council for Free Commerce (Consejo de Comercio Libre)

CCPP   Permanent Commissions (Comisiones Permanentes)

CCSC   Civilian Sector Coordinating Committee (Comité Coordinador del Sector Civil)

CEAR   Special Commission for Attention to Refugees (Comisión Especial para Atención a los Refugiados)

CERJ   Runujel Junam Council of Ethnic Unity (Consejo de Comunidades Etnicas Runujel Junam)

CGTG   General Coordinator of Guatemalan Workers (Coordinación General de Trabajadores de Guatemala)

CIN   National Interinstitutional Coordinator committees (Coordinadora Interinstitucional Nacional)

CLAT   Latin American Confederation of Workers (Confederación Latinoamericana de Trabajadores)

CNC   National Peasant Confederation (Confederación Nacional Campesina)

CNR   National Reconciliation Commission (Comisión Nacional de Reconciliación)

CNT	National Confederation of Workers (Confederación Nacional de Trabajadores)
CONAVIGUA	National Council of Guatemalan Widows (Consejo Nacional de Viudas Guatemaltecas)
CPR	Communities of People in Resistance (Comunidades del Pueblo en Resistencia)
CUC	Committee for Peasant Unity (Comité de Unidad Campesina)
CUSG	Guatemalan Confederation of Labor Unity (Confederación de Unidad Sindical Guatemalteca)
DCG	Guatemalan Christian Democratic Party (Democracia Cristiana Guatemalteca)
EGP	Guerrilla Army of the Poor (Ejército Guerrillero de los Pobres)
FAR	Rebel Armed Forces (Fuerzas Armadas Rebeldes)
FASGUA	Guatemalan Federation of Labor Associations (Federación de Asociaciones Sindicales Guatemaltecas)
FDP	Democratic Popular Front (Frente Democrático Popular)
FNO	National Opposition Front (Frente Nacional de Oposición)
FRG	Guatemalan Republican Front (Frente Republicano Guatemalteco)
FUN	National Front for Unity (Frente de Unidad Nacional)
FUR	United Front of the Revolution (Frente Unido Revolucionario)
GAM	Mutual Support Group (Grupo de Apoyo Mutuo)
GHRC	Guatemalan Human Rights Commission
IGE	Guatemalan Church in Exile (Iglesia Guatemalteca en Exilio)
INDE	National Electricity Industry (Industria Nacional de Electricidad)
INTA	National Institute for Agrarian Transformation (Instituto Nacional de Transformación Agraria)
MAS	Solidarist Action Movement (Movimiento de Acción Solidarista)
MDN	National Democratic Movement (Movimiento Nacional Democrático)
MLN	National Liberation Movement (Movimiento de Liberación Nacional)
NISGUA	Network in Solidarity with Guatemala
ORPA	Organization of People in Arms (Organización del Pueblo en Armas)
PAC	Civilian Self-Defense Patrols (Patrullas de Auto-Defensa Civil)

PAN	National Advancement Party (Partido de Avanzada Nacional)
PGT	Guatemalan Communist Party (Partido Guatemalteco del Trabajo)
PID	Democratic Institutional Party (Partido Institucional Democrático)
PMA	Mobile Military Police (Policía Militar Ambulante)
PN	Nationalist Party (Partido Nacionalista)
PNR	National Renovation Party (Partido de Renovación Nacional)
PR	Revolutionary Party (Partido Revolucionario)
PRI	Revolutionary Institutional Party (Mexico) (Partido Institucional Revolucionario)
PSC	Social Christian Party (Partido Social Cristiano)
PSD	Democratic Socialist Party (Partido Socialista Democrático)
PUA	Party of Anticommunist Unity (Partido de Unidad Anti-comunista)
RND	National Democratic Redemption Party (Redención Nacional Democrática, or La Redención)
RUOG	United Representation of the Guatemalan Opposition (Representación Unida de la Oposición Guatemalteca)
STINDE	Union of Workers of the National Electricity Industry (Sindicato de Trabajadores de la Industria Eléctrica)
TSE	Supreme Electoral Tribunal (Tribunal Supremo Electoral)
UASP	Unity of Labor and Popular Action Coalition (Unidad de Acción Sindical y Popular)
UNAGRO	National Agricultural Union (Unión Nacional de Agro-exportadores)
UNO	United National Opposition (Unidad Nacional Opositora)
UNSITRAGUA	Guatemalan Workers Labor Unity (Unidad Sindical de Trabajadores Guatemaltecos)
URD	Revolutionary Democratic Unity (Unidad Revolucion-aria Democrática)
URNG	National Guatemalan Revolutionary Unity (Unidad Revolucionaria Nacional Guatemalteca)
USG	Guatemalan Solidarist Union (Unión Solidarista Guatemalteca)
UTQ	Quetzaltenango Workers Union (Unión de Trabajadores Quetzaltecos)

1

Democracy and Violence

January 31, 1980, dawned a typically beautiful day in Guatemala City, a sprawling metropolis with more than 2 million of Guatemala's 9.2 million inhabitants. Before the sun would set dramatically over the towering volcanoes that fill the southwest skyline, that day would enter history as an infamous symbol of Guatemalan politics.

Guatemala's population is at least 60 percent indigenous.[1] The Maya live throughout the national territory, but the majority, and most identifiable and culturally strongest communities, are in the highland region north and west of Guatemala City. For most Maya, self-sufficiency consistent with their culture is economically impossible: landholdings are small and the land overused. Many families hire out as day laborers; for thousands this includes season-long migrations to Guatemala's Pacific- or southern-coast plantations or to coffee plantations.

In the late 1970s, many Mayan communities became more militant in demanding an end to centuries of oppression, petitioning for relief from landowners seizing their lands and from the military who protected those landowners by repressing Indians who spoke out. After several frustrating rounds of such activity, in January 1980, a delegation of about one hundred Indians from several communities in the Department (province) of El Quiché went to Guatemala City to seek redress from the government of General Fernando Romeo Lucas García.

The delegation's efforts were frustrated at every turn;[2] they were rebuffed in every attempt to meet with officials. On January 28, a group of the delegates seized two radio stations, broadcast their message and demands, and left peacefully, hoping to gain an audience with the government. But the government's response in the morning newspapers on January 31 was that it would not tolerate further disturbances by subversives or by rural groups being tricked by "subversive elements."

1

The Spanish Embassy

On the 31st, still hoping to gain an audience with the government, a group of thirty people, including about twenty of the Indian delegation from El Quiché, entered and occupied the Spanish embassy.[3] Armed with machetes and Molotov cocktails, the group took some ten hostages, including the ambassador and other embassy personnel and several former high-ranking members of the Guatemalan government, among them a former vice-president and a former foreign minister. Sympathetic to the Indians' plight and willing to intercede with the government on their behalf, Dr. Máximo Cajal y López, the Spanish ambassador, negotiated a peaceful solution to the intrusion, agreeing to communicate the Indians' demands to the government in exchange for the group's peaceful withdrawal.

Informed of these events, however, the government ordered police to surround the embassy and cut telephone lines to prevent further communication with the outside. Fearing the worst, since the police were threatening the embassy itself, the ambassador went to the doorway and demanded that the building's sanctuary be respected, especially since a solution to the crisis had been negotiated. The police responded by opening fire on the embassy. Thirty-nine people, including the hostages,[4] were burned to death in the explosions and all-consuming fires, apparently ignited by incendiary materials tossed into the building by the police.[5] There were two survivors, both badly burned. The Spanish ambassador escaped because he had been standing in the building's doorway when the fires broke out. Witnesses saw the police manhandling him after he ran from the building, before they recognized who he was. Gregorio Yuja Xona, one of the intruders, survived because he had been buried under a pile of bodies.[6]

Aftermath of the Massacre

In the weeks and months that followed, the effects of the Spanish embassy massacre rippled throughout the country, catalyzing ongoing processes of social and political change. Armed with a new awareness of national politics and economics, Indian communities began organizing to defend themselves against the Army. The events at the Spanish embassy marked the end of peaceful attempts by many popular groups to influence the government. Indian and *ladino*[7] communities alike began to integrate themselves into the resistance movement led by Guatemala's armed guerrilla groups. Recognizing the depths to which the Guatemalan government would sink to eradicate political dissent of any kind, many politically active individuals went into hiding or left the country.

Lines hardened as well among the elite minority who controlled the country. In the weeks following the embassy massacre, progovernment groups took clear steps to undermine social organizing. Business and agricultural associations, for example, placed large announcements in the press expressing support for the government's policies to eliminate "subversives." The press campaign included innuendoes against the Spanish ambassador, suggesting he had helped plan the embassy seizure and was therefore not entitled to any protection beyond that of a common criminal. International critics of the government's handling of the affair were labeled part of an international cabal, probably communist, seeking to destroy Guatemalan society. Officials of the U.S. Department of State who criticized the country's human rights violations were routinely described as paid collaborators of an international communist plot.

But the press campaign paled in comparison to military and police repression. Immediately after the embassy events, the Army intensified its patrols of city streets, raising the level of political tension. In the following months the military government escalated its violence, unleashing a wave of repression against professionals (especially lawyers), priests, university professors, reporters, and students who had shown sympathy for peasant or labor organizations. Before 1980, the violence had been directed mostly against visible political leaders. Now it spread to leaders and activists of the smallest popular groups and even to the masses of the population themselves. Death squads routinely and openly patrolled the streets. Though shocking, the Spanish embassy massacre represented only a small proportion of the political violence in Guatemala in 1980, when, by conservative estimates, some three thousand persons were killed for political reasons. Hundreds disappeared and others were tortured before their bodies were dumped in various locations around the nation. Dozens were machine-gunned in public, often on city streets during daylight hours.[8]

As grim as the 1980 data are, after that year conditions deteriorated even further. Systematic warfare came to Indian regions, as the Army expanded its counterinsurgency campaign against communities suspected of sympathizing with guerrillas. Between 1980 and late 1983, hundreds of villages were destroyed and thousands of Indians massacred or forced to flee, some to refugee camps in Mexico and elsewhere, some to the relative safety of urban slums, and some to a nomadic existence in the mountains. Hundreds of thousands of Indians were forced into civil defense patrols and/or "model villages." By 1984, large areas in rural Guatemala had become wastelands. The country had fallen into the abyss.

January 31, 1980, has come to symbolize the brutality of the Guatemalan government, at least of its police and military leaders. From this morass the nation somehow emerged in 1984 with new political institutions. Elections for a constitutional assembly were held, and a new constitution proclaimed. The military rulers agreed to "return to the barracks." Presidential, congressional, and municipal elections were held in the fall of 1985, resulting in the inauguration of a civilian president, the Christian Democrat Marco Vinicio Cerezo Arévalo, in January 1986. Municipal elections were held again in 1988, and in 1990, a second civilian president, Jorge Serrano Elías, was elected. Guatemala has apparently witnessed a dramatic transition from repressive authoritarianism, illustrated by the Spanish embassy massacre, through the democratic civility of the 1984 and 1985 elections, to a second election in 1990. This period merits serious study: how did such a transition happen, and what does it mean in terms of democratic development?

Democracy in Guatemala: Posing the Questions

Descriptions of such violence as described above are relevant to the analysis of an emergent democracy, because institutional change—such as the creation of free elections—must be studied in a broader sociopolitical context. The events and repercussions of the embassy massacre are more dramatic than most, but they illustrate the nature of Guatemalan politics and the extremism that so often characterizes political participation there. Most important, they become part of the real history of Guatemalan politics that all subsequent participants learn from or integrate into their planning.

The elections in 1985 seemed to reconstitute the electoral process in Guatemala, giving rise to several hypotheses about the status of democracy in Guatemala. The first position, expressed by the United States embassy at the time of the election, was that democracy had been achieved in Guatemala; it was declared a "post-transitional" case.[9] A second thesis— "Whoever is elected in Guatemala, the army wins" (Goepfert: 36)—suggests that Guatemalan "democracy" is a facade, consisting of superficial institutional changes with no meaningful change for society. In this view the overthrow of the capitalist system is a prerequisite for meaningful social change and hence for real movement toward democracy.

The thesis that Guatemala achieved true democracy in 1985 was rebutted by the newly elected president, Vinicio Cerezo Arévalo, who saw the elections that year as but a first step in the difficult process of creating a democratic society and political system. He acknowledged the weakness of the civilian government but viewed the future with cautious optimism because democratic procedures had been strengthened. These strengthened institutions would eventually lead to real civilian power, especially if "democratic values" could be acquired by the citizenry. At that time reform programs would be implemented.[10]

The second thesis, that achieving democracy depends on a revolutionary transformation of society's economic and social structures, appeals to many students of Guatemalan history, which is one of almost unbroken rapacity and greed implemented at the expense of the nation's working class and indigenous communities. But the revolutionary strategy is unappealing to many Guatemalans who paid an extraordinary price during the counterinsurgency violence of the early 1980s. Many Mayan communities, in particular, are determined not to be used as cannon fodder. Finally, the state is strong because of military technology and international aid programs, suggesting that the revolutionary model for achieving democracy could be even more costly in the future. Moreover, reformist politicians and popular organizations have a history of courageous and sometimes effective political action within the prevailing political economy, and their efforts should be incorporated into any systematic study of democracy in Guatemala.

A third thesis about Guatemalan democracy, loosely derived from the "transition to democracy" school, reflects President Cerezo's statements. This approach in part argues that creating electoral structures is a first step in a transition to a more democratized polity. Elections do not necessarily establish a democracy but are opportunities to create one from the crisis that produced the political opening.[11]

In sum, elections matter and need to be studied in terms of both their procedural dimensions and their aftermaths. They matter because they can lead presumably to public policies that respond to the majority of voters and their policy preferences. Although Guatemala appears to be quite democratic from the formal-legal data, additional data are needed about the procedural quality of the formally democratic structures, including data about human rights, public policies, and their societal impact.

Measuring Democracy

Politics is the exercise of power in the social pursuit of certain values.[12] Politics in dictatorships or democracies is the same in this regard, but the architecture of power differs widely. "Democracy" implies a widespread distribution of power, regardless of the particular institutional arrangements in any specific time and place. Widely distributed power in any society means public control of the state: citizens have the power to compel officeholders to act in certain ways. To measure the extent of this power, we need to look closely at political participation.

Political participation. Democracy depends as much on efficacious political participation as on the types of political institutions or social outcomes prescribed. Participation, whatever the level of political organization, includes not only how citizens influence society's distribution of goods, but also how those in power, including elites and governments, influence successful participation by the public. Governmental actors, like other participants, may try to inhibit the participation of others, and in extreme cases, "governments [may be] locked in some kind of struggle with their own people" (Adams 1979: 13).[13] Thus, patterns of political participation are excellent indicators of the distribution of power in a society, which in turn can measure the extent of its democratization.

Participation therefore is a concept that implies the study not only of political procedures but of public policy as well. The procedural dimension can be studied using the "liberal-representative" model of democracy, which focuses on:

1. Representational structures, including elections, that restrict the unfettered power of governing elites. Elections also reduce the direct power of citizens.[14] Vesting power in elected and appointed leaders inhibits tyranny by both elites and masses. At a minimum, there must be fair, periodic, and free elections, by which groups of people representing majorities, or at least pluralities, can regulate the flow of political power and decisionmaking in society.[15]
2. Civil liberties and civil rights that provide citizens the opportunity to organize to win office through elections and to influence government between elections. At a minimum citizens must be able to participate politically without being unduly restricted by the state. Moreover, the state should protect participating citizens from others who would seek to prevent their participation.
3. Constitutional provisions and public policies that protect "inalienable" rights, for example, "to life, liberty, and the pursuit of happiness." In theory, at least, these rights provide all citizens with opportunities to flourish individually.

Assessing the authenticity of elections as democratic events must take into account the context in which they occur. Herman and Brodhead identify six contextual dimensions as criteria that must be met for an election to be considered an authentic electoral event: (1) freedom of speech—including the opportunity to openly criticize governmental and other leaders; (2) freedom of media—including the absence of censorship and intimidation; (3) freedom to organize interest groups that serve as a medium for allowing "organized pressure on the state" and also serve to "restrain state power"; (4) the "absence of highly developed and pervasive instruments of state-sponsored terror"; (5) freedom to organize political parties and to field candidates; and (6) the absence of coercion and fear on the part of the general population (Herman and Brodhead: 11–14).[16] Taken as measures of procedures, each of these fits the liberal-representative model of democracy, but each moves beyond a narrow focus on electoral procedures and incorporates additional social and political elements that reflect the quality of other linkages, such as civil liberties, between rulers and citizens.

Even in a democratic context, however, the procedural dimensions of participation are not enough to meet the democratic standard. Impoverished majorities may have little power beyond that of consenting to the overall system and choosing among elites who differ in personal ambitions for holding office but pursue essentially the same social outcomes from it. The concept of democracy should go beyond procedural aspects of political life. Political participation means the exercise of power, but "power" must mean more than merely selecting leaders through voting.

Public policy. Effective participation should include influencing public policy through representative institutions or more direct forms of democratic participation that are characterized by mass mobilization. Participation, to be effective, should contribute to the democratization of society. To measure this, following Greenberg, we focus on questions of accountability and the policy impact of elections, seeking evidence that links voters with policies preferred by majorities. Greenberg sees a "democratic" election if:

> (1) candidates and parties . . . present clear policy choices . . . [on] . . . important issues. Elections . . . should be *competitive* and *nontrivial;* (2) Once elected, officials should try to carry out what they promised during their campaign; (3) Once elected, officials should be capable of transforming campaign promises into binding public policy; and (4) Elections should generally influence the behavior of those elites who are responsible for making public policy (Greenberg 1989: 177, italics in original).

Greenberg writes from the perspective of a "social democracy" model. And although his criteria relate to public policy, behind them is a concept of the state's role in guaranteeing citizens a genuine opportunity for self-development, consistent with the liberal tradition of individualism in Western thought. Democracy then becomes a means of human development, not merely a set of procedures that "allows the citizen only a passive role as an object of political activity" (Walker: 233).

Although political procedures are central to the social democracy perspective, their outcomes are equally important. Social democracy focuses on elections, political parties, and the rights that guarantee access to these procedures, but also on the majority's power to restructure society, with a corresponding redistribution of wealth in favor of the working classes. Democracy is "more than a set of rules of the game; it also encompasses a set of human purposes, embracing a broad vision of human development as its guiding principle" (Bowles and Gintis: 178).

Assuming participation is effective in convincing leaders to act in the majority's interest, democracy then must also include state control over society's resources, lest there be no substance to public control of government: public institutions must have the power to control the political economy.[17]

Complementing the macrosocial perspective, Bowles and Gintis also look
at this relationship at the level of individuals. Democracies, they assert,
should reduce the economic dependency of nonwealthy citizens, for such
dependency means more political power for those who control economic
resources, which reduces citizen capacity for democracy. This is clearly
problematic in a democracy, if not "antithetical to both liberty and popular
sovereignty."[18]

If wealth accumulations and social inequality produce economic
dependency for some individuals, then it is the duty of citizens, through
government, to intervene. Social democracy values the opportunity for
individual development more than the protection of individual tangible
property—indeed, that property itself, or at least the concentration of its
control among a few, can be the problem. Thus, social democracy affirms
the social utility of private property but only in the liberal sense: the justi-
fication lies in the benefits that accrue to individuals.

As with the dimensions of procedural democracy discussed earlier,
appropriate empirical indicators exist for measuring the quality of social
democracy. Gamer, for example, uses the concept of a "Stable Personal
Environment," defined as

> enough food to eat; health care; housing that is affordable and satisfying
> to live in; neighbors and cultural facilities with which individuals feel
> comfortable; a job offering a modicum of satisfaction, continuity, and
> above-subsistence income; and an educational system that can promise
> children the same advantages. A person with *no* monetary income can
> have this as well as one with high income: *the key lies in the balance of
> the parts* (Gamer: 8–9, italics in original).[19]

In this model, therefore, government programs for social reform are
important indicators of democracy in Guatemala, and these programs
should produce measurable results in the quality of life for the country's
impoverished majority. In short, in order for a society to be democratic
and its political process to be a stable and democratic one, government
should have a role in improving the quality of life of its citizens. In Guatemala this means that the "popular" sectors should show signs of progress.
Gamer's indicators, broadly reflecting the quality of life for poverty-
stricken citizens, offer a good standard against which to measure progress
between 1980 and 1992.

Beyond ethical concerns about the outcomes of political participation
lie empirical questions as well: democratic theory not only assumes certain
political arrangements and outcomes, it also assumes stability. It is ques-
tionable whether democratic procedures and institutions can survive
in grossly inegalitarian situations in which many citizens may find their
support for liberal systems weakened by the realities of economic neces-
sity. In Latin America liberal political systems have shown a degree of

immobilism that is quite acceptable to elites seeking to prevent change but intolerable to others who are pursuing social justice (Peeler: 152–153). The resulting high potential for social instability is a threat to liberal-representative political institutions and, ironically, to the economic wealth that liberal democracy is designed to protect.[20]

What this means, in effect, is that institutional opportunities for participation are necessary but not sufficient. Participation also should have a positive effect and lead to the desired results. Ultimately, the test of liberal democracy lies in the effectiveness of political participation by all actors. The "results" of participation, however, must be evident in substantive as well as more theoretical or procedural ways: those that increase social justice, for example, are more important for a transition to democracy than those that thwart reform. Ultimately, then, a transition to democracy depends not only on honest elections but also on human rights and movement toward social justice.

The questions of human rights and social justice are perhaps the most critical facing contemporary Guatemala, given not only economic inequality and its effects on political stability but strains on the global ecosystem as well. The country has a long history of struggle around issues of social justice. At various moments, democratic forms have been created, but democratic forms without social justice have not produced a stable society. A major question here is whether new forms of procedural democracy in place since 1984 have delivered, or can deliver, needed social reforms for Guatemala's impoverished masses within a reasonable time frame.

Conclusion

In theory, in a democracy the people are the government and government is "of, by, and for the people." The ideal of increased and effective participation remains critical to democratic theory. But direct participatory politics in large, complex societies is illusory in today's world. In practice, therefore, democracy has come to imply an egalitarian relationship between the people and their chosen governors, akin to a balance of power or détente between rulers and ruled. In turn, citizens support regimes when the state provides for the common welfare, as desired by citizens and as expressed in electoral behavior when this is possible.

Guatemala returned to constitutional government in 1985, under the leadership of President Vinicio Cerezo and the Christian Democratic Party. Has the quality of political participation improved in Guatemala since then? Have political participants enjoyed the protections implied by the phrase "constitutional government," or is the political arena characterized by an atmosphere of coercion and fear? Has the civilian government gained appreciable power over society's resources, relative to the military, for example? Is political power more widely distributed in 1992 than it was in 1980? How has the "Stable Personal Environment" of poor citizens fared? Is Guatemala making progress toward social justice? To answer these questions, it is necessary to examine carefully the beginning of Guatemala's transition to democracy in the 1980s and early 1990s.

While the concepts in this chapter establish a general context for the Guatemalan data, understanding Guatemala's transition process after 1985 requires some knowledge of the particular setting in which these events occurred. The events of January 31, 1980, for example, both reflect the past and help illuminate the future. Chapter 2 provides a general background of historical events and patterns that establish a relevant context for what has happened in the 1980s and early 1990s.

In the first part of this period, Guatemala lived through an unprecedented wave of terror and violence between 1980 and 1985. Chapter 3 studies elections in the country in the context of this political violence, culminating in the crisis that forced a coup d'état by the Guatemalan military in 1982. Chapter 4 continues the narrative after 1982, and provides background on the Guatemalan armed forces, since it is they who engineered the formal transition to democracy. Part of the military counter-insurgency strategy included elections, and this chapter studies that aspect of the military plan, the Constituent Assembly election of 1984, and the presidential election of 1985.

Chapters 5 through 8 examine the presidential administration of Vinicio Cerezo and the Christian Democratic Party (Democracia Cristiana Guatemalteca—DCG), focusing on economic and fiscal policy (Chapter 5) and the activities of the popular sectors, including not only their demands but the government's responses (Chapter 6). Chapter 7 returns to the question of the quality of political participation by examining human rights under Cerezo.

Chapter 8 looks at all these themes during the late Cerezo administration, summarizing its successes and failures, then focuses on the 1990 campaign that elected as president Jorge Serrano Elías of the Solidarist Action Movement (Movimiento de Acción Solidarista—MAS). The first two years of his administration are covered in Chapter 9 with the multi-thematic approach used for the Cerezo period. Combining these findings with the concepts here, Chapter 10 concludes with thoughts on the continuing struggle, and prognosis, for democracy in Guatemala.

Notes

1. Naming this group is a sensitive question for outsiders. The aboriginal pre-Columbian peoples of the region have been called *primitivos*, *naturales*,

"indigenous," "native Americans," and of course "Indians." This last appellation is consistent with the preference of Rigoberta Menchú (as reported in Frank and Wheaton: 21, note 1). More recently, the word *Maya* is used to describe these groups. In this text, I will use several terms, trying to avoid unnecessary repetition while remaining mindful of the sensitivities of the people under study. For an essay focusing on the epistemological and political implications of "naming" in Guatemala, see Shapiro.

2. For example, when they met with a sympathetic attorney in Guatemala City, police kidnapped the attorney while the meeting was going on. Still alive, he was thrown out of a speeding car that same afternoon on a busy downtown street. He had been tortured and died soon after.

3. The account of events leading up to and including the events at the Spanish embassy on January 31, 1980, is based on accounts in the Guatemalan press, interviews with associates of one of the victims, and personal observation. Useful published summaries can be found in *Green Revolution* 37, no. 5 (Sept. 1981): 20–28; Burgos-Debray: 183–187; and Davis and Hodson: 49. For a detailed description of the day's events, including especially the activities of the various police and security organizations involved, see "Massacre." For details on background leading up to the incursion into the Spanish embassy by the Indian delegation and their supporters, see Ismaelillo: 4–5. For a description focusing on the massacre's impact on alliances among rural and urban opposition groups, see Frank and Wheaton: 57.

4. Among the victims was Vicente Menchú, from the municipality of Uspantán. Menchú was the father of Rigoberta Menchú Tum, who was awarded the Nobel Peace Prize in October 1992 (discussed in Chapter 9).

5. Filmed by television news teams, these events were shown on national television later that afternoon. Guatemalans viewed grisly scenes of roaring flames and charred bodies. It is worth noting in passing that one aspect of violence is terror. Political violence in Guatemala is rarely subtle: it is open and committed with impunity.

6. The fate of the two survivors of the embassy massacre is as symbolic of Guatemala in the early 1980s as the main events themselves. Initially, both were taken to a leading private hospital for treatment, Ambassador Cajal López because of his status and Yuja Xona because the ambassador insisted upon it to protect Yuja's life. Although the hospital was heavily guarded by police, Yuja Xona was kidnapped and dragged from the hospital the following morning. Within days, his tortured body was thrown on the campus of the University of San Carlos, the national university, with a message threatening similar treatment for the Spanish ambassador himself. As for Cajal López, a rotating group of ambassadors and other international officials kept a vigil at his hospital room to prevent his kidnapping. After a few days, in spite of his injuries, Cajal López left the hospital to convalesce at the U.S. ambassador's residence. When he left the hospital, the ambassador was accompanied by several other diplomats who specifically requested that there be no police protection.

7. The word *ladino* is used to describe Guatemalans of mixed Indian and Caucasian origin and even Indians who have left their communities and adopted "Western" dress and the Spanish language.

8. Throughout 1980, the Guatemalan press routinely published pictures of corpses and individuals who had disappeared, often accompanied by emotional pleas from families seeking information about their relatives.

9. The embassy position is from a statement issued to the Guatemalan press. The posttransitional classification was made by Carl Gershman, president of the

National Endowment for Democracy, in a speech at the International Congress of
the Latin American Studies Association.

10. For a full-length treatment of Guatemalan politics that reflects this perspective, see Fauriol and Loser (1988). A group of scholars representing the Latin
American Studies Association includes this perspective:

> With the 1985 election, Guatemala began what President Vinicio Cerezo
> calls a "transition to democracy," a process of building institutions and
> processes of political participation within a traditional liberal, represen-
> tative constitutional framework (LASA: 16).

11. The purpose here is not to review or discuss the extensive literature that
has emerged since the 1980s on the "transition to democracy." For examples of
this literature, see Booth and Seligson, eds. (1989); Tulchin, ed.; Caviedes; Drake
and Jaksic, eds.; González; Diamond, Linz, and Lipset, eds.; and the series of volumes edited by O'Donnell, Schmitter, and others. For an essay that sees U.S. foreign assistance and programs such as the National Endowment for Democracy as
essential to the promotion of transitions to democracy, see Diamond.

12. I am indebted to my colleague Bill Hudson for his help with this discussion of democracy.

13. Adams further sees participation as actions that may be

> designed to realize the best interests of the actors through immobilizing
> the efforts of those who have interests putatively contrary. Participation
> must then be seen not only as a positive effort by citizens or the govern-
> ment to realize their own interests, but also as equally positive efforts to
> inhibit or obstruct the realization of the contrary interests of others
> (Adams 1979: 14).

14. Jeane Kirkpatrick, former U.S. ambassador to the United Nations and
advisor to President Reagan, provides an excellent perspective on elections:

> Elections . . . are the central institution of democracy. . . . Democratic
> elections are competitive, periodic, inclusive, and definitive. . . . Demo-
> cratic elections produce representatives that are chosen by their people
> whom they are to represent. Democratic elections guarantee that laws
> will not be made simply in the name of a community but with the consent
> of the community. No substitutes are acceptable. . . . Democratic elec-
> tions ensure that the goals of government are consistent with those of a
> majority of citizens (Kirkpatrick: 2–3).

15. Drake and Silva provide a properly skeptical approach about both the origin of elections in authoritarian systems and the role elections play in producing
more democracy in such settings:

> The dictator's dilemma of staging and manipulating a credible election
> bedevils most authoritarian regimes. Elections concocted for legitimation
> may unintentionally become instruments for expanding liberalization—
> and eventually initiating democratization. . . . They provide a powerful
> (if minimal) vehicle for the government's adversaries to voice demands
> (Drake and Silva: 3, 5).

16. Herman and Brodhead seek to show that some elections are held to "demonstrate," to the American public in this case, that certain foreign regimes are worthy of U.S. economic and military assistance. In their view these "demonstration elections" often disguise the most undemocratic regimes imaginable. This international relations aspect of their argument is not relevant to my description of Guatemalan elections. Rather, I use their set of indicators to measure the immediate context of electoral events, so that we can distinguish between authentic electoral contests and events designed primarily to sway public opinion. The point is not to apply impossible standards to Guatemalan political life but to provide empirical indicators that can serve as a basis for comparisons and a better understanding of Guatemalan political behavior.

17. Bowles and Gintis, stressing individual development as the goal of state activity, suggest that private property should be controlled by collective democratic political action: inasmuch as capitalist economic processes are social processes, the economy should be controlled democratically. Public control over wealth is desirable, and the role of the state in controlling economic activity should be expanded. Whether this has occurred in Guatemala in recent years is of course a major question here.

18. Bowles and Gintis eschew "specific institutional prescriptions," but they argue that their four propositions

> point unmistakably toward the democratization of the economy, the attenuation of economic inequality, the democratization of the learning process, and the promotion of what Hannah Arendt calls "new public spaces for freedom" (Bowles and Gintis: 205).

19. The purpose of introducing this concept is not to insist that Guatemala achieve this standard before it can be judged "democratic." Few countries would pass so stringent a test. Rather it is to provide a referent against which to measure movement. The questions are whether Guatemala has made significant progress toward achieving this standard and the consequent implications for democracy.

20. This is not a new view in Central American political analysis; Martz concludes his early survey of the region:

> Unless the widespread causes of suffering are remedied, . . . no one can prophesy the magnitude of the inevitable disaster. The critical moments are arriving—the tide of Central American history is sweeping toward desolation if not complete destruction (Martz: 26).

More recently, Seligson (1987) asserts:

> Central American nations seem bent on avoiding the major structural changes that are needed to reduce inequality. . . . It is a safe bet that unless the existing policies are reversed, one can expect continuing unrest and political violence (Seligson: 187).

2

Economic and Political Development to 1980

Is it illusory to imagine that a transition to democracy can occur in Guatemala? Are there democratic elements in Guatemalan history that are relevant to its reality in the 1990s? Historical evidence about the quality of political participation and levels of social justice illustrate the context confronted by political actors at the beginning of the 1980s.

Pre-Columbian Period

Reasons for admiring the achievements of the Maya, Guatemala's earliest known inhabitants, are abundant.[1] Far from being a primitive society, except in some dimensions of technological knowledge, the Maya were considerably more advanced in many ways than the Spanish who conquered them. They are known for their architectural monuments, their extraordinary knowledge of astronomy and mathematics, their preoccupation with time, and their agricultural prowess.[2]

An important characteristic of Mayan social life was the relatively egalitarian distribution of social production, at least as reflected in nutritional conditions. Although not idyllic, life for the majority was not desperate either. The rural-subsistence sector of the economy, comprising the vast majority of the people, had reasonable access to productive land (Jonas 1974a: 95). Even though some production was taken by elites through taxes and tributes, enough remained so that adequate nutrition with a varied diet was the norm (Jonas 1974a: 95–96; Behar: 114–119).[3]

There is little extant information about Mayan political institutions, but their political economy must be included among their achievements. The available information about their politics suggests that their political economy reflected a balance of power between rulers and ruled, although procedures for selecting leaders may not have conformed to what observers would today call pluralist democracy. Mayan society was not devoid of elite domination, but the rulers' dependence on their communities for sustenance produced a society characterized by considerable social justice. Their realm endured for centuries, and their social and intellectual achievements were based on a productive and reasonably efficient political economy.[4] Ultimately, the Maya did not survive as an independent population because of environmental problems and foreign conquest.

The Spanish Conquest

The Spanish Conquest decimated Mayan society through at least three ways: the violence of warfare, disease, and cultural disruption. Warfare may have led directly to the death of as many as four to five million Indians.[5] The violence of warfare, though bad enough, was the least severe of the three aspects of the conquest in its impact (Veblen: 88). Disease and cultural disruption were more serious.[6] Forced migrations during the early colonial period caused both high mortality and declines in nutrition. The tremendous population decline in the highland regions[7] of Guatemala meant a shortage of labor to exploit the newly acquired grants of land and resources awarded Spanish conquerors. A consequence of labor scarcity was the creation of huge landed estates and debt-peonage structures to regulate Indian labor for the benefit of the conquerors (Lovell 1982: 103; Moors: 67–68). The Spanish superimposed a new elite on Mayan society, one that used Guatemala's land and labor to produce wealth not only for itself but also for Spain.

Although there were elements of feudal culture during this period, feudalism was not the basic economic mode of production. From the beginning of the colonial period capitalistic entrepreneurs engaged in export agriculture (Woodward: 60–61). By the 1700s, the Spanish (Bourbon) rulers were stressing exports and the profitability of the colonies, especially in relatively less well developed Central America. Spain viewed the colony as a source of wealth for itself, and Spanish colonists, the Creoles, were concerned with their own profit, not with the overall development of Guatemala (Jonas 1974a: 107). The conflicts between the needs of Spain and those of the colonists—between the mercantilist capitalists and the "liberal" capitalists, as it were—eventually helped create two political movements among the elite in Guatemala: Liberals, who generally favored commercial development, and Conservatives, who wished to remain more "feudal" (Woodward: 60–61).

The specifics of the relationships between Spanish and Creole rulers and the Indian population varied during the colonial period, but oppression was a constant (Jonas 1974a: 108–114). The role of labor throughout the colonial period was based on economic utility, not on legal status. Given the demographic realities of the period and the fact that economic conditions determined the need for labor, elites of both political tendencies used public policy to help meet their needs, since market incentives were not adequate (Mörner: 83–84). Administrative and religious "reforms" increased the numbers of ladinos in Indian regions of Guatemala, contributing to widespread rebellions by the native population until after independence in the 1820s (Carmack: 147–148). In sum, Spanish colonization produced a systematic and largely uninterrupted decline of the quality of life for most indigenous people. Guatemala still has not regained some of the qualities of social development that were the norm for the Maya.

Independence Period

Independence for Central America was part of Mexico's independence efforts in the early 1820s.[8] Guatemala was part of the Central American Republic that broke away from Mexico later in the decade. At the outset, the republic was governed by the Liberals, and the brief history of the federation reflected tensions between Liberals and Conservatives, as well as regional tensions among the five provinces (today separate nations), whose boundaries had been inherited from colonial times. In Guatemala Conservatives seized power from the Liberals in the 1840s, using Rafael Carrera's army, largely made up of Indians fighting because of previous encroachments by Liberals (Jonas 1974a: 126).

The major agricultural export until the early nineteenth century had been indigo. After this crop faded in commercial importance, it was replaced by cochineal, another natural dye. After independence in the 1820s, cochineal grew in importance until, by the 1850s, it accounted for "roughly 79 percent of the total value of Guatemalan exports between 1851 and 1855, with indigo accounting for another 15 percent" (Woodward: 64). The invention of chemically based dyes in the middle 1850s meant the end of Guatemala's reliance on these two agricultural products.

Coffee had been cultivated since the 1840s, but its measurable impact on exports emerged in the early 1860s, under Conservative administrations (Woodward: 65–67). It became the leading export crop in the second half of the nineteenth century. By the 1860s, ownership of coffee-producing land had already become more concentrated in Guatemala than anywhere else in Central America. In spite of the fact that smaller producers were more efficient (in terms of production per hectare), overall production totals showed more statistical concentration in Guatemala than elsewhere in the region (Paige: 157–158). The key to this concentration of wealth lay in the monopolistic control of the coffee industry by a small number of processing plants (*beneficios*) and licensed exporting houses. In short, the political economy continued to show signs of dependence on international markets in spite of, or because of, independence.[9]

Throughout the first fifty years of independence, Guatemala's economy reflected changes in the external markets for agricultural exports more than it reflected ideological and political differences between the two oligarchic political parties, the Liberals and the Conservatives, who shared an elite consensus on the export orientation of the economy. Although Liberals of the day were perhaps more ideologically inclined to mouth the rhetoric of free-market capitalism, the orientation of the political economy reflected the opportunities and limitations of Guatemala's dependence on external markets and its domestic labor supply, regardless of ideological and cultural differences between Liberals and Conservatives.

Independence in the 1820s removed the political limitations that the Spanish Crown had imposed on the local elite, opening up new trade opportunities. Conflicts between Liberals and Conservatives in the period were political, however, not economic. At least until 1871, and perhaps later, the economic system and class structure showed remarkable continuity. Despite fluctuations in export crops and differences in elite ideological affiliations, the overall structure of the political economy changed little from that inherited from the colonial period. From early on, the economy was a "capitalist" system that showed many nonmarket characteristics. This mercantilistic, state-regulated style of capitalism dominated Guatemala until the 1944 October Revolution (Alvarado: 137).[10]

Liberal Reforms

By 1870, coffee had become a major international commodity. Guatemala was exporting coffee successfully, but many of the potentially best coffee lands were inaccessible—they were owned by Indian communities or controlled by the Catholic church. Moreover, because Indians lived successfully on their communal lands, or often were protected on church lands, the labor supply was inadequate for the fast-growing coffee export industry. In the late 1870s, Liberals under the leadership of Justino Rufino Barrios legislated changes to overcome these limitations. These policies, collectively called the Liberal Reforms, sought to control land and labor and to develop export agriculture, especially coffee, by reorganizing the nation's resources.

The first major changes were laws that eliminated communal holdings and created mechanisms by which the new "private land" of the Indians could be "acquired." To implement this, the Liberals did not expropriate the idle lands of Conservative oligarchs, even in cases when this land had been seized illegally during earlier Conservative regimes (Cambranes 1985: 242). Nor did they indiscriminately seize lands held idle by the church, although the church was traditionally allied with the Conservatives and a political and ideological rival of the generally anticlerical Liberals.

They also did not redistribute lands already owned by the state, which would have made the reform measures less oppressive socially and politically.

Instead, they seized the communal property of the Indians. By displacing potential workers from their secure environments on communal lands, the Liberal government created conditions—reinforced by other laws—that ensured an adequate labor supply. As a result, the Liberals gained the support of other elite sectors, which was vital if the Indian communities were to be successfully subjugated to these "reforms" (Cambranes 1985: 242–247). Elite consensus made domination of the working classes a less difficult process.

A second major change was a series of new laws that increased the supply of cheap, reliable labor for the coffee growers (Jonas 1974a: 137–138).[11] Vagrancy laws, for example, made workers available as cheap or free labor for plantation owners. A third major component of the Liberal Reforms involved concessions to foreigners, especially German nationals and immigrants, who eventually dominated the coffee industry (Woodward: 71). When price fluctuations forced some coffee growers to sell their land to creditors, one result was increased German ownership of land (Frank and Wheaton: 18). The state provided fiscal incentives and credit for modernizing production, as well as basic infrastructure for transporting products (Jonas 1974a: 132).

In sum, the Liberal Reforms assured that more of Guatemala's land would be accessible for coffee cultivation, that an adequate supply of labor would be available, and that fiscal and other state policies would support the development model. The success of these policies meant that within a few years, Guatemala's coffee oligarchy had consolidated its economic power. Land and labor institutions had been reorganized to stimulate export production, and the result was both greater economic development and greater social inequity.[12]

During this period internal dynamics were set in motion that remain the key to understanding politics after 1980: first, an economy producing wealth for a small minority through dependence on exports and foreign capital; second, a political system relying heavily on the rhetoric of classical liberalism, hence one that might be consistent with the forms of liberal democracy; and third, a continuing reliance on the military to suppress resistance by groups that suffered as a result of change.[13]

Besides changes in the dynamics of production and the continuing pauperization of Guatemalan workers, the Liberal Reforms produced other changes with long-lasting legacies. One result of successful economic development, for example, was the growth of a middle class that demanded increased access to political power, which neither the Liberal nor the Conservative oligarchy favored (Woodward: 72). The resulting tensions were resolved temporarily after the October Revolution of 1944, which ushered in a decade of changes favoring the middle classes.

The Decade of Spring: Unsuccessful Reform

Since the Spanish Conquest in the sixteenth century, Guatemala's history has shown an increasing concentration of wealth and of social control over labor in the hands of a small elite, as well as consistent declines in quality of life for the Indian as well as non-Indian working sectors.[14] By the early twentieth century North American investors had become major participants in Guatemala's export-oriented economy and in the political system needed to maintain that economic orientation. The United Fruit Company, for example, dominated transportation and the banana industry, helping to create the stereotype of the "banana republics" for Central American politics.[15] When market fluctuations made economic growth difficult during the depression of the late 1920s, the dictator Jorge Ubico increased the native oppression by reinstituting vagrancy laws and simultaneously creating the National Police to enforce them (Frank and Wheaton: 19).

In spite of such efforts, by the 1940s the changes that had produced economic growth after the Liberal Reforms had run their course and were now producing economic stagnation. Owners of coffee-producing lands resisted fundamental changes in the economic arrangements, nevertheless. Middle-class reformers, relying on the rhetoric of both democracy and nationalism, overcame this resistance and instituted another series of reforms that re-oriented the use of Guatemala's economic resources. The 1944 revolution, sometimes called the October Revolution, produced a series of changes that lasted until the U.S. Central Intelligence Agency helped engineer the overthrow of the Guatemalan government in 1954.[16]

The roots of the October Revolution lay first in the middle classes' growing desire for access to the political process and second in the economic stagnation that had characterized Guatemala since its export economy collapsed at the onset of the Great Depression in 1929. Stagnation during World War II led to increasing frustration among the middle class. Although some elements of the military resisted the rebellion, many younger officers lent their support: the three-person junta that emerged in October 1944 included two colonels, Francisco Arana, who tended to represent the pre-1944 traditional Army, and Jacobo Arbenz, who represented the reformist, modernizing, nationalist movement within the military (Poitevín: 51–52).

The new leaders based their movement on the ideas of freedom and democracy espoused by Franklin Delano Roosevelt and on the example of social reforms promulgated during the presidency of Lázaro Cárdenas in Mexico from 1934 to 1940 (Gordon: 50). Juan José Arévalo, a schoolteacher who had spent years in exile in Argentina, was elected president and took office in 1945. Even though his "spiritual socialism" included political, social, and economic agendas (Jonas 1974a: 151–155), he did not radically depart from the norms of Western development. To the contrary, he sought to build democracy and dismantle years of dictatorship by enfranchising citizens and working toward social liberation of the poor, especially the Indians.[17]

The Arévalo government created structures and institutions that encouraged the mobilization and participation of "popular" groups.[18] For example, it gave legal support to cooperatives and labor unions as well as organizations of professionals and business people. Rural workers and peasants were given legal protection: the rights of working-class people to vote, unionize, bargain, and strike marked their first participation in national political life. By 1950, the government had established a social security system for health care. In rural areas the government aimed at integrating the Indian communities into national political life as participants for the first time. Arévalo eliminated the semifeudal systems of peonage and forced labor and established judicial procedures to ensure protection of workers' rights. The Law of Forced Rental, for example, obliged large landowners to lease uncultivated land at low rates to landless campesinos.

This was not an idyllic, unblemished transition to democracy, however, because of hostility from elite groups and some sectors of the Army. The Arévalo government itself was not totally committed to participation by the people and used the specter of right-wing reaction to urge moderation in participation. Government pressure, and in some cases repression, was brought against independent labor organizing in the early days after the October Revolution (Dalton: 450–457).

Yet on the whole, Arévalo's program was Guatemala's equivalent of the New Deal. Perhaps mild by current U.S. standards, his programs were more serious in the Guatemalan context, and they threatened elements in the oligarchy and the military's conservative wing. In spite of the tensions caused by these modernizing reforms and the many coup attempts against him, Arévalo was the first Guatemalan president to finish a constitutional period of government. His successor was Colonel Jacobo Arbenz Guzmán, who took office after the election of 1951. Although the balloting was quite honest by Guatemalan standards, the victory was tainted because Arbenz's principal opponent, Colonel Arana from the 1944 junta, was assassinated under suspicious circumstances.

President Arbenz sought to build upon earlier reforms by further mobilizing the still largely excluded Indians and rural working class into the national political community. Arbenz based his political reforms on economic ones, as did John Kennedy in his Alliance for Progress that would follow in less than a decade (Jonas 1974a: 156–158). Arbenz believed, as Kennedy later expressed, that democracy could work only if economic justice provided land for destitute rural workers and social and economic justice for urban workers.

The centerpiece of Arbenz's program was his agrarian reform, the famous Decree 900, which expropriated unused land and compensated the landowners. The United States later encouraged precisely this type of agrarian reform throughout Latin America under the Alliance for Progress in the early 1960s. But in the 1950s, land reform seemed radical, and this one touched U.S. corporate interests: a major target was the United Fruit Company, which held vast areas of unused land. In Guatemala in 1952, no agrarian reform could have been successful without affecting some of the company's property.[19]

Arbenz promoted economic growth that was primarily capitalist but nationally controlled (Jonas 1974b: 47–50). During the Decade of Spring the number of individuals who enjoyed an "inalienable right to property" was expanded to include at first the new commercial and urban groups, and later, under Arbenz, rural smallholders. The regime was more democratic and nationalistic in orientation than earlier governments, but only within the limits of the dialectic with the agro-exporting traditionalist sector. No revolution in the Marxist sense took place, that is, no hint of changes in the mode of production or of the destruction of one social class by another. The revolutionary decade barely altered the basic capitalist nature of the Guatemalan economy, which once again revealed remarkable continuity, the pattern since the Spanish Conquest.[20]

The period from 1944 to 1954 seems revolutionary because Guatemala moved toward political democracy and socioeconomic reform. As in earlier periods, the state was the prime instrument in producing social and economic changes. New institutions allowed many citizens previously excluded from politics to participate efficaciously for the first time. The nation made great strides toward achieving a democratic society and political system, moving "further in the direction of liberal democracy than many other Latin American countries" (Blasier: 63).

Arbenz's efforts to move Guatemala toward a more nationalist economic development were supported by the nationalist sector in the military but opposed by the traditional sector, which saw itself as guardian of the existing order. Part of the urban business community favored the reforms that would expand domestic markets and diversify the economy, but the traditional coffee oligarchy preferred the export orientation of earlier periods. Not unexpectedly, the traditional oligarchy particularly opposed any policy that increased the political or economic power of newly mobilized rural groups. The oligarchy thus fought both the increased power of urban labor and the mild land reform—and its historical control over land and labor made it a formidable opposition. What would have been the ultimate results of the Arévalo-Arbenz experiment within the framework of capitalist structures is not certain, for it ended with the counterrevolution of 1954.

Counterrevolution

The counterrevolution of 1954 had both international and domestic elements. The international picture is described well elsewhere: after a long, sustained campaign by the United States government and the United Fruit Company to destabilize and isolate the government of Guatemala, a CIA-trained group led by exiled Colonel Carlos Castillo Armas invaded eastern Guatemala, and the Arbenz government fell some days later.[21] The goals of U.S. policy are fairly clear and well documented. Nonetheless, it is important not to overestimate the effect of U.S. efforts at the time, nor to underestimate the role of domestic forces in this situation. The October Revolution of 1944 had been supported by urban middle-class capitalists who wanted more power over the economy. Policies that achieved this goal, and hence improved economic opportunities for Guatemala's urban, middle sectors within a capitalist framework, produced substantial domestic support.

Reforms aimed at domestic owners of industrial and agricultural wealth, however, diminished middle-class support for the reformist movement. Conflicts arose when newly integrated groups at the top of the reform movement—the middle classes and military officers—felt threatened economically by redistribution of property and politically by the democratic pressures of mass mobilization.[22] These sectors began forming new alliances with sectors of the traditional oligarchy, as well as with the United States, to search for an alternative path to economic development (Alvarado: 137). The success of the counterrevolution is probably due far more to these domestic dynamics than to international pressures.

Political and Economic Change After 1954

The counterrevolution of 1954 produced many economic and political changes. Before 1954, Jacobo Arbenz had moved Guatemala's economy away from its export orientation and dominance by foreign companies, specifically the United Fruit Company. His program helped create a business sector that would, in effect, compete with the traditional oligarchy. Arbenz espoused a program of economic modernization with state assistance, in this sense not unlike the programs of the Liberal Reforms of the 1870s. The model was capitalist but, unlike the Liberal Reforms, also included socioeconomic reforms as part of building a strong economy. Arbenz's approach was "economic modernization with social reform."

By 1954, therefore, the dominant sector of society was more heterogeneous economically than the coffee-based oligarchy of the pre-1944 era had been. This diversity increased as governments after 1954 encouraged industrialization and agricultural diversification into cotton, sugar, and cattle, and opened Guatemala to foreign investment in such diverse industries as banking, mining, food processing, pharmaceuticals, oil refining, paper, and steel tubing. Among these upper-sector groups, not surprisingly, conflicts arose over government policies, for example tax policy, infrastructure expenditures, and tariff protection. Powerful private associations formed to protect the economic interests of their members. The 1954 counterrevolution was designed to reorient the Guatemalan economy toward exports, but at the same time it had no intention of abandoning the goals of economic modernization and development. Despite the conflicts between new and old economic elites, all were willing to agree on one crucial point: land reform was out of the question. After 1954, the "Guatemalan model" became "economic modernization *without* social reform."

Politically, Guatemala regressed into waves of repressive violence. Because of the social and political progress that had been achieved in the previous decade, restoring the political status quo meant both major changes and high levels of violence to enforce them. Violence was necessary, ironically, precisely because the previous decade had seen the development of democratic practices: members of politically active labor unions, peasant cooperatives, and some of the political parties now had to be excluded. Castillo Armas led Guatemala into a period of repression more intense than any other preceding it, except the Spanish Conquest. Perhaps no other historical period illustrates so clearly the idea that state repression is political participation by elites intent on eradicating or preventing democracy.

The "antireforms" of the Castillo Armas government included repeal of universal suffrage, cancellation of the registrations of 533 unions, and revision of the nation's labor laws to make effective labor organizing impossible (WOLA 1983: 8; Jonas 1974e: 74–75; and Schlesinger and Kinzer: 221). The number of organized workers dropped from over 100,000 in 1954 to fewer than 27,000 in 1955 (Jonas 1974e: 75). Land reform was reversed: peasant beneficiaries were dispossessed and their land returned to previous owners. Less than .5 percent of the approximately 100,000 beneficiaries under Arbenz remained on their lands by the end of 1956 (Adams 1970: 400).

During the first few years of the period, economic performance was disappointing (Adams 1970: 149–155; Jonas 1974a: 177–184; and Jonas 1974e: 81). Before 1961, U.S. economic assistance programs in Latin America were extremely modest, but after the Cuban Revolution John Kennedy proposed the Alliance for Progress, which shifted U.S. policy toward direct governmental assistance for Latin America. In Guatemala new capital was used to promote a strong export orientation, to push for economic integration throughout Central America, to stress agricultural and industrial diversification, and to fund the development of infrastructure

(Brockett 1984b: 372).[23] This major change in U.S. policy helped spur improved macroeconomic performance. The decade of the 1960s was a period of economic growth: real GNP grew at about twice the rate of population growth until the late 1970s (WOLA 1983: 2; and World Bank: 27). New export commodities flourished.[24]

Sustained economic growth did not mean similar progress toward social reform, however. During the same period, productive resources were becoming more concentrated and social indicators declined. The Guatemalan government made little effort to reverse either trend; indeed, state policy abetted both tendencies. The concentration on export crops also led to a decline in the production of basic foodstuffs and a need to import rice, beans, and corn.[25] The loss of peasant landholdings was matched only in part by increased demand for wage labor on cotton and other plantations. By the late 1970s, hundreds of thousands of peasants were migrating annually to find low-paying temporary work under harsh and often dangerous conditions (WOLA 1983: 3). The wages of those with work were meager, and rural unemployment reached 42 percent by the 1970s (Brockett 1984a: 492).[26]

With public policy generally redistributing resources in favor of the wealthiest sectors, very little of the prosperity generated by renewed economic growth trickled down to the nonbusiness and nonelite sectors of society.[27] By the mid- to late 1970s, Guatemala had the second worst index of malnutrition for children under the age of five years: 81.4 percent of all persons in this category suffered from malnourishment in Guatemala.[28] There were equally distressing data on many other indicators as well. Illiteracy rates were high: 69 percent of the rural population—82 percent of the Indian rural population—was illiterate. But school enrollments were low: 44 percent of all children—76 percent of rural children—were not enrolled in school (Davis and Hodson: 21). Health care statistics were the worst in Central America.[29] Overall, then, the situation for the poor sectors of Guatemalan society was deplorable in terms of social justice.[30]

Furthermore, the period from 1954 to the late 1970s showed continuing decline, not evolutionary progress or even stagnation. Throughout this time, public policy made the social situation worse, not better.[31] At various times during this period, and with varying degrees of effort, the United States attempted to promote reforms in Guatemala, including tax and agrarian reforms and support for cooperatives, but these reform efforts routinely failed. Agrarian reform was scarcely mentioned, perhaps because of its association with the Arbenz regime, despite U.S. suggestions that agrarian reform was necessary. Agro-exporting landowners not only resisted land reform, they actually dispossessed peasants from their existing holdings. Tax reform proposals, which initially received wide publicity, were abandoned when the elites protested. In spite of the absence of reforms, U.S. assistance was never curtailed, and by the mid-1960s the United States ceased using foreign aid to push for social reform (Jonas 1974c: 105–106). With the assistance of the Alliance for Progress, a largely self-sufficient rural peasantry had been converted into a rural proletariat, subject to the vicissitudes of world demand for Guatemala's export commodities and to the vagaries of local elites controlling the plantations.

Communal Activism: The Tradition of Participation

This brief historical summary has touched on many of the major events that shaped Guatemala's political and economic dynamics before 1980. One additional cultural tradition must be highlighted and added to the context. The tradition of democratic communal activism has immense significance in any attempt to understand the quality of political participation in Guatemala in the 1980s.

Guatemalans, especially in rural areas, have a long history of community-level participation in developmental activities. Communal activism, problem-solving activities in which poorer groups work in their own communities to improve standards of living in specific ways, has long been characteristic of rural Guatemala. Community-level participation has been especially successful in the indigenous regions, for several reasons. First, the cultural worldview (including resistance to outsiders) and the Mayan tradition of decentralized control over local affairs reinforced the idea of community action to solve local-level developmental problems. Second, the Catholic church, through its Catholic Action program (an organized movement that is usually conservative), has fostered local organization for self-help since at least the 1940s, often causing confrontations with traditional Indian leaders, especially after the repression of the late 1950s (Adams 1970: 278–286; IGE 1987: 8–11; and Arias).

Third, after the 1954 counterrevolution, with its anticommunist ideology, religious groups were invited to send missionaries to Guatemala to help institutionalize this anticommunist process. These mostly conservative groups successfully integrated both the rural and urban poor—including Indian communities—into cooperatives, religious organizations, neighborhood organizations, literacy classes, and other activities that promoted effective local-level participation. From the perspective of the United States, Guatemala had been reclaimed from communism in 1954, so the Alliance for Progress programs of the 1960s included assistance for rural cooperatives. Finally, communication with outsiders through missionaries and Peace Corps volunteers, education in urban centers, and direct electronic connections with the outside—the age of the transistor radio—all led to demands for social modernization and stimulated communal activism (Frank and Wheaton: 29–36).

After the earthquake of 1976, when it became clear that the government was unwilling or unable to cope with the social and economic results of the disaster effectively, local citizens sought assistance on their own, by organizing reconstruction committees throughout the nation. These local-level committees successfully dealt with international agencies directly to obtain supplies and manage relief and reconstruction efforts (Davis and Hodson: 15). These successes, plus the relatively nonviolent government of General Laugerud in the 1974–1976 period, resulted in a growing sector of rural and urban poor who were well organized and participant, almost exclusively at the local level and almost exclusively in "nonpolitical" ways: that is, their participation had little or nothing to do with the electoral or party process.

Since at least the period beginning with the 1944 revolution, then, outside agencies and local communities have worked together in hundreds, perhaps thousands of local-level projects to improve the Indian's quality of life in areas such as health, education, agriculture, and cooperatives. Outside agencies included religious missionaries and various nongovernmental private voluntary organizations (PVOs), as well as the major U.S. commitment of Peace Corps and USAID programs beginning in the 1960s (Davis and Hodson: 1, 14). Within Guatemala's history, therefore, is a vibrant legacy of communal activism: citizens directly participating at the local level in making decisions about issues that affect their lives.

Solving local problems is obviously important to the individuals and communities involved, but these activities take on additional significance for political participation and for democratic development.[32] Communal activism is a long-standing and successful tradition in Guatemala, and understanding current attempts to build democracy requires awareness of this important dimension. The tradition of communal activism suggests that if there is a genuine political opening, the country will move toward democracy. Unfortunately, Guatemalan history reveals a second pattern of participatory behavior that is antidemocratic: violence to prevent or destroy organizing within the popular sector.

Conclusion

Even the most casual observer of Latin American history and politics can recognize that Guatemala has been an extremely violent nation for several decades.[33] Although many Latin American societies have suffered repressive violence, usually under the guise of "national security," no other American nation has suffered so intensely nor for so long as has Guatemala. Political violence there has been common, pervasive, sometimes appearing to be endemic, and always sinister.[34] To be understood properly, this violence must be studied in the context of economic change, as a form of political participation; it is the product neither of the psychological aberrations of madmen nor of a generalized culture of violence. It is, unfortunately, often a rational response to the circumstances in which political actors find themselves.

Guatemalan history clearly shows such circumstances. Economically, the historical dynamics are clear: the nation's prevailing economic model is oligarchic capitalism strongly dependent on resources that the state commands. Government is a major actor because the economic model requires it to be so, not because the state is responding to the citizens' demands as a whole. The social context is equally clear. As the decade of the 1980s opened, socioeconomic conditions in Guatemala were abominable for at least three-fourths of its inhabitants. Modernization in the economic sector had led to the destruction of communities as well as the impoverishment of most workers. The increasing orientation of the economy to exports began to render most citizens unimportant, except as cheap labor: given widespread poverty, people become increasingly irrelevant.

Politically, Guatemala's history shows a continuing struggle around these issues. Given poor socioeconomic conditions and a penchant for democratic action in the populace, even slight political openings produce a surge in political participation by popular groups attempting to place their needs on the social agenda. With few exceptions, the government's responses to these surges have not included a public policy of redistribution but usually, instead, one of repression, sometimes violent. With little room for reform within the system, rebellion and insurgency have frequently been chosen as rational options by progressive citizens. Conversely, with little room to maneuver on the international economic scene, Guatemala's elites have shown no tolerance for social reform domestically and have frequently used violent repression as a rational strategy for survival. As the potential for rebellion has increased, so has the elite's need to rely on violence, rather than systemic legitimacy, to maintain dominance.

The result is chronic instability: popular resistance to social injustice means that elite dominance has been and will remain precarious. Throughout Guatemalan history and especially since 1954, worsening situations generated by the model of economic growth without reform have generated popular pressures for change. The very economic structures that have provided wealth for elites have also produced opposition: social injustice has led to a steady flow of demands for the redress of grievances, not to apathy. But historically, the government has not been able or willing to stabilize the political system through public policies that generate legitimacy for the system—theoretically the normal pattern in liberal societies.

Many state policies have had an impact on political participation and the democratic participatory potential of nonelite sectors of society. Elite policy decisions and behavior affecting the quality of political participation are important elements, but a complete analysis of the quality of democratic politics must include the nonelite segments. In Guatemala, the potential for democracy has been strongest in the popular sectors. The most discontinuous period in modern Guatemalan history, the Decade of Spring following the 1944 revolution, illustrated the democratic potential of the majority of Guatemala's citizens. The need for counterrevolution and violence demonstrated how compelling the pressure from below for democracy has been.

With this difficult and complex historical context in mind, the stage is now set for an in-depth analysis of Guatemalan politics since 1980. In this analysis we will look for hopeful signs that indicate improvement in the quality of political participation and civil and human rights for more citizens, positive movement on socioeconomic questions and social justice issues, and other indications that the state is becoming more responsive in its public policies to the majority's wishes and needs. Given the dual traditions of communal activism and political violence, the critical question is to determine which of these prevailed during the terms of Guatemala's civilian presidents, Marco Vinicio Cerezo Arévalo and Jorge Serrano Elías.

Notes

1. Portions of this chapter appear in slightly different format in Trudeau and Schoultz.
2. For a fascinating series of essays about the Mayan orientation to time, see Bronk. On the overall achievements of the Maya, Girard writes the following:

> The Mayan capacity for abstraction produces universal admiration, for they outdid all other peoples of the New World, as well as the Egyptians, Babylonians, Chinese, Persians, Greeks, and Romans. . . . They had adjusted their annual calendar to the rhythm of the seasons before Julius Caesar. . . . They were the best astronomers of both worlds until the end of the Middle Ages (quoted in Cambranes 1986b: 62).

3. There was no word for infant malnutrition in the detailed Mayan medical lexicon (Tejada Valenzuela: 103–108).
4. For more detailed treatments, see García Bauer: 19–54; Cambranes 1986: 61–77; and Jonas 1974a: 94–100.
5. The figures are attributed to Bartolomé de las Casas, the Dominican known as the "Defender of the Indians." They perhaps exaggerate the extent of the direct impact of warfare, but accurately reflect the overall population decline in this period (Veblen: 92; Lovell 1982: 110). The Spanish conquistador Alvarado wrote that "huge numbers of Indians were killed during this extended period of conquest" (Veblen: 90).
6. The first great plague to invade the region actually preceded the physical arrival of the Spanish in Guatemala and may have reduced the Indian population by up to one half (Veblen: 89; Lovell 1982: 108–117).

7. As one example of depopulation, one Guatemalan region, considered typical in its demographic history, took until 1950 to return to the population levels that had inhabited the area before the Spanish Conquest. The population declined for over 150 years after the conquest, bottoming out in the late seventeenth century after a decline of about 90 percent (Lovell 1982: 108, 117–118). Veblen reports that highland Guatemala returned to its pre-conquest population levels sometime in the middle of the twentieth century, which would indicate an Indian population of about 3 million at the time of the conquest (Veblen: 98).

8. For more detailed studies of this period, see Pinto Soria; and Jonas 1974a: 115–127.

9. Other crops illustrate these dynamics as well. For example, given the drop in the value of natural dyestuffs in the 1850s, and the gap until the rapid growth of coffee production in the 1860s, one would expect some economic and political dislocations in Guatemala in this period. The potential negative effects of this lag were avoided because of the Civil War in the United States, which increased demand for Guatemalan cotton in the mid-1860s. In 1865, cotton produced 19.2 percent of the total value of Guatemala's exports (Woodward: 64, 68). A few years later cotton was again insignificant as an export, not to revive again until after World War II.

10. For a more detailed survey of this period and this perspective, see Jonas 1974a: 126–127. Her summary:

> Ultimately, "development" under the highly educated, "progressive" criollo, [Liberal] Gálvez, was not strikingly different from the "reaction" under the illiterate, proletarian "caudillo," [Conservative] Carrera. . . . By the 1860's political independence had made very little structural difference in Guatemala. The colonial economy and class structure had taken new forms, but in essence remained intact (Jonas 1974a: 130–131).

11. Paige provides this overall perspective:

> Guatemala . . . is unique in the elaboration of an institutionalized system of labor power backed by both the informal armed power of the coffee planters and the formal armed power of the state (Paige: 168).

12. For an extremely detailed and well-documented analysis of the period and its historical antecedents, see Cambranes 1985. Also see Jonas 1974a: 133 ff.; and McCreery. For a briefer analysis see Frank and Wheaton: 18–19, who summarize the period thus:

> The Liberal period therefore established the basic structures of modern Guatemala: a small oligarchy and a mass of landless or land-poor laborers; a strong, centralized state which provided the elite with the needed services and labor; and economic dependence on foreign investments and interests (Frank and Wheaton: 18).

13. Woodward's summary of the legacy of the Liberal Reforms is that they "produced wealth for the few and poverty for the masses in the twentieth century, making inevitable the conflicts that our own times have inherited" (Woodward: 73). Though certainly not the only factor in explaining rebellion, impoverishment is a major factor. See Booth and Walker, especially chapter 5, for a model based on this factor.

14. Increasing poverty for the masses became the norm. For example, daily wages, expressed as corn prices, showed that the earning power of workers dropped by one-third between the decade of the 1880s and the period from 1920 to 1939, from about 7.5 pounds of corn per day of work to between 4 and 4.5 pounds (Woodward: 73).

15. In coffee, German investors continued to expand: "by 1914, Germans owned nearly half of the land on which coffee was grown" (Frank and Wheaton: 18). By 1926, only 7.3 percent of Guatemalans owned land. The dominance of foreign investors and the high concentration of land reinforced the relationships between land and labor that had been refined by the Liberals in the 1870s (Frank and Wheaton: 18).

16. There are excellent studies of this period in Handy; Blasier; Jonas 1974a; Immerman; and Schlesinger and Kinzer.

17. For more detailed descriptions of these efforts, see Blasier: 54–64; Immerman: 44–57; Schlesinger and Kinzer: 25–42; Melville and Melville: 27–39; and Poitevín: 51–53.

18. The phrases "popular sectors" and "popular organizations" commonly refer to those sectors of Latin American society that are neither elites nor part of the middle sectors, loosely defined. The word "popular" is taken directly from the Spanish word used to describe these groups and has no sense of "popularity," unlike the English cognate. Because such large portions of the lower classes are chronically unemployed or functioning at the margin of the capitalist, cash economy, it makes sense to refer to these groups as popular, rather than to call them the working class. Moreover, this is the appellation most commonly used in Latin America.

19. In 1953, Arbenz announced that his government would redistribute 234,000 acres of United Fruit Company land, none of which was being cultivated. At the time, the company was cultivating only 139,000 of its more than 3 million acres, which constituted 42 percent of the nation's arable land (LaFeber: 118; Schlesinger and Kinzer: 75–77; Melville and Melville: 61–63; and Jonas 1974a: 158–160). For more complete treatments of this critical episode, see LaFeber; Schlesinger and Kinzer; Melville and Melville; Jonas 1974a; Blasier; and Immerman.

20. Jonas 1974a: 166–169 offers a similar argument. Elsewhere she concludes: "The economic measures of the revolution did more to *spread* private property than to abolish it" (Jonas 1974b: 52, italics added). According to Galeano: 51: "The agrarian reform law laid down as its basic objective *the development of the peasant capitalist economy and the capitalist agricultural economy in general*" (italics in original).

21. For detailed versions of these events, see Immerman; and Schlesinger and Kinzer. For shorter versions, see Blasier: 159–177; and Jonas 1974f: 57–73.

22. Extensive mass mobilization in rural areas during the early 1950s may have developed into a threat to private property, i.e., may have *become* revolutionary in an economic sense. Certainly this potential threat was part of the basis of opposition by opponents of the Arbenz regime, some of whom probably perceived rural organization as threats ipso facto.

23. For a detailed account of this process, see Jonas 1974d: 86–103.

24. Between 1961 and 1973, arable land devoted to export crops increased by 6.5 percent annually, but for food crops by only 1.7 to 2 percent. Exports increased dramatically; this was a period of sustained, successful economic growth:

Between 1960 and 1974, . . . the value of Guatemala's five major agricultural export crops increased from $105.3 to $367.5 million During this period, Guatemala's agricultural-export economy, as measured by average annual increases in production, outperformed 22 other countries in Latin America, including Mexico, Colombia, and Brazil (Davis and Hodson: 46).

25. Guatemala was almost self-sufficient in production of corn during the 1950 to 1954 period, but the counterrevolution that reversed the Arbenz land reform also disrupted production to the extent that major importing of corn began in 1955 and continued through at least the mid-1970s (Villacorta Escobar: 78).

26. In 1980, USAID identified the "very low wage rates paid by commercial agriculture and an extremely low minimum wage established by the government" as the principal causes of Guatemalan poverty (USAID, cited in WOLA 1983: 6).

27. In 1970, an AID-sponsored study concluded that:

all the data that have been reviewed on production, yields, farm size, income and employment indicate that the income position of small farmers has deteriorated considerably since 1950. . . . Over large areas of the central region, per capita production is surely falling, and total production may be falling as well (Fletcher et al.: 196).

Another study concluded that growth "has not resulted in any substantive increase in the internal market or in the economy's capacity to absorb available labor" (CSUCS: 121).

28 Of these approximately 800,000 children, some 56,000 were listed as Gomez III–level malnourished, indicating severe malnutrition. The proportion of Guatemala's malnourished children in this "severe" group was third highest in Latin America: 5.9 percent of Guatemala's children from zero to four years of age were *severely* malnourished, almost twice the proportion for El Salvador, for example (IADB: 19). See reference to Tejada Valenzuela, note 3 above, for an ironic contrast.

29.

Based on such figures as number of physicians per 100,000 inhabitants, numbers of licensed and auxiliary nurses, dentists, and hospital beds, and percent of government health expenditures per capita, Guatemala ranks below all other Central American countries (Davis and Hodson: 21).

30. In the late 1970s, life expectancy was low and skewed: ladino life expectancy was 60.7 years, but Indian life expectancy was 44.5 years (Ruiz de Barrios Klee: 5). In terms of income, for example, dividing the rural population of Guatemala into quartiles reveals that the cost of the *minimum* adequate diet— $278.75 in 1975—exceeded the per capita income of *all four* quartiles. The minimum diet in this period cost more than the per capita income of about 70 percent of all Guatemalans, rural and urban (Amigo: 125).

31.

State policies have tended to exacerbate the historical inequities of the Guatemalan agrarian system and have done almost nothing to alleviate the conditions of hunger and misery of the poor (Davis and Hodson: 46).

32.

The very acts of planning, resource development, and cooperation required to carry out such projects can leave residues of organization, interaction patterns, participatory skills, and problem-solving models that further political development (Seligson and Booth 1979: 7).

33. Guatemala's unfortunate place in the history of political violence in the hemisphere has had even linguistic consequences. Guatemala is generally held to be the source of the Spanish words for "disappeared" and "to disappear" a person. Guatemala has also contributed the Spanish word *rematar,* which translates literally as "to re-kill." The word is used to describe situations in which victims of failed assassination attempts are visited a second time, in hospitals, for example, so that the assassination can be finished successfully.

34. That this pattern is a modal response is reflected in President Jorge Serrano's reference to a "culture of violence" as an impediment to successful negotiations with the URNG insurgents in 1992, discussed more fully in Chapter 9. See LATimes 9/19/91: 1A for a similar conceptualization.

3

Elections and the
State Crisis of the 1980s

Democracy in terms of the quality of participation is reflected in electoral behavior as well as in civil liberties and human rights. Conventional indicators for the procedural aspects of democracy, then, are data on elections and voting, political parties and party systems, civil liberties and human rights, and formal-legal data. These last include information about legal structures and the formal status of voters and political parties, which are important indicators of the structural limits on, and opportunities for, political participation.

At the formal-legal level Guatemala has been a "democracy" since at least 1945, with regular elections held since then, as well as several functioning political parties and other accoutrements of procedural democracy. Guatemala's party system has been a multiparty one for most of the same period. Constitutional provisions from the documents of 1945, 1965, and 1985 all provide guarantees for electoral and party behavior. The Constitution of 1965, for example, guarantees the existence of opposition parties and contains detailed provisions to protect civil rights and liberties that permit groups to organize and participate in electing officials. The constitution acknowledges the existence of human rights and provides procedures to defend them.[1]

Beyond the formal-legal level, however, the picture is not so clear. Keeping in mind criteria borrowed from Herman and Brodhead and from Greenberg (see Chapter 1), this chapter examines Guatemalan elections up to the election of March 1982, which precipitated the military coup that led to Guatemala's formal transition to democracy in 1985, and reveals the importance of a broad contextual approach to the study of elections and political participation.

Elections: 1954–1982

The first electoral event after the successful 1954 counterrevolutionary invasion was a validating plebiscite organized shortly after Colonel Carlos

Castillo Armas took power. In this referendum, held during the wave of repression associated with his regime, citizens voted orally in the presence of security personnel. Given the procedural qualities of the referendum, the absence of alternative candidates, and the general climate of fear in Guatemala at the time, it is not surprising that Castillo Armas received 95 percent of the vote. It is also fairly clear that this "election" does not indicate any movement toward democracy. Subsequent elections, however, are much more complex in their results.

The first contested elections after 1954, in effect two rounds of struggle, took place in 1958 and 1959, after the assassination of Castillo Armas in 1957. (See tables 3.1 and 3.2 for results of several elections before 1982.) Both campaigns featured only groups that had opposed the Arbenz government. The "official" party, the National Democratic Movement (Movimiento Nacional Democrático—MDN), later the National Liberation Movement (Movimiento de Liberación Nacional—MLN), nominated Miguel Ortiz Pasarelli. His opponent, General Miguel Ydígoras Fuentes, was a staunch anticommunist who had lived in exile during the Arbenz administration but who had been rejected by the United States as a suitable leader for its 1954 invasion.

The 1958 voting returns were fraudulent: Ortiz and the MDN claimed victory, but Ydígoras urged public marches and demonstrations to prevent the fraud (Handy: 151–153). The chaos prompted a compromise, a second round of elections. In this round the MDN changed its candidate, nominating José Luis Cruz Salazar, a military officer during the Arbenz government who had served briefly in the first junta after the 1954 *golpe* and then had been Guatemalan ambassador to the U.S. Ydígoras carried the election in this second round but not without renewed accusations of fraud, this time on the part of the defeated MDN.

Miguel Ydígoras Fuentes's party, the National Democratic Redemption Party (Redención Nacional Democrática—RND, or simply La Redención) was almost purely a patronage structure and had no programmatic line other than vocal anticommunism; this was also the line of the defeated MDN. His government was extremely corrupt and ineffective: "Ydígoras' ineptness succeeded only in exacerbating the frustrations of progressives and conservatives alike" (Weaver: 72). The corruption contributed to factionalization and frustration in the military. One faction, led by progressive, nationalist officers, attempted a coup d'état in 1960, which eventually developed into an insurgency campaign in the middle and late 1960s. Tensions also built within the military over the use of Guatemalan territory to train the forces that eventually invaded Cuba in the *Playa Girón* (Bays of Pigs) operation.

Eventually, in 1963, these tensions culminated in a successful military coup led by Colonel Enrique Peralta Azurdia and his "moderate" faction of

Table 3.1   Presidential Election Results, 1945–1978

Year	Registered Voters	Votes Cast	Percentage Abstaining	Winner's Ballots	Winner's Percentage
1945	310,000	296,214	4.5	255,700	82.5
1951	583,300	407,663	31.1	266,800	45.7
1958	736,400	492,274	32.1	191,000	25.9
1966	944,170	531,270	43.7	209,400	22.2
1970	1,190,449	640,684	46.2	251,100	21.1
1974	1,568,724	727,174	53.6	299,000	19.1
1978	1,785,764	652,073	63.5	262,900	14.7

Sources: "Elections in Guatemala": 5; Inforpress 1985: 26

Table 3.2   Presidential Election Results by Party, 1957–1978

Year	Candidates	Party	Percentage of Vote
1957	Miguel Ortiz Pasarelli	MDN	62.0
	Col. Miguel Ydígoras	RND	38.0
1958	Col. Miguel Ydígoras Fuentes	RND	38.8
	Col. José Luis Cruz Salazar	MDN	28.1
	Mario Méndez Montenegro	PR	27.0
1966	Julio Méndez Montenegro	PR	44.4
	Col. Juan de Dios Aguilar	PID	31.7
	Col. Miguel Angel Ponciano	MLN	23.9
1970	Col. Carlos Arana Osorio	MLN/PID	42.9
	Mario Fuentes Peruccini	PR	35.7
	Maj. Jorge Lucas Caballeros	DCG	21.4
1974	Gen. Kjell Laugerud García	PID/MLN	41.0
	Gen. Efraín Ríos Montt	FNO	36.0
	Col. Paíz Novales	PR	23.0
1978	Gen. Romeo Lucas García	PID/CAN/PR	41.0
	Gen. Enrique Peralta Azurdia	MLN	33.0
	Gen. Ricardo Peralta Méndez	DCG	26.0

Key to Party Acronyms

CAN	National Authentic Center (Central Auténtico Nacional), originally the Central Aranista Organization (Central Aranista Organizado—CAO)
DCG	Guatemalan Christian Democratic Party (Democracia Cristiana Guatemalteca)
FNO	National Opposition Front, including DCG, United Front of the Revolution (Frente Unido Revolucionario—FUR), and Revolutionary Democratic Unity (Unidad Revolucionaria Democrática—URD)
FUN	National Front for Unity (Frente de Unidad Nacional)
MDN	National Democratic Movement (Movimiento Nacional Democrático)
MLN	National Liberation Movement (Movimiento de Liberación Nacional)
PID	Democratic Institutional Party (Partido Institucional Democrático)
PR	Revolutionary Party (Partido Revolucionario)
RND	National Democratic Redemption Party (Redención Nacional Democrática)
UNO	United National Opposition (Unidad Nacional Opositora), includes DCG and a moderate faction of the MLN (PNR).

Source: Adapted from Handy: 283–284.

the Army (Handy: 152–155; Weaver: 66–67). The coup put an end to the chaotic period after 1954, and Peralta Azurdia, as chief of state, ruled by decree for the next two years. Holding himself aloof from partisan politics, he led the country through a process of constitutional reform and elections, using the specter of guerrilla insurgency to extract U.S. military assistance, which was largely used to reorganize and modernize the armed forces. In 1965, a new constitution was promulgated and a new electoral process created, with elections scheduled for 1966.

A Civilian President

By the 1966 election Guatemalan elections had been widely discredited,[2] yet that election was the first procedurally honest one in Guatemala after the 1954 counterrevolution. A reformist civilian, Julio César Méndez Montenegro, was the candidate of the Revolutionary Party (Partido Revolucionario—PR), a party that sought to identify itself with the Arévalo and Arbenz governments by characterizing itself as the "third government" of the 1944 revolution. The United States backed Méndez's bid against two military candidates, and once the balloting was over, Washington announced it would not support any attempt to annul the election (Melville and Melville: 189). The Méndez victory offered the U.S. the possibility that the reformist development strategy envisioned in the Alliance for Progress could be implemented in Guatemala. The military, at least on paper, would return to the barracks after the election.

But although a civilian reformer taking office after a fair counting of the ballots seemed a positive step after military rule, a closer look reveals the real limits of civilian power in relation to the strength of the military. For example, the 1965 Constitution had restricted parties with "exotic ideologies"—such as social democracy and the Christian Democrats—and outlawed left-wing opposition, which limited effective political participation by groups and parties supporting serious reforms (Black: 21).[3]

Moreover, the only parties allowed to participate in addition to the PR were the MLN, the rightist oligarchic party that emerged after 1954, and the Democratic Institutional Party (Partido Institucional Democrático—PID), the party of the armed forces. Even the PR itself had shifted to the right in the late 1950s when its leader at the time, Mario Méndez Montenegro, "purged the entire left wing of the party" (Jonas 1974a: 196). Julio Méndez Montenegro became the candidate only after his brother Mario had been assassinated. From the beginning, then, the electorate's choices were narrowly constrained and the "reformist" credentials of the PR open to question.

Once elected, the Méndez government was severely limited. First, Méndez was not allowed to take office until he agreed to guarantee the military "a free hand in counterinsurgency, autonomy in such matters as selection of the Defense Minister, Chief of Staff, budgets, etc." Méndez also had to promise "to exclude 'radicals' from the government, but not to retire too many generals" (Jonas 1974a: 195). Second, threats from the oligarchy prevented him from carrying out even relatively mild, U.S.-supported tax reforms, let alone take the initiative on more serious land reforms (Jonas 1974c: 104–108). Perhaps most serious, Méndez was powerless to stop a new wave of repression unleashed by an anxious military and the paramilitary death squads controlled by the oligarchy.

In short, an honest election in 1966 did not guarantee even procedural democracy, let alone social justice, regardless of whatever reformist intentions Méndez Montenegro professed. In fact, the net impact of the Méndez period was a decline in the quality of life for Guatemala's majority, even as macroeconomic growth created new wealth for the middle class and the elite. The overall structural situation remained intact, while social indicators shifted in the direction of more inequality. Though the presidency of Méndez Montenegro was characterized by an autonomous, reorganized military in power, the example of the relatively open campaign by the PR inspired progressive members of the middle class to organize reformist parties, including the early Christian Democrats, the United Front of the Revolution (Frente Unido Revolucionario—FUR), and the Democratic Socialists (Partido Socialista Democrático—PSD).

The elections of 1970, 1974, and 1978, which with only one exception were contested solely by military candidates, represented contests between military factions and their civilian allies, sometimes including members of progressive parties like the Christian Democrats and others (Handy: 166–180). The 1970 election was rife with fraudulent procedures, including buying votes; issuing false identification documents; social pressure, especially on the large haciendas; ballot recounting and re-marking; and preelection fraud centering on illegal registration and harassment of opposition candidates (Thesing: 20–22).[4]

In 1974, General Kjell Laugerud García was imposed as president in a fraudulent election generally thought to have been won by the Christian Democratic candidate, General Efraín Ríos Montt. After that election Ríos Montt became Guatemala's ambassador to Spain.[5] One DCG leader admitted that "in Guatemala, it is useless to think of governing, except as the result of a political decision by the Army" (Black: 31).[6]

The 1978 election was subject to similar sorts of manipulation. As the returns were televised on election day, General Lucas García appeared to be finishing third of the three major candidates, with the winner the former dictator General Peralta Azurdia, whose candidacy was supported by the MLN party. The televised vote count was interrupted, and after several days of meetings it was announced that Lucas García had been certified

as the winner (Aguilera Peralta 1978). The MLN party "won" the largest
bloc of seats in the Congress, however.

The Crisis of the 1980s

It is difficult to overstate the severity of the crisis facing Guatemala in the
early 1980s. As the 1970s came to a close, economic growth slowed.
Squeezed by international financial and investment pressures and by petro-
leum prices, beset by declining commodity prices for its exports, and bur-
dened by the costs of waging war on its own citizens, Guatemala faced a
severe economic crisis. Warfare had erupted in rural areas by 1980, largely
as a reaction to the military's violence after the 1976 earthquake. Tourism,
a major source of foreign exchange, declined precipitously after 1979
because of the political violence.

In the late 1970s, the Army found itself competing not only with the
bulk of the population that was living in economic and social misery but
also with other sectors of the economic elite and the civilian middle
class. The cleavages became especially contentious by 1980 because of
the combination of a prolonged economic crisis and the drying up of foreign sources of capital, plus the fact that many Army officers had
become major economic players themselves during the 1970s (see Chapter 4).

Rural Insurgency

By 1980 or 1981, the military's campaign of violence in the Mayan highlands had produced some ironic repercussions. In its rural operations the
Army justified its acts as a campaign against a communist insurgency
inspired by Soviets and/or Cubans. In fact, the guerrillas were few in number when the wave of repression began around 1976. The guerrilla activity
that had emerged in 1975—led by some of the survivors of the movement
in the 1960s—was at first confined to Indian highland areas of northern
El Quiché Department, notably in the Ixcán and Ixil regions.

Military repression of reformist efforts and community organization,
however, led to widespread mobilization: to protect themselves from the
landowners and the military, the Mayan communities began to organize
for self-defense. One result of government violence in Indian regions,
therefore, was the politicization of indigenous communities, which often
led to their incorporation into the armed insurgency. Victimized by the military and lacking alternatives for economic self-improvement, Indians increasingly turned to armed opposition, swelling the ranks of the guerrilla movement. This process almost always occurred *after* government repression and

attempts to eliminate successful programs of communal activism, not before. In this sense, the Army's campaign was a cause of the insurgency, not a response to it; the insurgents were recruited because of military repression, not by ideological conviction. On the whole, native resistance was a creature of state repression, not its cause (Concerned Guatemala Scholars: 47–54).[7]

Three important insurgency groups emerged at this time. The largest, the Guerrilla Army of the Poor (Ejército Guerrillero de los Pobres—EGP), had formed in 1972, and by 1975 it began to attract peasant Indian support in the Ixcán region (Payeras; and Black: 72–78). By 1980, the EGP was operating in several departments and was able to field fighting units composed of significant numbers of Indians. The Organization of People in Arms (Organización del Pueblo en Armas—ORPA) first appeared publicly in the late 1970s, after it had already become a major factor in the region around Lake Atitlán as well as in other areas. The third major group in the early 1980s was a regeneration of one of the 1960s' groups, the Rebel Armed Forces (Fuerzas Armadas Rebeldes—FAR), which for a time was allied with a faction of the Guatemalan Communist Party (Partido Guatemalteco del Trabajo—PGT). Each of these groups blended some form of Marxist analysis with demands for the end of discrimination based on race. Each claimed to support democratic political structures and pledged to respect religious preferences.

In the early 1980s, guerrilla units were strong in the northwest and west, and on the plantation lands of the southern coast. The EGP and ORPA guerrilla units were largely composed of Indians. Nearly all the combatants had originally been mobilized into political action during the 1975–1980 period as members of the popular organizations (Black: 102–107). In 1982, these guerrilla organizations proclaimed their unity in a statement issued under the banner of a new coordinating group, the National Guatemalan Revolutionary Unity (Unidad Revolucionaria Nacional Guatemalteca—URNG).[8] Before the escalation of the military's counterinsurgency campaign around 1980 and 1981, the insurgency presented a serious threat to the Guatemalan state.

Urban Confrontation

In the cities a new generation of political leaders had matured by the mid-1970s, and moderately reformist political parties began to organize. From 1976 to 1980 marked growth occurred in several political movements. Besides the labor unions two major political parties, both representing center-left perspectives, began to organize in earnest. The Democratic Socialist Party and the United Front of the Revolution each sought reforms that reflected programs begun during the 1945–1954 Decade of Spring.

During the Laugerud administration, both parties worked to gain legal status, but they achieved this only after General Lucas's election in 1978.

The relatively peaceful interlude during the Laugerud administration revealed the possibilities, even if limited, for democratic political participation. When elite policies of violence and repression were relaxed, popular organization was forthcoming. Unfortunately, their resurgence was not enduring. Even during the Laugerud administration, and certainly with the beginning of the Lucas García regime in 1978, Guatemala again returned to the darkness of systematic repression, as an armed, hostile minority imposed its will on the nation.

A wave of urban and rural violence reached fever pitch during the Lucas García administration, with violence directed at three sets of individuals.[9] The first two included national political figures and leaders of intermediate organizations, such as labor, student, and peasant groups. Although both sets were selectively targeted, the second experienced an expanded scope and scale of violence. In addition, violence was directed at the rural populace generally, as in village massacres. Each of these types of violence is examined below.[10]

In urban areas violence against political party and labor union leaders increased dramatically after the fraudulent election of General Romeo Lucas García in 1978. Guatemala's two centrist-reformist political parties, the PSD and the FUR, were crushed following the 1979 assassinations of their leaders, former Foreign Minister Alberto Fuentes Mohr and former Guatemala City Mayor Manuel Colom Argueta, respectively. The grassroots leadership of the center-right Christian Democrats was decimated: 150 murders of party organizers in 1980–1981 silenced all but a handful of party activists.[11]

Perhaps because of its visibility and central role in urging social change and economic reform, organized labor suffered greatly from political violence during this period. For example, 110 "regional and national trade union leaders" and 311 peasant leaders were assassinated in 1980 alone (WRH, 2/24/81: 1). Two specific incidents illustrate the dynamics of state terrorism during this time.

The 1980 May Day labor parade was conducted peacefully, amidst antigovernment chants and the spraying of graffiti slogans on walls along the parade route (*Guatemala News* 5/9/80: 7). Moreover, the parade was legal: although the government had delayed the permit procedures, labor groups were able to secure them. Military security was high, especially in the vicinity of the National Palace, the parade's final destination. In spite of the public security presence—or perhaps because of it—thirty-one deaths were reported in connection with the parade, and almost all the victims were students or workers, including one man killed by armed men in civilian clothes, at a rally in the park facing the Palace.[12]

The second and similar incident illustrates more clearly the role of public security forces in political violence. In June 1980, some sixty armed "unknowns" led an assault on the national headquarters of a legal, registered labor federation, the National Confederation of Workers (Confederación Nacional de Trabajadores—CNT), located on a main avenue in downtown Guatemala City near the National Palace. The invaders blocked the avenue, redirected traffic, and then used a vehicle to break in the building's door, all of this during daylight hours. Twenty-seven union leaders, assembled for a meeting in the building, disappeared in this mass kidnapping.[13]

In rural areas the Army and landowners reacted even more violently.[14] After the 1976 earthquake landowners clearly began to view organized popular groups as threats to their domain. The structure of repression in rural Guatemala passed from local landlords to the direct presence of the military at about the time of the 1976 earthquake. At that time, using "social confusion" and the need for law and order during reconstruction efforts as pretexts, the military began to move forcefully into areas of rural conflict, regions in which landlords had not been able to root out development programs or in which resistance to landlords could not be eliminated.

Beginning then, and with increasing fury after 1978, the Guatemalan Army unleashed a wave of violence directed at popular groups of all types. Repression levels grew dramatically, especially in the Indian highlands of western Guatemala and in the plantation areas of the southern coast, culminating in the massive counterinsurgency program of the early 1980s. Thousands of rural poor were victims. In the years between 1975 and 1985, violence far exceeded the repression campaigns after 1954 and during Méndez Montenegro's term in the late 1960s.

The State Crisis

By 1980, repression had reached unprecedented levels in urban areas, both statistically and in terms of a generalized climate of terror. Few reformists were participating openly in Guatemalan politics. Major parties that might have been considered progressive, moderate, or centrist suffered crucial setbacks during the first years of General Lucas García's presidency. In addition to the assassinations of primary leaders such as Fuentes Mohr of the PSD and Colom Argueta of the FUR, the Christian Democratic Party (DCG) lost dozens of its local and national leaders during this period. Labor, professional, and educational groups were brutally repressed.[15] Guatemala was becoming an international pariah because of its terrible human rights record.

Besides its repressive behavior, the Lucas García administration (1978–1982) was corrupt and proved unable to sustain the levels of economic growth and political stability that the nation needed. Although it shared those characteristics with earlier regimes—Ydígoras had been corrupt and economically ineffectual and Arana had certainly been repressive—President Lucas took Guatemala to new extremes in state violence, including not only the assassinations noted but also widespread massacres of Indian villages suspected of supporting the armed insurgency.

Under Lucas García, the state faced a triple crisis. In addition to the economic crisis, there was one of legitimacy at the international level. Even the promilitary Reagan administration was finding it difficult to provide military aid to the Lucas García group, in large part because of the extreme human rights violations and the reactions to these in the U.S., including Congress. Third, an internal political crisis had developed as a result of the growing guerrilla insurgency, which was a significant military threat by 1981. In society at large, increasing levels of hardship for the majority meant even lower levels of legitimacy or general support for the system. Lucas's response to all symptoms of this crisis was to escalate state terrorism.[16]

The leaders of the ruling coalition from 1978–1982, General Lucas García, Jorge García Granados of the PR, and Minister of the Interior Donaldo Alvarez Ruíz of the PID, were also partners in financial deals, including major landholding in the Northern Transversal Strip, Guatemala's primary colonization area during the 1970s (Pinzón: 14). Lucas and Alvarez reportedly coordinated the government's political repression apparatus (Amnesty 1981). This melding of state—the "legitimate" use of coercive force—with personal economic ambitions exacerbated tensions.

Combined, these dynamics increased pressure from other factions of officers within the military and led to more factionalization within the elite outside of the military itself. The guerrilla insurgency caused younger military officers to become increasingly dissatisfied both with the corruption of the upper echelons and with the fact that they, the younger officers, were bearing the costs of the counterinsurgency campaign, the excuse responsible for the foreign aid the generals—and some civilians—were stealing.

Crisis and the 1982 Election

The presidential election of 1982 can only be understood in the context of this multifaceted crisis. The first phenomenon to note is that in the face of this crisis, the Lucas García group decided not to abandon the presidential palace. The governing group formed a coalition, the Democratic Popular Front (Frente Democrático Popular—FDP), consisting of the PID and the PR, the vehicles of Alvarez Ruíz and García Granados, respectively. The coalition nominated one of the clique's members, General Aníbal Guevara, a former minister of defense, to run for the presidency.

The 1982 election campaign, like many others that preceded it, gave the appearance of pluralistic competition in a multiparty system.[17] In fact, superficially, the 1982 campaign seemed even more democratic than earlier events, for only one of the four major candidates was a military officer. In addition to General Guevara, the other candidates were Alejandro Maldonado, of the United National Opposition (Unidad Nacional Opositora—UNO), Mario Sandoval Alarcón, of the MLN, and Gustavo Anzueto Vielman, of the National Authentic Center (Central Auténtico Nacional—CAN).

The MLN was a party of the extreme right, and while formally in the opposition, it was part of the dominant coalition of political forces, at least ideologically. The party had a large bloc of seats in the Congress and several of its members served on government committees and commissions. In addition, probably not by coincidence, its leadership was relatively free from constant assassination attempts. For 1982, the MLN nominated its perennial leader, Mario Sandoval Alarcón.

The CAN, the party of General Carlos Arana Osorio, a former president, nominated a civilian candidate, Gustavo Anzueto Vielman. CAN had allied itself with the official government coalition in the 1978 national elections and had been rewarded with one of the better "perks" in Guatemala: control of the highway department. This control helped CAN do well in the local-level elections of 1980, and having this base of public support was part of the rationale for offering its own candidate in 1982. A separate candidacy for the CAN suggested political division in the military but did not indicate serious ideological opposition.

The "ideological opposition" in the 1982 campaign came from a coalition of several groups. The UNO's candidate was Alejandro Maldonado of the National Renovation Party (Partido de Renovacón Nacional—PNR). Like the CAN, the PNR had supported the government's coalition in 1978. Maldonado, although perhaps genuinely offended at the excesses of the Lucas administration, had represented Guatemala internationally during earlier periods of repression and therefore could hardly be seen as an ideological opponent of the elite. His party, in fact, was originally a "moderate" offshoot of the extreme right-wing MLN.

The Christian Democrats were in an awkward position before the 1982 election. On the one hand, the party had a "reformist" agenda, advocated certain social reforms, and persistently attacked the government's role in political violence. But on the other, dissent was a costly path to follow. The DCG has long been a victim of government and right-wing violence, and its participation in electoral events has been related to its rate of victimization. For example, after the party's success in the 1980 municipal elections, especially in rural Indian areas in which the military government had relatively less support, dozens of its local-level leaders were killed.[18]

In short, the DCG found itself on the horns of a dilemma. By participating in the election campaign, the party ran the risk of political assassination as dissidents. Not participating, however, would have been seen as
an attempt to de-legitimize the government, which would produce even
greater risks, especially for local-level party leaders. The party chose to
participate and joined the UNO coalition, delivering major voter support.
Opponents of the regime were critical. Christian Democrats were accused
of being an important source of support for the regime, since their participation within the system would significantly legitimize the regime while
generating few reforms (Solórzano Martínez 1980: 32–33).

Other opposition parties played minor roles. The FUR and the PSD
were parties that favored reforms, such as honest elections in a violence-
free atmosphere, and freedom for labor to organize. FUR was a legal, registered entity and was therefore guaranteed certain civil rights, but the
party had paid a high price for its participation: besides the assassinations
discussed earlier, Francisco Villagrán Kramer, vice-president of Guatemala and a former FUR member, had been forced to resign and go into
exile in 1980, after criticizing the military and Guatemala's human rights
record. The PSD was technically a party "in formation," meaning the government had not yet ruled on the PSD's request for legal recognition as a
party. The PSD also had been severely repressed, with its leaders killed or
in exile. Neither party was able to participate openly in the 1982 election
because of the violent atmosphere, but both issued frequent denunciations
at home and abroad.

By election time, nearly a dozen parties had assumed a direct role,
either nominating a candidate or joining a coalition to support one of the
major candidates. Prospects for the centrist or prochange parties were very
dim, however, for their leadership resources had been decimated during
the Lucas García administration and their participation proscribed by violence. The campaign had a distinct right-wing flavor, in spite of the presence of the Christian Democrats, the least rightist of the major parties

None of these opposition groups, taken individually, presented a particularly serious obstacle to the government. Some were ideologically
aligned, others had downplayed their policy agendas in favor of pragmatic
considerations, still others had been successfully repressed. Taken
together, however, the opposition was a double-edged sword for the ruling
faction. The appearance of pluralism was important for regime legitimacy,
but the prospect of losing an election was anathema to the ruling clique's
agenda of personal ambitions.

It was difficult to determine the real electoral power of the major parties. In a straw poll of several thousand voters, conducted before the election and published in the Guatemalan press, Alejandro Maldonado, the
UNO candidate, won almost ten thousand votes, compared to eight thousand plus for Anzueto Vielman of the CAN. More dramatic, the "official"

candidate, General Guevara, and the extreme right-wing candidate of the MLN, Mario Sandoval Alarcón, trailed far behind. Regardless of the precise accuracy of the straw poll, these figures showed that the ruling coalition would have fared relatively poorly in a free, honest election. Clearly, signs of defeat were in the air for the government.

In the end corruption won out. Given the crisis situation and the personal corruption of the Lucas group, the official election results were not surprising: the Supreme Electoral Tribunal (Tribunal Supremo Electoral—TSE) declared General Guevara the winner. The tabulation was generally considered fraudulent. The losing parties protested the event, and Guatemala witnessed the unusual spectacle of a joint protest march by parties as disparate as the extreme right-wing MLN and the moderates and progressives of the DCG.

Continuing economic decline, the real threat of the insurgency, and widespread disgust over human rights abuses all exacerbated social tensions, which were not resolved by a fraudulent election, a tactic that had been successful since at least 1956. Public opposition within Guatemala, combined with international criticism of the election's procedural aspects, quickly made the situation untenable for the military as a whole. The specter of a military victory by the guerrilla insurgency added fuel to the escalating conflagration within the political system.

By March 1982, then, the Guatemalan political system was facing its most serious crisis ever. Open dissension existed even within the military. Internationally, the Reagan State Department had referred to the government as "a bunch of thugs." Guatemala was a pariah nation. President Lucas García had been intransigent in the face of most international pressures, perhaps following the long tradition of nationalism in the Army, but the economic crisis and the insurgency led other factions to fear for the system's survival. Lucas García's manipulation of the 1982 election was merely the final straw and did nothing to improve the situation. Indeed, it accelerated the deterioration of the process: having adopted a strategy of repression and lacking the co-opting capacity of a structure such as the Mexican Revolutionary Institutional Party (PRI) to pay off dissidents, General Lucas was unable to sustain the fraud.

Just two weeks after the 1982 election, on March 23, a military coup led by a coalition of young military officers and some elements of the MLN party seized power, installing retired General Efraín Ríos Montt at the head of a three-person junta.

Conclusion

Guatemala's recent history includes several examples of elections and of vigorous party activity. Some of these elections were fraudulent, some were relatively honest in a narrow procedural sense, including the 1966 election of Méndez Montenegro.[19] Behind these indicators of democracy—elections, a multiparty system, and constitutional clauses guaranteeing democratic procedures—the reality was more complex. The fraud that has been characteristic of most presidential elections in recent Guatemalan history is only one element of the picture. Even during the reformist civilian administration of Méndez Montenegro, the consistent dynamic was growth of the military officer corps' political and economic power relative to other organized sectors of society.

Moreover, although political parties functioned throughout the period, their role was circumscribed in important ways. First, elections themselves were often primarily struggles among elite factions, including military officers at times, rendering the popular mobilization role of parties relatively useless. When opposition parties acted as if they were *not* mere trappings of a fraudulent democracy, by intimating that elections be mechanisms of popular sovereignty over the public-policy process, for example, dominant groups usually took steps beyond electoral fraud, including state violence, to ensure their position in society. Political violence has been an inevitable part of an electoral system designed primarily to legitimate a nondemocratic society while helping elites resolve conflicts within their own sectors of society.

Except in the sense of formal-legal requirements, then, most of Guatemala's elections up to 1982 did not move the polity toward the democratic ideal. The claim is easy to sustain when there is obvious fraud and intimidation of voter; few objective observers would see much democracy, no matter how they were to define the term, in such circumstances. But the quality of democracy is harder to assess when formal-legal standards are met, arguably the case in the 1966 election, for example. In this case, the weight of procedural honesty on election day itself is outweighed by the context. Concerning the Decade of Spring described earlier, observers label Juan José Arévalo's term in office as "democratic" not because of an honest election ipso facto, but because of the political and social reforms that took place after the election. The same standards applied to the Méndez administration after 1966, however, show democracy wanting.

In 1982, by drawing as much political power to its inner circle as possible, the ruling clique not only had weakened the state but had eroded whatever democratic possibilities might have been available to political actors. From the perspective of political participation, elections in this period were clearly antidemocratic events. These cases are especially important in view of the 1985 election, which was scrupulously honest in the eyes of most international observers (see Chapter 4).

The military coup of March 1982, symbolizes the nadir in the recent development of the Guatemalan state. Without legitimacy, internationally and domestically, the government could only rely on coercion to shore up its corrupt regime. But the guerrillas of the URNG had demonopolized armed power in the country. With the economy in great trouble and the very structure of the state threatened, the ruling clique led by General Lucas García nevertheless sought to use the mechanisms of electoral fraud to remain in power, further weakening the nation.

After the coup the Army's agenda was complex, encompassing military action as well as renewed economic involvement, but much of the public persona of the military centered on the "tutelary" role of the armed forces, whose stated mission was to create genuine democracy. The tutelary, prodemocracy role played by the Army is the principal topic of Chapter 4.

Notes

1. For an analysis of the 1985 Constitution, see Linares Morales.
2. In 1966, one study's summary said: "Guatemalan elections are characterized by varying degrees of fraud and violence" (ICOPS: 12).
3. The 1965 Constitution

laid the groundwork for a "limited democracy" with closely circumscribed political party activity and an institutionalized ritual of elections. Any threatening opposition outside an Army-decreed spectrum was constitutionally banned. . . . [It] restricted such "exotic ideologies" as social democracy and Christian Democracy (Black: 21).

4. Thesing's study revealed that some 60,000 false documents were involved in the presidential election of 1970, which equals almost 10 percent of the actual votes deposited.
5. Rumor, always a critical part of day-to-day politics in Guatemala, has it that the general was given a handsome cash settlement in exchange for his quiet retreat from the domestic scene. One still hears stories of his treachery to the parties that supported him in the 1974 election.
6. The Christian Democratic leader, Daniel Barillas, was assassinated in 1989.
7. A typical reaction:

Initially, many people [in San Felipe] simply wanted to remain uninvolved. The actions of the government, however, persuaded them that this is no longer possible. People . . . now recognize the extreme need for change. This, combined with their increasingly desperate economic conditions, makes them feel that the guerrillas may offer some hope. Where else are they to turn? Government bombs dropping on Indian homes, or Indian families set on fire by Guatemalan soldiers, create quick converts to the guerrillas' cause (quoted in Davis and Hodson: 12).

8. The "Unity Statement," which calls for an end to the "economic and political domination of the repressive wealthy, both national and foreign, who rule

Guatemala," can be found in Black: 183–185; and in URNG: *Guatemala: The People United.*

9. This typology is based on the analysis of attorney Frank R. LaRue, a Guatemalan labor lawyer and representative of the United Representation of the Guatemalan Opposition (Representación Unida de la Oposición Guatemalteca—RUOG).

10. A complete chronology of Guatemala's political violence is not within the scope of this study. Reports and statistics on political violence are published in a variety of sources, including publications of Ceri-Gua and Agen-SIAG, and newsletters from such groups as the Washington office on Latin America, the Council on Hemispheric Affairs, Amnesty International, NISGUA (The Network in Solidarity with Guatemala), the Guatemalan Church in Exile (IGE), Americas Watch, and others. For regular periodical chronologies of political violence in the 1960s up to the late 1970s, see the magazine *Panorama Político* (primera época), published until its editor, Ricardo Galindo, disappeared in 1980. For an overview of the human rights situation in the early 1980s, see Karp; and Trudeau 1982 and 1983. For fairly detailed chronologies of violence in the period from 1976 through about 1985, see Davis and Hodson: 47–52; and Benton et al. See Black for a detailed study of this period up to about 1983. See Simon for a detailed analysis of more recent political violence and its aftermath, and see WOLA 1988, 1989a, and 1989b for more up-to-date examinations. Information in the following pages relating to political violence is compiled from these and other sources. Information specific to 1980 is compiled from similar sources, plus the author's eyewitness experiences and interviews.

11. Among prominent political party exiles was Francisco Villagrán Kramer, a reformist civilian who had been elected vice-president of Guatemala in 1978. Villagrán resigned his position in 1980, after he had dissented publicly from a policy decision to construct a highway system clearly designed to benefit Army generals at taxpayer expense. He resigned while he was in Washington, not in Guatemala.

12. One report on the parade describes violence that was typical at this time:

> At least nine members of the newly-formed union at the Ray-O-Vac battery plant were also kidnapped—some right out of the ranks of the parade, and others on their way home after the march. Three of the youths were found with signs of torture on their bodies, all shot to death (*Guatemala News* 5/9/80: 7).

13. No less than three separate branches of the government's security forces, staffed by at least several hundred police, detectives, and military personnel, had headquarters within four blocks of the CNT headquarters. One of the three, the headquarters of Comando Six, the National Police nonuniformed detectives and narcotics divisions, was almost directly across the street from the scene of the events. Several hundred soldiers were barracked behind the National Palace, about two blocks away. The furthest of these three headquarters, a major police station, was no more than four or five minutes' walking distance from the scene of the crime. Although the mass kidnapping took about twenty minutes to execute, no public security force responded to appeals for assistance. None of the twenty-seven persons kidnapped has ever reappeared. Amnesty International (1981: 12) provides another description of this mass kidnapping, including personal data on one of the victims.

14. For detailed summaries and analyses of this violent reaction by the government and elites, see Davis and Hodson; for details from the perspective of the Indian communities themselves, see Rarihokwats; and Frank and Wheaton: 69–82, 92. For a systematic analysis of earlier political violence, especially in rural Guatemala, see Aguilera Peralta et al. 1981. Black presents the best overall summary of the increasing militarization of rural Guatemala beginning in the early 1970s.

15. Parties of the right, although not immune, typically were affected much less seriously by this repressive violence. One exception involved Jorge Torres Ocampo, a leading member of the extreme right MLN party, who was assassinated in a hail of machine-gun fire near downtown Guatemala City in 1980, shortly after he published a booklet that criticized the military government and the United States for not doing more to eradicate poverty and injustice, which Torres Ocampo saw as the fundamental causes of rebellious insurgency in Guatemala. But generally, assassinations of right-wing politicians were much less frequent during the 1980s.

16. For a detailed look at this pattern of using violence to sow fear, see Figueroa Ibarra (1991), both of whose parents were assassinated in 1980.

17. This account of the 1982 electoral period is based on interviews and press and newsletter accounts from a variety of sources.

18. It has long been conventional wisdom about Guatemalan party politics that a price is paid for the right to dissent openly, even within the party system—witness the connection between the registration of the Democratic Socialist Party and the assassination of its leader, Fuentes Mohr, and between the registration of the FUR and the subsequent assassination of its leader, Colom Argueta. Indeed, during the 1982 campaign itself, right-wing/government terrorists at one point assaulted the DCG's party headquarters in the center of Guatemala City, in a daytime machine-gun attack (*Guatemala News* 2/20/81: 1, 7).

19. Another example is the municipal-level elections held in April 1980. Space limitations prevent a longer analysis of these elections, which were fascinating if only because of the multiplicity of party coalitions among strange bedfellows. The larger dimension, however, was the fact of the horrific violence then engulfing Guatemalan society, a dimension that clearly outweighed the relative purity of the voting process itself.

4

The Military
as Democratizers

Our goal has been to reverse the logic of the military strategist von Clausewitz, that is, in Guatemala, politics should be the continuation of war.

—Hector Gramajo

The Guatemalan political economy continued to decay in the early 1980s, and the 1982 election, which symbolized that decay, finally led to an abrupt change in political leadership. The military dictators Generals Ríos Montt and Mejía Víctores, who followed Lucas, pursued restorative measures, and the elections of 1984 and 1985 culminated in the inauguration of a civilian Christian Democratic president, Vinicio Cerezo Arévalo, in January 1986. As these elections were one part of an explicit counterinsurgency strategy, it seems appropriate to study them in the context of the development and recent activities of the Guatemalan armed forces.

Among many imaginable impediments to democracy in Guatemala, the military is conventionally singled out as a major "problem." The overwhelming physical presence of the Army, the historical record, and the cultural tradition of "Hispanic authoritarianism" all seem to imply weak democratic structures. On the other hand, apologists cite many contributions by the military: protection of national security and "law and order," suppression of subversion, and even its impact as a modernizing agency. Supporters note that the Army has provided skilled personnel in many administrative areas and has consistently provided entrepreneurial talent that has helped the state develop economically while allowing middle-class officers to prosper individually.[1]

The principal argument, though, is that the military's impact on democracy is an indirect contribution. Although the military may not be democratic in its internal values, it is a modernizing institution, perhaps the only such institution that can guarantee the development of democracy.

Moreover, in societies characterized by widespread disorder such as Guatemala, the military may be the only institution capable of restoring order. This modernized version of the Hobbesian argument suggests that the military's intervention allows democracy to flourish by creating social order. This is a key factor in the study of Guatemalan democracy, for at no time in recent decades have the armed forces been far from the presidential palace.

Whatever the initial assumptions, the military is a key institution. The concentration of political power in one small sector of society seems to be the antithesis of democracy. Indeed, liberal notions of popular sovereignty and representation demand as widespread a distribution of at least electoral power as possible. Has the tutelary activity of the Army had such a pro-democratic impact? Examining salient events from its history establishes a context to focus on the activity of the military between 1982 and 1985, during which the officer corps led two successful military coups and reestablished constitutional government. In addition, data on the 1984 national elections for a constituent assembly, and those of 1985, for president and Congress, are included.

Early Development of the Guatemalan Military

Liberal Reforms

The use of armed force to implement disruptive social and economic change and inhibit resistance to those changes is not a new dynamic in Guatemalan politics. The elite minority has consistently used violence both to enforce change and to prevent reforms aimed at reducing its privileged status. The institutional development of the military parallels many of the economic and political developments previously described.

The period of the Liberal Reforms, for example, symbolizes in one respect the triumph of export capitalism in Guatemala, but it also symbolizes the consolidation of state power over the national economy. The reforms were as much a process of reorganizing the elite as one of seizing property to increase coffee production. The growth of the military was a major part of the reform process as a necessary concomitant of increased state disruption of Indian communities on behalf of "free-market liberals" who wished to export coffee. Three primary aspects of the Liberal Reform period were redistribution of land, regulation of labor, and incorporation of foreign investors. The fourth major component was professionalization of the Guatemalan Army, which for the first time became an arm of the state rather than of individual landowners or political groups.

The disruptive changes of the Liberal Reforms led to political tensions, and increased poverty of the landless peasants, most of whom became part of a forced-labor system, led to unrest. Indian resistance was widespread and constant, but the symbiotic linkages between economic elites and working masses were structural, not personal, and hence very stratified.[2] As a result, repression of dissidents was economically beneficial in the short run. Numerous coercive tactics—dissolution of villages, forced relocation of groups, seizure of land, and systematic violence— were effective in crushing and then discouraging peasant revolts. For example, the newly professionalized Army, now loyal to the national government rather than to regional *caudillos,* repressed a major rebellion in the municipality of Momostenango (Department of El Quiché) in 1875 (Handy: 69–71).

In spite of short-run successes in suppressing resistance, a common pattern in Guatemalan history, the Liberal Reforms revealed the long-term need for a major military organization. Exacerbating oppressive conditions while leaving the poor no political recourse resulted in the long run in social movements that could not be controlled by individual landowners. Although the Army went through different stages of development after the 1870s, its main function remained relatively consistent from the colonial period through 1944: to regulate society so that labor and capital resources would remain primarily available to the powerful agricultural elites. As the political economy became more centrally coordinated, the military became a national, professional institution. As with other aspects of the Liberal Reforms, the legacy of these changes survives as a major institutional obstacle to democracy in the 1990s.

The October Revolution: 1944

The military clearly dominated during the Ubico period before 1944, as a personalist arm of the dictator himself. After the October Revolution, Juan José Arévalo's presidency had profound implications for the armed forces. Nationalistic pride, competition with entrenched military leaders from the earlier Ubico period, and the opportunity to benefit from a rejuvenated economy led to solid military support for the reformist movement among much of the officer corps: the Army participated actively in developing the new political institutions.

Among its early reforms, the new civilian government in 1945 took steps to "rationalize," in the Weberian sense, the relationships between the military and civilian regimes. The goal of civilian reformers was to distance the military from active interference in civil political matters, especially the politics of presidential selection. Their aim was to avoid more dictators like Ubico, who perpetuated themselves in office through control of the Army. To achieve this separation, the civilian government paid a price: the autonomy of the Army as an internally self-governing institution.

As part of the arrangements after 1945, the Army high command selected its own chief of staff from a list of three nominees submitted by the president. Moreover, only the Congress, not the president, could remove the chief of staff, although the president continued constitutionally to be commander-in-chief of the armed forces. Finally, and ultimately most important, the Army was given authority to act as the interpreter of national values and to evaluate other political actors' conformity to these values (Cruz Salazar: 11). The Army ostensibly exchanged an active day-to-day role in politics and public administration for a role as final arbiter of national politics. In effect, the Army was given an independent existence, built into the new constitution.[3]

Economic modernization and expansion in urban areas provided new opportunities for officers, a process that was functionally similar to the "opening" of rural Guatemala during the Liberal Reforms of the previous century. While some officers profited from new access to both economic wealth and political control of the state, others became increasingly disgruntled allies of the traditional oligarchy, which had been weakened by the government's relative de-emphasis of exports in its model of economic growth.

The rivalry between the two military members of the 1944 junta, Colonels Jacobo Arbenz and Francisco Arana, led each to build separate power bases. On the one hand, factional divisions in the Army helped President Arévalo survive the many attempted *golpes* during his administration. But the same divisions meant a continuing major role for the military in social and political life (Handy: 111–113). Civilian ascendancy in presidential politics was short-lived: the two colonels became the major candidates in the early stages of the next presidential campaign. Colonel Arana's assassination in 1949 deepened the factional differences within the Army and exacerbated tendencies toward polarization in the political system.

After 1950, the quickened pace of social and economic reform under Jacobo Arbenz aroused stiff resistance from vested interests. During this period the military was divided among several disparate but not necessarily mutually exclusive tendencies: (1) opposition to reforms that seemed to threaten the dominance of the oligarchy; (2) reformism of the Arbenz faction; (3) nationalism, arising in the face of increasing pressure from the United States; (4) anticommunism; and (5) putschist impulses from disgruntled officers removed from their traditional and customary access to wealth and power (Weaver: 64; Handy: 272–273). It was this fifth tendency, wrapped in the ideology of the fourth, that the United States used as the basis for the 1954 counterrevolutionary invasion led by Carlos Castillo Armas. Factionalism helped undermine Guatemala's democratic experiment by contributing to the success of the 1954 counterrevolution.

Developments After 1954

When the Castillo Armas invasion triumphed, the Army was rife with division, an effect of the factional tendencies described above. Yet this was precisely the moment when the elite needed a strong military to move Guatemala back to the political status quo ante. As a result of the institutional weakness of the military, coercion became less centralized; the counterrevolution saw the reemergence of private, paramilitary organizations. Moreover, the middle classes and urban groups had made major strides in political and economic development before 1954, contributing to a more open and competitive system. In short, the aftermath of the overthrow of President Arbenz was political instability, marked by elite factions seeking to reorient the economy and consolidate their own position in the new order. Not immune to these pressures, the military clearly declined in status relative to its position before 1944.

With the resurgence of the export-driven, state-assisted model of "growth without reform" after 1954, popular resistance became an increasingly common irritant to economic elites, leading to opportunities to renew the central role of the armed forces. After 1954 and especially after 1960, in response to these dynamics the military underwent major changes in three areas: institutional unity and cohesion, military efficiency, and the economy, where it emerged as a principal economic and political actor. Foreign military assistance was a major ingredient in all three of these.

The United States had provided military assistance to Guatemala since 1954, but after the attempted coup of 1960, aid increased dramatically. By 1961, the Alliance for Progress, designed to encourage social reform while simultaneously providing counterinsurgency assistance to prevent "another Cuba," offered increased military assistance to Guatemala. A major civic action program was begun there, the first such program in Latin America (Sharckman: 194).[4] But disunity and corruption in the Army rendered U.S. military assistance relatively ineffective. The more "professional" or "modern" sectors of the armed forces, led by Colonel Enrique Peralta Azurdia, harbored a general feeling of disgust for corruption in government and in particular within the Army. Peralta seized power in a coup in 1963.

Although the catalyst for the coup that ousted President Ydígoras may well have been the imminent return to Guatemala of former President Arévalo,[5] the stated goals of the coup leaders included, not surprisingly, the suppression of communism and the prevention of civil war (Black: 20). But from the Army's perspective, the coup was primarily an attempt to rescue the military institution from its own decay and dissension and to resolve factional problems among the elite. While head of state, Colonel Peralta Azurdia sought to unify the military by stressing administrative reforms. This coincided with the official U.S. position at the time, which was to make militaries more professional and hence less likely to become involved in politics (Sereseres: 199). The bulk of U.S. military assistance before 1965 was oriented toward these technical and administrative goals (Sereseres: 238–239). Although his administrative reforms made him acceptable to the U.S., Peralta Azurdia did not pursue the counterinsurgency campaign against guerrillas in eastern Guatemala with much enthusiasm (Black: 20–22, 69).

Given the recent success of the Cuban Revolution in 1959 and the more recent failure of the Bay of Pigs invasion of Cuba in 1961, the United States had international security goals along with its desire to professionalize the Guatemalan armed forces. Peralta's conservative approach toward the guerrillas did not meet with U.S. approval. Military assistance for counterinsurgency training had increased over the pre-1959 levels, perhaps because of the 1963 coup, but major military aid did not flow to Guatemala until about 1965, when plans for a new constitution and election of a civilian government had been put into effect (Sharckman: 195–196). These included electing a civilian president who would have little control either over the military or over a planned major counterinsurgency effort aimed at guerrillas in eastern Guatemala, the effort Peralta had pursued without enthusiasm.

President Julio César Méndez Montenegro, elected in 1966, indeed had very little control over the armed forces. After Colonel Carlos Arana Osorio was placed in charge of the counterinsurgency program in 1966, U.S. military assistance reached its highest levels (Sharckman: 194–195). At the same time, the United States financed and supervised the "modernization" of Guatemala's police, most branches of which were directed by the military (WOLA 1983: 9).[6] Both the United States and the Guatemalan officer corps were pleased with the outcomes:

> With one simple tool, a counterinsurgency campaign, the civilian government was able to maintain its precarious political position for the entire four year term by providing the military institution with a professional task and by securing outside resources that would be used to maintain the loyalty of the two most important supporters of the Méndez regime (Sereseres: 71).

In sum, the net effect of military modernization, of increased professionalism, and of copious U.S. assistance, was institutional unity and military efficiency. Greatly helped by U.S. assistance, "the Army was fast becoming . . . the only credible political force in the country" (Black: 23). After having degenerated into factionalism and disarray in the years after the 1954 CIA coup, the military recovered its unity and efficiency after 1962, in the process becoming a formidable fighting force, able and willing to wage war on its own people in the name of national security. It quickly became clear that the Army viewed political opponents with democratic or reformist tendencies as threats to its own security. The military's aggressive expansionism had profound consequences for Guatemala's political economy in the next decades.

The Military and the Political Economy

The modern political ascendancy of the military had begun as early as 1950, during the administration of Colonel Jacobo Arbenz. But control over the political system became institutionalized only after the 1963 Peralta coup. By 1965, the military had generated a new constitution and overseen elections. Between the 1963 coup and the 1970 election, the Guatemalan military officer corps benefited as much as any single institution in Guatemala from the economic growth of the 1960s, as officers gained access to resources from the Alliance for Progress and became entrepreneurs. The Army became a major supporter and beneficiary of economic growth, but it also became an impediment to the development of democratic institutions. The interplay between this rejuvenated military force and continuing pressures for social change and political reform produced a decade of oscillating waves of violence and relative tranquility.

During the 1960s, the Army consolidated its political position in the Guatemalan spectrum, and during Colonel Carlos Arana's presidency, after 1970, the military consolidated its position economically. Although corruption had always been rife in the Army, in the early 1970s military officers became business entrepreneurs as well. Military policy melded the state with the economic interests of individual military officers, using the threat and application of force to acquire wealth. As the military was taking advantage of U.S. military assistance to turn itself into a formidable internal security force, it was also using its political control of the government and of U.S. economic aid to become an economic elite. As long as economic growth continued, no significant opposition by civilian economic elites to the military's encroachment arose, nor any significant internal factional strife within the Army itself (Black: 26–27).

In spite of occasional reverses, the development of the military reveals fairly steady, unilinear movement: the armed forces have grown more and more powerful as a political organization over the decades. The continuity in the process by which the Army has aggrandized its position since the 1944 middle-class October Revolution is much more apparent than the occasional backsliding. Very little in recent history suggests that the military had relinquished any significant political power by 1980. On the contrary, it had consolidated itself economically, first by protecting the wealth of the oligarchy, then by taking advantage of economic growth to become an economic elite itself, both rural and urban, and finally by taking steps to weaken the social and political power of the nonmilitary economic elites.

Making Guatemala Safe for Democracy—Part I

The period between 1979 and 1982 revealed the development of a major crisis for the Guatemalan state. Throughout this period one major obstacle to the success of the Army's counterinsurgency campaign was the venality of the military faction in power under General Romeo Lucas García. This was resolved by the military coup that installed retired General Efraín Ríos Montt.

The messianic Ríos Montt had been the candidate of the Christian Democrats in 1974.[7] The coup shifted power within the military and, as a result, produced change in the military's political strategy. The foreign assistance needed to sustain the national economy, and the military's economic position within it, could be obtained only if lip service, at least, were paid to international pressures on protecting human rights, ending corruption in government, and fashioning a transition to democracy by holding honest elections. The new junta immediately pledged to guarantee all three. After the coup became a fait accompli, all the major political parties, who of course had resented the fraud in the 1982 election, endorsed the change in political leadership.

Ríos Montt was installed as chief of a three-person junta but soon became sole head of state. Power rested with an Army faction representing younger officers opposed to military and civilian corruption, even though generally antidemocratic. This group grudgingly recognized the need for formal democracy, if only to tranquilize international and domestic opponents of the regime. Ríos portrayed himself and the Army variously as avenging angels, as concerned parents who, perhaps reluctantly, felt compelled to discipline and punish their children, or as winners in the struggle against communism. Messianism was characteristic not merely in the conjoining of Christian morality with acknowledged mass violence, but even in requests, for example, that bureaucrats openly pledge to end corruption and to wear buttons confirming their pledge.

The state terrorism that had prevailed during the Lucas García regime soon declined in Guatemala City and other urban areas, a welcome improvement. But Ríos Montt established "tribunals of special jurisdiction," which held secret, summary military trials. Executions of suspected "enemies" continued. Repression in rural areas rose to a fever pitch, including massacres of whole villages. Popular organizations were practically eliminated. Under the Army's *fusiles y frijoles* (guns and beans) campaign, its counterinsurgency plan expanded from concentrating on the military campaign against the insurgency to establishing a series of controls over the rural civilian population.[8] Indians were removed by force from some villages, and others were reorganized into "development poles" similar to the "strategic hamlets" program in Vietnam, where the military provided food in exchange for quiescence. The Indians were virtually imprisoned, their movements carefully restricted, and independent organization forbidden. During this period some four hundred villages were destroyed, an estimated half-million people were forced to live in development poles, and all males in the highland conflict zones were conscripted into civil defense patrols (Krueger and Enge: vi–vii).[9]

As this scenario of repression was escalating, the formal political system was changing as well. To Ríos Montt, preparing Guatemala for new elections meant purging the system. The government announced several new conditions that effectively reduced the formal level of democratic participation in the system. The changes quickly alienated much of the political party spectrum. The honeymoon between political parties and new military rulers ended quickly, because of electoral politics, not rural repression.

First, Ríos Montt's new law of political parties sought to weaken the established political parties, using the half-true rationale that the party system had to be opened up to all political persuasions. All parties were officially disbanded. Any group could form a new political party by meeting new organizational and signature provisions, according to a set timetable. A group could become registered as a "party in formation" or as a "civic committee," with only five hundred signatures. The new provisions reduced the number of signatures needed for final legalization from fifty thousand to four thousand. The resulting proliferation of registered groups came as no surprise, much to the chagrin of the established parties (see Table 4.1). The Army portrayed its party reorganization as a return to democracy, even as it weakened organized sectors that could mobilize public opinion within the electoral process.

Second, the new election calendar quickly became a bone of contention, for most newer groups wanted to postpone elections in order to establish themselves. The established parties, especially the well-organized MLN, wanted elections as quickly as possible, to capitalize on their momentum after the failed electoral fraud of March 1982, and their successful participation in the Ríos coup. The Christian Democrats again found themselves torn between two rationales, as they had been in the 1982 election campaign. The party needed time to rebuild after the repression of the previous few years but at the same time feared the proliferation of parties.

A "law of spectrum location" had been helping the DCG before this period. With no true leftist organizations surviving within the party system during the Lucas García regime, the DCG had found it easy to be moderate

Table 4.1   Registered Party Committees, 1984 Election

	P?	4%?		Party Committee
1	N		ACR	Revolutionary Civic Action
2	Y	N	AD	Democratic Action
3	Y	Y	CAN	Authentic Nationalist Center
4	Y	N	CND	National Democratic Coordinator
5	Y	Y	DCG	Guatemalan Christian Democracy
6	Y	N	FCD	Democratic Civic Front
7	Y	N	FDP	Popular Democratic Force
8	N		FN	New Force
9	N		FPO	Organized Popular Force
10	Y	N	FUN	Front for National Unity
11	Y	N	FUR	United Front of the Revolution
12	N		MDN	Nationalist Democratic Movement
13	Y	N	MEC	Emerging Movement for Concordance
14	N		MIDEH	Indigenous Humanist Democratic Movement
15	Y	Y	MLN	National Liberation Movement
16	N		PAR	Party of Revolutionary Action
17	N		PC	Catholic Party
18	Y	N	PDCN	Democratic Party of National Cooperation
19	Y	Y	PID	Institutional Democratic Party
20	N		PIN	Party of National Integration
21	N		PJS	Socialist Justice Party
22	N		PLO	Orthodox Liberal Party
23	Y	Y	PNR	National Renovating Party
24	Y	N	PP	Populist Party
25	Y	Y	PR	Revolutionary Party
26	N		PSC	Social Christian Party
27	N		PSD	Democratic Socialist Party
28	Y	N	PUA	Party of Anticommunist Unification
29	Y	Y	UCN	Union of the National Center
30	N		UNE	Party of National Equicratic Unity
31	N		UPN	National Patriotic Union
32	N		URD	Democratic Revolutionary Unity
33	Y	N	ANP	Progressive National Alliance
34	Y	N	OCAS	Peasant Organization for Social Action
35	Y	N	COZAUN	United Zacapa Committee

Notes: P?: Did the registered party committee actually participate in the 1984 election?
(Yes or No); 4%?: If the party participated, did it receive a minimum of 4 percent of the
vote—the minimum if its status as a registered party was not to be cancelled? (Yes or No)
Source: Adapted from Rosada Granados 1985: 37–38.

and still wear the progressive mantle. New party-registration laws meant
that the vacuum to the left filled rather quickly, and some of the new
groups were defectors from the DCG—the Social Christian Party (Partido
Social Cristiano—PSC), led by Dr. Carlos Gehlert Mata, for example. The
PSD, whose leader Mario Solórzano Martínez returned from exile, offered
another left-of-center alternative.

Third, Ríos Montt pursued his campaign against political parties in
other directions as well. Using corruption as the excuse, he eliminated all

civilians from executive government positions. He removed all elected mayors, most of whom had been elected in the relatively honest municipal elections of 1980, and replaced them with military officers. Another decree permitted the head of state to act as legislative as well as executive power, removing the major political parties from this avenue of political participation as well. For parties, the atmosphere was uncertain to say the least: Ríos Montt frequently harangued the parties as historically corrupt institutions that were representative neither of the wishes nor the needs of the citizenry. Civilian political leaders had little left except the somewhat dubious prospect of future elections.

Not surprisingly, the civilian middle-class elites, who originally had seen the 1982 coup as a way to return to power under a new regime promising honesty, opposed much of Ríos's political platform. After a year and a half in power, Ríos Montt's exotic messianism had alienated most sectors of the ruling class. The hierarchy of the Catholic church had become alienated by his strident proselytizing on behalf of the Protestant, born-again evangelical sects. Moreover, Ríos Montt's legitimacy as a guarantor of foreign economic assistance had become jeopardized by both his eccentricities and the extraordinary levels of violence in rural areas. Like his predecessor General Lucas, Ríos had become an embarrassment to the ruling class, apparently unable to sustain the system. On August 8, 1983, General Ríos Montt departed as he had arrived, in a military coup, this one led by General Humberto Mejía Víctores.[10]

Making Guatemala Safe for Democracy—Part II

The 1983 coup led to a decrease in born-again evangelism as a political style but had little or no impact on the government's policy of responding to political pressure with brute force. Mejía continued to apply the same brutal counterinsurgency techniques as his predecessor—crop burning, massacres in villages suspected of guerrilla sympathies, forced resettlement into camps, and forced service in paramilitary civil patrols.

During the Lucas García administration and the two military dictatorships that followed it, repression in rural areas was truly astonishing. By 1984, mass killings had become a regular occurrence. Vast areas were virtual wastelands.[11] Perhaps more than 50 percent of the 2.58 million Indian residents of the highlands were severely disrupted by the violence, that is, they disappeared, were murdered, forced to relocate into model villages and/or forced to work and participate in civil patrols, or fled as refugees (Frank and Wheaton: 92). The juvenile division of the Supreme Court estimated that one to two hundred thousand orphans and forty-five thousand parents were killed between 1978 and 1985 (Simon: 86).[12] The violence included explicit disruptions of the cultural integrity of the Indian communities. The Army shut down indigenous-language radio stations and isolated high school and university students and other urban professionals from the rural population, especially in Indian areas. A government-sponsored "literacy campaign" has been described as "a farce and as a means of identifying rural leaders for kidnappings and assassinations" (Davis and Hodson: 21).

Additional political and economic impacts resulted from development agencies that were either closed or disrupted—leaving local members cut off from resources and protection—as well as land ownership patterns and food production that were severely disrupted when individuals fled, losing their land, perhaps never to get another chance to own land again. Refugees flowed to cities to live in volatile slums, or they fled the country. Cooperatives stopped functioning because leaders were killed and monies routinely robbed. Curfews in rural areas prohibited public gatherings, which meant that the total fabric of opportunity for democratic participation was disrupted (Davis and Hodson: 11, 19–27; WOLA 1988: tables, 93–98). In terms of development efforts, the violence showed an unmistakably clear pattern of increased inequity and agony in rural society.

Repression in the highlands in response to communal activism had been a constant after 1954, but levels had fluctuated in response to surges in successful communal activism. State terrorism and elite violence in general intensified if groups represented a threat to elite economic privilege. Violence was part of an economic struggle, not the result of a "culture of violence." Repression was designed to suppress an emergent citizenry, thereby reducing the potential for democracy. The wave of rural violence in this period, directed largely against communal activism efforts, produced a series of terrible impacts on all dimensions of rural Guatemalan society, including religion, family, and the economy (Davis and Hodson: 19–27).[13]

Creating Electoral Procedures

The first two phases of the military's counterinsurgency plan—the military campaigns of the early 1980s and the militarization of the countryside by 1984—had successfully weakened the insurgency. The third phase of the plan was to increase legitimacy for the regime in the face of human rights violations and economic failures, and the vehicle for achieving this was the re-establishment of constitutional government with free elections.

Part of the goal of the strategy was international legitimacy, a major prerequisite for foreign aid and in turn a prerequisite for economic development. International legitimacy could be enhanced not only by holding elections but by guaranteeing procedural purity. Moreover, given the notoriety earned by the Army's activities through 1984, legitimacy could also be increased if a civilian were elected, one seen as a reformer or, better still, as an antagonist of the Army.

In the political arena public debate over the organization and scheduling of elections resumed with the Mejía Víctores coup in 1983, but in general, the structures and calendar inherited from Ríos Montt remained intact, with some modifications. After "consulting" with party leaders in late 1983, General Mejía decreed new electoral laws, to take effect in January 1984. The new election procedures included the following:

1. A deadline of April 30, 1984, was imposed, by which time political parties would have to meet the new registration requirements, including the signature rules described above as well as other provisions, such as establishing a minimum of fifty local organizations in at least twelve of Guatemala's twenty-three departments. Parties were also required to hold departmental and national conventions to select candidates for the Constituent Assembly.
2. The election for the Constituent Assembly was scheduled for July 1, 1984; the assembly would take office on September 15, 1984.
3. While requirements for creating a new party were considerably more lax than previous rules, parties were faced with the new requirement of obtaining at least 4 percent of the vote in the 1984 Constituent Assembly election or automatically having their registration rescinded.
4. The Constituent Assembly would consist of eighty-eight seats. Of these, twenty-three were considered "national" seats. Parties were expected to nominate slates of national candidates, for whom votes would be cast in all electoral districts of the country. The remaining sixty-five seats were to be elected from departments, with the number of seats varying with the population of the department.
5. Only parties still registered after the 1984 elections could participate in the 1985 elections for president, Congress, and municipal offices.[14]

The future Constituent Assembly's legal mission and real power had been debated for several months before the promulgation of these electoral laws. Many of the political parties saw the assembly as a sovereign body, with authority to take any action it deemed proper, including naming a provisional president. The regime's position was that the exclusive duty of the assembly was to prepare a new constitution and that no legal power existed for any other activity beyond elaborating a law of habeas corpus. The military's position prevailed.

Once the electoral laws had been proclaimed and put into effect, parties turned to the task of meeting the new registration requirements. By

May 1, 1984, nineteen groups had met the requirements for the 1984 Constituent Assembly election (see Table 4.2). Of the nineteen, only five as of
May 1, 1984, had succeeded in offering a full slate of candidates in all
departments of the country. One slate was an alliance between the CAN
and the MLN. The other four parties were the PR, the DCG, the PNR, and
the UCN. The PID and the PUA also ran at the national level but without
full slates.

The UCN had recently been formed by Jorge Carpio Nicolle, publisher of the daily newspaper *El Gráfico,* and was the only national party
that had not existed as a major party in the 1982 presidential election. In
other words, the lineup of major parties in Guatemala shifted only slightly
as a result of the new rules imposed by the military. Generally, the traditional parties had survived, in spite of factionalization.

Legalized Repression

Changes in electoral procedures were one response to the lack of international legitimacy; another was the Army's strategy to legitimate its military activities by legalizing, in effect, three of its de facto counterinsurgency structures and tactics. Each of these changes reduced the need for
open military repression, while at the same time providing the appearance
of new levels of popular participation and democracy.

The first was the Civilian Self-Defense Patrols (Patrullas de Auto-
Defensa Civil—PAC). In most rural areas where the Army was active,
membership and rotating tours of duty in the PACs were mandatory for all
males. The civil patrols, whose membership was estimated at between
750,000 and 850,000 by 1984, ostensibly served the purpose of protecting
local villages from guerrilla attacks. But the real purpose of these ill-
equipped patrols was social control; they were a means to account for and
regulate the whereabouts of villagers.[15]

The second institutional mechanism, which complemented the first,
was the creation of model villages as part of the poles of development program.[16] The military described this plan as one of coordinated development aimed at bringing social progress and basic quality-of-life improvements to highland areas marked by isolation and extreme poverty. In fact,
in addition to offering military officers control over adjacent agricultural
lands and individuals desperate for work, the basic intent of these villages
was counterinsurgency by means of population control.

The third mechanism for maintaining military control over rural Guatemala
was a structure to regulate political affairs and development assistance, the
National Interinstitutional Coordinator committees (Coordinadora Inter—institucional Nacional—CIN), established in each department and presided
over by military-zone commanders. The CIN coordinated and regulated all

Table 4.2   Registered Parties and Party Leaders, 1984 Constituent Assembly Election

Parties of the "Moderate Left":

1. United Front of the Revolution (Frente Unido de la Revolución—FUR), César Toledo Peate.
2. Guatemalan Christian Democratic Party (Democracia Cristiana Guatemalteca—DCG), Vinicio Cerezo Arévalo.
3. Democratic Action Party (Acción Democrática—AD), Leopoldo Urrutia Beltrán.
4. Popular Democratic Force (Fuerza Demócrata Popular—FDP), Francisco Reyes Ixcamey.
5. Revolutionary Party (Partido Revolucionario—PR), Napoleón Alfaro.

Parties of the "Moderate Right":

6. Populist Party (Partido Populista—PP), Acisclo Valladares Molina.
7. National Renovation Party (Partido Nacional Renovador—PNR), Alejandro Maldonado Aguirre.
8. National Center Union (Unión del Centro Nacional—UCN), Jorge Carpio Nicolle.
9. National Unity Front (Frente de Unidad Nacional—FUN), Gabriel Girón Ortiz.
10. Emerging Concordance Movement (Movimiento Emergent de Concordancia—MEC), Colonel Luis Francisco Gordillo.

Parties of the "Extreme Right":

11. National Democratic Coordinator (Coordinadora Nacional Democrática—CND), General Aníbal Guevara Rodríguez.
12. Institutional Democratic Party (Partido Institucional Democrático—PID), Oscar Humberto Rivas.
13. Authentic National Center (Centro Auténtico Nacional—CAN), Mario Aguilar Arroyo.
14. Anticommunist Unification Party (Partido de Unificación Anticomunista—PUA), Leonel Sisniega Otero.
15. National Liberation Movement (Movimiento de Liberación Nacional—MLN), Mario Sandoval Alarcón.

Other Parties:

16. Democratic Party of National Cooperation (Partido Democrático de Cooperación Nacional—PDCN), Nery Noel Morales Gavarrete.
17. National Progressive Alliance (Alianza Nacional Progresista—ANP), Mario Castejón García.
18. Peasant Organization for Social Action (Organización Campesina de Acción Social—OCAS), Mauricio Quixtán.
19. National Integration Party (Partido de Integración Nacional—PIN), Jorge Antonio Castillo C.

Sources: Parties 1–15, including the typology and classification: *Guatenoticias* 4/1/84: 6; Parties 16–19: PDCN: *Prensa Libre* 5/1/84; ANP, OCAS, and PIN: *El Gráfico* 5/1/84; *Inforpress* 5/4/84: 54–55.

normal civil governmental functions under direct military supervision, to "reduce corruption and increase efficiency." The CIN became in essence a parallel government, allowing the military to continue to dominate even though Guatemala would return to "civilian rule" (Krueger and Enge: 53–59; VM 1/7–13/85: 6; and GNN 4/85: 5, 8).

Like civil patrols and model villages, the CIN inhibited independent community organization and local control over local political affairs. The military clearly perceived local self-help organizations and communal activism as threats and sought to ensure that the "democratic opening" of 1985 and the civilian government inaugurated in 1986 would not threaten military dominance. In short, the Army was able to create structures that would allow itself a fairly unfettered hold on the rural areas it felt were threatening. By 1984, the military's three mechanisms for social control had created an environment in which fear, terror, and totalitarian control replaced murder as the primary mechanism for social domination. In 1985, these mechanisms were integrated into the new constitution by military decree, in effect legalizing the repression.

Beyond the general climate engendered by this overwhelming presence of the Army, several specific examples of military involvement in the period before the elections further compromised the quality of the process. The first followed from the civil defense patrols. The government announced that the patrols were not military institutions and that therefore the members would vote. Since, in May 1984, the total number of voting citizens was about 2.3 million, this meant that a body of voters as large as the patrols could affect the outcome of the election, if those votes were to be excluded, controlled, or miscounted. In response to public concern, the Army pledged not to interfere in this aspect of the voting.

Second, all mayors were now military appointees, meaning that military officers would preside over ballot counts in their localities. This issue, inherited from the Ríos Montt period, led to concern that the Army could manipulate vote counts in situ. The military responded by announcing a nonmilitarized counting of the ballots. A third issue arose from the Army's obvious physical superiority and infrastructural sophistication, especially in isolated, rural areas: the possibility of fraud occurring during the transportation of ballots. In March 1984, the Army responded that the military would provide security at polling places but would not transport any ballots.

Although the military was taking steps to guarantee an honest election process, it clearly had no intention of diluting its control over the zones of conflict. The electoral process "cleansing" under the Ríos Montt and Mejía regimes had a clear goal of international legitimacy,[17] not the creation of any mechanism reflecting popular sovereignty. Social democracy, based on social justice considerations, was not part of the official agenda, and repression continued to stymie political action outside of the limited electoral structures. In sum, the general context setting the stage for the 1984 and 1985 elections was violent and uncertain.

Elections: 1984 and 1985

The campaign period for the Constituent Assembly election was very vociferous, but none of the principal parties took clear positions on concrete issues (Rosada Granados 1985: 24). Given the historical context of human rights violations and the presence of a very powerful military, it is perhaps understandable that only a very tame opposition surfaced at this time. Yet, the absence of serious discussions in an election campaign meant voters had fewer substantive choices and, in effect, less potential power over decisionmakers. In July 1984, voters elected eighty-eight members to the new Constituent Assembly. The Christian Democrats won twenty seats, compared to twenty-one for the UCN, the newly organized centrist party, and twenty-three for an alliance of the MLN and its fellow party of the right, the CAN. The remaining seats were distributed among seven other parties (see Table 4.3).

Table 4.3 Constituent Assembly Election Results, 1984

Party	National Votes	% Votes	N	Departmental Votes	% Votes	D	T
DCG	326,064	16.4	6	261,207	13.1	14	20
UCN	273,744	13.7	5	278,740	14.0	16	21
MLN/CAN	249,712	12.5	5	260,466	13.1	18	23
PR	146,092	7.3	2	179,199	9.0	8	10
PNR	133,680	6.7	2	126,021	6.3	3	5
PID	106,188	5.3	2	109,905	5.5	3	5
PUA	61,116	3.1	1	53,385	2.7	0	1
FUR	45,677	2.3	0	45,490	2.3	0	0
MEC	42,764	2.2	0	43,753	2.2	0	0
FUN	40,488	2.0	0	47,366	2.4	1	1
Other	110,029	5.5	0	147,762	7.6	2	2
Valid Votes	1,535,554	77.0		1,553,274	78.0		
Null Votes	300,513	15.0		296,076	15.0		
Blank Votes	158,866	8.0		143,044	7.0		

Notes: "Other" combines totals for seven minor parties and two party coalitions. OCAS and the DCG/PNR coalition won the two seats in that category. "N" signifies number of assembly seats won at the national level; "D" signifies the number at the departmental level; and "T" is the total number of seats won. Party acronyms are spelled out in Table 4.1.

Source: Based on Rosada Granados 1985: 39, which is based on data from Guatemalan Supreme Electoral Tribunal.

Fourteen political parties participated at the presidential level in the 1985 election (Embassy of Guatemala: 1; Stix et al.), supporting one of the eight candidates (see Table 4.4). In addition to the presidential election, organized on a plurality and runoff basis, a new Congress of one

Table 4.4   Presidential Elections, First-Round Results, 1985

Party	Candidate	% Votes
CAN	Mario David García	6.29
MLN/PID/FDP	Mario Sandoval Alarcón	12.52
PNR	Alejandro Maldonado Aguirre	3.15
PUA/FUN/MEC	Leonel Sisniega Otero	1.90
DCG/FDC-5	Vinicio Cerezo Arévalo	38.59
PDCN/PR	Jorge Serrano Elías	13.80
PSD	Mario Solórzano Martínez	3.42
UCN	Jorge Carpio Nicolle	20.28

Notes: Number of potential voters: 3.95 million (est.); number of registered voters: 2,753,572; total ballots cast: 1,887,232; nullified ballots: 144,392 (7.65% of total votes); blank ballots: 81,535 (4.32% of total votes); valid ballots: 1,661,305 (88.03% of total votes; 42.06% of total number of potential voters). FDC-5 is a coalition of small progressive parties that formed for this election only. Percentages in Column 3 are based on valid votes. Party acronyms are spelled out in Table 4.1.
Source: Compiled from data in Embassy of Guatemala.

hundred members was elected, seventy-five of these by electoral districts corresponding to Guatemala's twenty-three departments, and twenty-five elected at-large on a national basis. At the local level 328 municipalities held elections for mayors and municipal councils.

During the presidential campaign of 1985, again none of the candidates broached issues of corruption or of human rights violations by the military. None suggested that such violators be punished for past crimes or proposed a dialogue with the insurgents. All contenders pledged not to pursue major socioeconomic reforms, and all acknowledged the special status of the military. Differences of style and rhetoric appeared, but few major programmatic differences on nontrivial issues of policy. The campaign resembled a "beauty contest" (Gleijeses: 22–23).[18]

In the presidential election itself, no candidate gained a majority of the vote, but Vinicio Cerezo of the Christian Democrats outdistanced Jorge Carpio Nicolle of the UCN, with almost 39 percent of the vote to Carpio's 20 percent (see Table 4.4). As no candidate had a majority, a runoff between those top two candidates was scheduled for December 8, 1985. In the congressional elections, the Christian Democrats won a slim majority of seats (CAR 11/8/85: 1–2) (see Table 4.5).

Between the two rounds of the presidential election, political debate centered on two issues. The first was an allegation by the MLN that the first round of voting had been fraudulent. This contention was rejected by the Supreme Election Tribunal. The second centered on the runoff instructions for the losing parties to give their adherents. The PSD, PR, and PNR announced their support for the Christian Democrats. Except for the MLN, the parties of the right released their voters, suggesting that they vote for

Table 4.5 Congressional Election Results, 1985

Party	% Votes	N-Seats	D-Seats	T-Seats
DCG	34.58	11	40	51
UCN	20.58	5	17	22
PDCN/PR	13.53	4	7	11
MLN/PID	15.27	3	9	12
CAN	6.26	1	0	1
PSD	3.66	1	1	2
PNR	4.23	0	1	1
PUA/MEC/FUN	1.43	0	0	0
FCD	0.21	0	0	0
Totals	99.95	25	75	100

Notes: Total percentage is not 100 due to rounding. Percentages are based on valid votes.
Party acronyms are spelled out in Table 4.1.
Source: Based on data in Rosada Granados 1986: 14, 18.

the candidate of their choosing. After the MLN's allegations of fraud had been rejected, its leadership urged its voters to cast blank or null ballots (VM 11/6/85: 3–4; and 11/12/85: 3–5). During the runoff period the UCN campaign was essentially that the Christian Democrats were likely to try to establish a one-party dictatorship and that the DCG was part of the "international Left" (VM 11/12/85: 3–4).

Vinicio Cerezo and the Christian Democrats won the runoff election handily, winning 68 percent of the vote. With Cerezo's inauguration in January 1986, Guatemala returned to civilian government for the first time since 1970, when President Méndez Montenegro left office. According to an international delegation observing the process, the election campaign, balloting, and vote counting appeared to have been in accordance with Guatemalan electoral law. The election was "procedurally correct" (Booth et al.: vii–xvi) but openly antireformist: besides campaigns devoid of serious substantive issues, both the Army and business leaders from the private sector—specifically the Council of Commercial, Industrial, and Financial Associations (Cámara de Asociaciones Comerciales, Industriales, y Financieras—CACIF)—made clear that they would not tolerate reform proposals after the inauguration.[19]

In the final analysis it is difficult to measure the success of the electoral process within the atmosphere of counterinsurgency. Vote totals were higher than in elections from previous decades.[20] The high turnout and the party results coincide with the military's political program, designed to reduce the power of traditional right-wing parties and maintain a relationship with a moderate but nonthreatening civilian sector (Rosada Granados 1986: 10–11). By these indicators the election was a success for the military.

The same results, however, can be interpreted as a negative public reaction to the military. The results, including the turnout, did not indicate support for the DCG or UCN platforms and programs, which were not particularly clear to begin with, so much as votes against the traditional right and the violence and authoritarianism of the Army. There was a clear coincidence of preferences between much of the voting public and the dominant faction of the military to the extent that both desired to reduce the political influence of traditional right-wing parties and oligarchy.

Three years later, in April 1988, municipal-level elections provided more data (see Table 4.6). Participation was low, and perhaps more politically expressive than the government and the Army would have hoped for. Direct absenteeism was high: 57 percent of the registered voters did not vote. This "apathy" was described by both the right and the left as symptomatic of the public's displeasure with unfulfilled promises of the government, that is of the ruling Christian Democrats. The guerrilla insurgency leadership (URNG) had urged that citizens either vote for progressive candidates or, in situations where there were no progressive candidates, not to vote or to deliberately invalidate their ballots. In fact, of the 1,251,517 votes cast, 743,997 (59.45 percent) were subsequently declared invalid (VM 5/88: 5–6).

In spite of these figures, it is difficult to differentiate between anger directed at the DCG itself and expressions of discontent with the overall nature of the political economy. Voting results show a mixed degree of support for the government and the DCG (see Table 4.6). All of the major political parties lost ground in the 1988 elections, winning control of fewer municipal governments than they had won in the 1985 elections, although the declines were not substantial. The DCG had won control of 54 percent of the municipalities in 1985, and 51 percent in 1988, for example, and the UCN's percentage declined from 21.3 to 20.6 percent, suggesting that for those voters who participated in a "conventional" way, party loyalty remained relatively consistent. For the parties of the far right, however, results were less encouraging: the MLN-PID coalition had won in thirty-nine municipalities in 1985, but prevailed in only twelve in 1988. Civic committees, local-level groups of nonaffiliated citizens, won control of twelve mayoralties in 1988 (VM 5/88: 5–6).

Conclusion

The 1984 and 1985 elections look quite democratic by many conventional indicators. There were no military candidates, and several political parties participated, including even the Democratic Socialist Party. The Christian Democrats, who won, were widely considered to be reformists. All three

Table 4.6   Municipal Election Results, 1985, 1988

Party	% of Valid Vote 1988	1988 Victories	1985 Victories
DCG	36.7	140	148
UCN	24.0	56	58
MLN/PID (1985)	—	—	39
MLN	5.1	12	—
PID	0.3	1	—
PDCN/PR (1985)	—	—	13
PDCN	2.0	3	—
PR	6.9	9	—
MAS	1.7	2	—
PSD	1.6	1	1
CAN	0.5	2	4
PNR	0.5	0	4
UNO	0.3	0	0
MEC	0.1	0	0
FUN	0.1	0	0
Totals	79.8	226	267

Notes: Total number of contests is 272. Valid votes do not total 100 percent because local-level civic committees and several coalitions of rightist parties have been excluded. Civic committees won 12 mayoralties and rightist coalitions won 34.

Source: Based on data in *Vistazo Mensual,* 5/88: 5–6.

rounds of voting were characterized by procedural honesty. This analysis would be more or less consistent with the position of the U.S. government at the time: the 1985 election, if not the final step in establishing democracy in Guatemala, was certainly a major and important step in that direction, especially in comparison with earlier electoral episodes. President Cerezo himself was more careful, noting that the military was still very powerful, but he nevertheless portrayed his administration as a democratic regime beginning to have an impact in the country.

A procedurally correct election, with open participation of opposition parties, is a key component of the liberal-representative model of democracy, but the context of elections in the 1980s raises questions about whether liberal-representational criteria were met. State violence had abated during the campaign for the Constituent Assembly in 1984, but increased during the 1985 electoral campaign. In addition, continuing rumors of possible coups, the weakened state of several political parties, the general disregard for human rights, a violent Army intervention on the campus of the national university, and the continuing economic and social crisis together produced a less-enthusiastic campaign than might have been expected for a country returning to democracy. Moreover, the institutional role of the Army in rural areas, not to mention in other walks of economic and political life, served to reduce public confidence in the honesty of the upcoming elections. Finally, skepticism was widespread about the real strength of whatever government would emerge from the elections (Rosada Granados 1986: 5). In sum, the immediate context of the electoral events was problematic at best and thoroughly antidemocratic at worst.

Guatemala's human rights record between 1975 and 1985 was as bad as any in the hemisphere, negatively affecting political participation. Electoral and party structures notwithstanding, the climate of the election period was one of violence and fear, though perhaps mixed with hope. The net impact of years of repression was that the quality of elections in 1984 and 1985 was seriously diluted. In one view, in fact, holding an election under the existing circumstances in 1984 and 1985 was a "deception" that had the effect, perhaps unintended, of inhibiting Guatemala's transition to democracy (Stix et al.).

The question, then, is not whether elections ipso facto mean democracy exists but whether policies that create elections as part of a counterinsurgency plan can lead to a more democratic environment. Insisting that no change resulted from these elections is as inappropriate as insisting that the historical pattern was broken by the Cerezo election. Guatemala's 1984 and 1985 elections must be understood as the public policy of elites with faltering power who were seeking to reestablish a state responsive to their interests. Perhaps in spite of the counterinsurgency aspect of the elections, democratic growth was possible after these elections as a direct result of them and the return to constitutional rule.

Evidence for verifying that possibility is not merely in the electoral procedures themselves but in the quality of political participation and the policy performance of the Cerezo government following the elections. Finally, the Army's democratizing role is a question that can be answered only partially without additional data on the performance of the Cerezo administration after 1985 and the Serrano administration after 1990.

Notes

1. Some even point to the direct positive impact of the military on Guatemalan democracy. One perhaps whimsical example is the colonel who remarked during the municipal-election campaign in 1980 that the Army should reduce each field to single candidates in order to prevent the dissent that weakens democracy. Another example is the statement by a U.S. State Department official, who acknowledged that the military had fraudulently intervened in Guatemala's 1978 election to impose General Romeo Lucas García but went on to assert that this intervention had prevented the electoral victory of Mario Sandoval Alarcón of the National Liberation Movement, a proviolence leader of the extreme right and enemy of liberal democracy.

2. Every landless peasant needed the nearby landowner, because of vagrancy laws and debt-peonage arrangements instituted by the Liberals. But although every landowner needed labor, he did not need any specific individual peasant.

3. Although many dimensions of sociopolitical change are central to the Decade of Spring, Cruz Salazar sees the changes in the military's role as the major discontinuity with earlier periods, the one indicator that the 1944 movement was revolutionary and not merely a continuation of business as usual: "It's perhaps in the question of the armed forces where the process of change is most evident" (Cruz Salazar: 11).

4. "Civic action" is the use of the military in projects aimed at social and economic infrastructure projects, such as road building. Part of the rationale for civic action was political: projects sought to gain public support for the military, although their long-run impact was to create economic opportunities for military officers and to facilitate subsequent militarization of rural areas.

5. Former President Arévalo was scheduled to run in the 1963 elections. Secret U.S. "permission" for the coup apparently was based on fear of Arévalo: it was assumed he would win a free election (Black: 20).

6.

In 1957 the AID Office of Public Safety began a training program for the Guatemalan National Police. Twenty-four Americans began patrolling with the National Police and the judiciales—the political police—on a daily basis. From 1957 until Congress abolished it in 1974, the program pumped $4.4 million into the Guatemalan police, trained 425 agents in the U.S., and provided extensive supplies of arms, anti-riot equipment, and communications and transportation technology. . . . Among other services, AID set up the police training center . . . [and] organized and equipped the PMA ([Ambulatory Military Police—Policía Militar Ambulante] the units hired out to landlords and to suppress campesino unrest) (WOLA 1983: 9).

7. Between the 1974 election and the 1982 coup, Ríos had become an active, born-again Christian evangelist and brought this style of politics to government, including weekly sermons on national television. See the video *When The Mountains Tremble* for some examples of this style. The same video includes an interview with a second member of Ríos Montt's junta, Colonel Maldonado Shaad, who is dressed completely in white during his interview. Maldonado's responses illustrate another dimension of the military's style.

8. Rabine describes the three phases of the counterinsurgency plan developed in the early 1980s:

(1) the forcible separation of the guerrilla insurgency from its base among the rural indigenous population through massacring and terrorizing that civilian population (Victory '82); (2) the creation of social, political, and economic institutions to replace the shattered fabric of indigenous life (Stability '83); and (3) the legitimation of these institutions through a return to civilian forms of government (Institutional Renewal '84) (Rabine: 61).

For a detailed study of all three phases of the counterinsurgency plan, see "Contrainsurgencia": 5–23. In an interview in 1987, an official of the U.S. embassy in Guatemala acknowledged that the electoral process was part of a counterinsurgency orientation, inasmuch as the Army now recognized that it could not maintain order in Guatemala by itself and needed civilian assistance. For a contrary view asserting that the recent elections are *not* part of a counterinsurgency strategy but a new beginning for Guatemala, see Fauriol and Loser 1985 and 1988.

9. The patrols, development poles, and other institutional structures that were part of the counterinsurgency plan are discussed more fully later in this chapter.

10. Ríos had been quick to describe his ascension to power in 1982 as "an act of God," but he was curiously silent about his removal from office.

11. See Krueger and Enge; and WOLA 1988. One fairly typical report of Army violence illustrates the type of repression aimed at Indian communities:

> On July 19, [1981,] army troops marched on a tiny San Miguel Acatán village, Coyá, and opened fire on the people. The villagers tried to defend themselves with sticks and stones, but, by then, army trucks had already brought 200 soldiers into San Miguel and the original troops in Coyá were backed by helicopter support. At noon, a combat plane joined the helicopter in machine-gunning and bombing the residents. One survivor testified that the army killed 150 to 300 people in Coyá. According to the government, the Army had discovered "a school for communist indoctrination" in the village and 25 "subversives" had been killed (Davis and Hodson: 3).

12. Many observers have used the word "genocidal" to describe this rural wave of violence because the combined physical and cultural disruption has centered on Indian areas. The callousness of the government during the period is reflected in the words of a North American observer, an early supporter of the Ríos Montt military coup, who testified in Congress in support of a bill to send military aid to Guatemala during this time. In his remarks he stated that the use of the word "genocide" to describe the antisubversion campaign was not accurate, since (to paraphrase his remarks) more Indian children were being born each month than were being killed. This statement did not appear in the printed record of the hearing.

13. Forced to leave because of the repression, one departing development worker described the changes:

> When I first arrived, there was no killing. Just a cohesive community structure based on trade and improved cooperative action, with regular festivals and public gatherings to enjoy life and to worship. Their desire to meet Americans and travel to see their own nation, even if on foot, was great. They wanted to learn to read and to obtain new skills in the schools so as to improve their well being. Now, no one wants to talk to strangers, travel, gather to pray, learn new skills or to read. Everyone groups their families indoors as much as possible and asks not "Will I be killed by the army?," but "When will I be killed by the army?" (quoted in Davis and Hodson: viii).

Another description:

> People are fearful of holding meetings, particularly of cooperatives, which President Laugerud García (1974 to 1978) appeared to promote. Many leaders became known and very visible, and many of them are dead today. In the Ixcán area . . . , the army has now destroyed most of the cooperatives and killed many of their leaders. In other areas, there has been a conscious effort by the government and the army to dismantle cooperatives and to eliminate their leaders (quoted in Davis and Hodson: 17).

14. The best single source summarizing formal-legal as well as contextual information about the Constituent Assembly election in 1984 is the work of Héctor Rosada Granados. Much of the data here comes from his publications.

15. For detailed accounts of the PACs, see Americas Watch 1983; and Krueger and Enge: 23–26. For an example of how the stated purpose of PACs was taken as the real purpose, even in the "responsible" media, see CSMonitor 12/13/83: 5. For an especially poignant description of civil patrols as a mechanism of social regulation, see Paul and Demarest. As we shall see in Chapter 9, the PACs remain a major part of Guatemalan life and a major and difficult issue on the political agenda in 1992.

16. For a thorough analysis and description of this program, see IGE 1984 and 1986; and Krueger and Enge: 17–52. For evidence of U.S. fiscal and ideological support for the program, see GNN 12/84: 7; and Enfoprensa 12/7/84: 4. For documentation of the church's opposition, see VM 3/18–24/85: 3.

17. One indicator of this was the military's frequent claim that an international campaign to discredit Guatemala was continuing, ignoring the progress made in holding elections and returning to democracy.

18. Rosada Granados provides a concise summary of the situation at the time of the elections:

> The election campaign drew to a close with political party pronouncements that had no organic relationship with the nature of the internal crisis Guatemala was suffering. There being no differences between the positions of the [major] parties, citizens dealt with proposals that were ambiguous and abstract, and that were of little significance for an electorate that needed specific responses and clear orientations. Immersed in this confusion and skeptical about the elections in the face of predictions that there would be massive abstentionism, Guatemalans went to the polls (Rosada Granados 1986: 5).

19.

> Spokesmen for both the Army and the private sector made it clear . . . that fundamental reforms would not be tolerated, and that the new government's economic policies would have to fit within strict limits. The head of CACIF, the political arm of Guatemala's private sector, made it clear . . . that any move by the new civilian government to initiate land reform would be intolerable (Rabine: 62–63).

20. Rosada Granados's data are slightly different than those in Table 4.4, but the pattern is similar. He reports that of the total number of votes cast (1,907,771), 12 percent of the voters (228,771) deposited a null or blank ballot. Of the 3.8 million eligible to register to vote, 27.5 percent (1,045,399) did not register. Of those registered (2,754,601), 39 percent did not submit a valid vote: either they did not vote at all or they voted with a blank ballot or their ballots were nullified. The total number of valid votes (1,679,000) comes to 44 percent of the eligible population of 3.8 million (Rosada Granados 1986: 9).

5

Economic Policy During
the Cerezo Administration

Vinicio Cerezo's Christian Democratic Party had several professed goals when he took office in January 1986, including generating renewed economic growth, moving the nation toward democracy, and staying in office through the term. DCG goals also included social reform, as seen both in their overall ideology and in many public statements that committed the government to aiding the poorest sectors of society. This chapter centers on two major themes: (1) the economic and social context in Guatemala at the time of President Cerezo's inauguration; and (2) the government's fiscal and economic growth policies and their impact on measures of socioeconomic progress.

If economic growth is the primary goal for economic elites, social reform is an important goal for popular-sector groups. One test of democracy, then, is in terms of political conflict around the mix of policies that led to the accumulation of capital for economic growth versus policies that led to the distribution of wealth via social reform. If we view policy outputs as a competition between the traditional minority holding power and the popular organizations seeking to use the political access promised by the new democratic forms of government, we can evaluate the strength of Guatemalan democracy.

Policies to produce growth and generate investment capital during the Cerezo administration included a renewed orientation to an export model of growth, attempts at tax reform and budgetary conflict resolution, and pursuit of neoliberal measures in general. This chapter focuses on these policy areas and Chapter 6 will focus on demands for social reform from the popular sectors and the government's policy responses.

Economic Conditions and Policy Responses

Stable economic development has eluded Guatemala for decades, although economic growth took place during much of the period. In the past three decades the economy has suffered from an oscillating cycle of bursts of prosperity and periods of stagnation or decline, sometimes as a result of domestic public policy but often as a result of the vagaries of the international economy. The country has traditionally depended on outside markets both as a destination for its commodities and as a source of capital and other necessary imports. Guatemala has long had an economy driven by exports, particularly agricultural commodities such as coffee, cotton, sugar, bananas, meat, and cardamon. In the 1980s, it became an exporter of crude oil as well.

Since the early 1980s, achieving any growth at all, let alone sustained development, has been the main challenge for economic policymakers. Economic growth averaged 7 percent per year from 1970 to 1980, but between 1981 and 1984, GNP per capita declined by 15.5 percent. The growth rate was zero in 1984 (*Guatemala!* 5/85: 3).[1] One consequence was the lack of revenue for government programs, from counterinsurgency to subsidies for development to social services. Equilibrium among contending factions has been maintained over the decades, but the insurgency of the 1980s drove costs of government upward at a time when economic growth was declining. The result was a serious crisis in the political economy.[2]

After 1981, the Quetzal began to lose its value relative to the dollar, with which it had been on equal par value for several decades. By 1985, it had declined to $.50, a 100 percent devaluation. Exports increased 5 percent in 1984 over 1983, but still the growth rate was zero.[3] Deficits forced the government to sell some 20 percent of Guatemala's gold reserves during this period, in spite of foreign assistance from the United States and several European institutions. The foreign debt had grown from $239 million in 1976 to $2.4 billion in 1984 and $2.9 billion in mid-1985 (*Guatemala!* 5/85: 10).

International financial pressures, including suggestions from the International Monetary Fund, led the military regimes of Ríos Montt and Mejía Víctores to attempt a tax increase for civilian elites to help pay for the counterinsurgency war. Until then, the Army and the government had been diverting much of the international assistance received to military spending, leaving fewer resources for customary expenditures, including social spending and subsidies for the system's economic growth. Because of the deficits, the IMF had some input in this decision. Although IMF strategy usually involves cutting social spending in order to shift revenues to growth activities, in Guatemala social spending was so low, and social needs so high, that the IMF solution essentially consisted of increasing government revenues—although the social-spending policy was assailed publicly. The pressures on Guatemalan leaders were real; the IMF had withheld funds from an earlier agreement with Guatemala because the government was not meeting IMF's guidelines (*Guatemala!* 5/85: 3).

Taxation Policy

Taxes long have been an inflammatory issue in Guatemala. For decades, the elite successfully resisted all serious attempts to tax their assets. As of the early 1960s, for example, income tax applied only to profits from business activities, with no tax on "purely personal income" (Sommerfield: 68). A progressive personal income tax was enacted in 1963, "after nine unsuccessful attempts in the previous ten years" (Sommerfield: 183). In 1983, Ríos Montt proposed a 10 percent value-added tax (IVA) on all commercial transactions. Opposition to this proposal from the civilian elite was part of the reason Ríos was overthrown in August 1983. General Mejía Víctores, his successor, imposed the IVA, but at 7 percent, resulting in further declines in quality of life as increased costs were passed on to consumers even while unemployment increased (*Guatemala!* 5/85: 9).

Mejía Víctores also proposed other fiscal policies, including additional tariffs on some imported goods, new taxes on exports, and a 30 percent increase in interest rates. Elite resistance to these proposals was swift and successful. General strikes—lockouts—were threatened. Mejía withdrew the measures and fired his finance minister, Colonel Figueroa Villarte (*Guatemala!* 5/85: 3).

Because the domestic market continued to be devastated by the economy and counterinsurgency violence during this period, Guatemala was forced to rely on exports, even more than in the past, to solve its development problems. Of the $482 million received in loans in 1985, half went to the agro-exporting sector, and this, coupled with the low wages paid by landowners, allowed them to compete internationally in spite of weak markets in that arena. Industrial owners fared less well, getting only subsidies for cheap electricity and for fuels, which did not offset the high costs of imported raw materials (*Guatemala!* 5/85: 10). Increasing foreign debt, the continuing fiscal deficit, weak currency, and poverty and unemployment combined to make development of an internal market as the basis for sustained economic growth difficult.[4]

The tax program implemented in November 1987, for example, included a proposed property tax, with the amount to be assessed on the basis of self-valuation (*"auto-avalúo"*).[5] There were protests from the right, including the MLN party and CACIF, which saw this measure as a precursor to land reform. Normally pro-DCG Indians in the highland municipality of Totonicapán also protested (GNIB 1–2/88: 12). Minister of Defense General Héctor Gramajo appeared before an assembly of leading civilian elites to seek approval for the concept of the entire society supporting the counterinsurgency, and specifically to ask them to approve new taxes and new minimum wages being proposed by the government. The leader of the military's "reformist" wing sought elite support for steps to pay what the Christian Democrats were calling at the time the "social debt." In response, private leaders rejected the plan and continued refusing to pay higher wages (VM 6/88: 3).

As of early 1987, the Christian Democrats felt that the tax reform situation had been resolved to the detriment of the business elite; the party believed the reforms were progressive and that elite sectors had been defeated in their attempts to prevent them. An opposing point of view, however, suggested that in fact the military was acting to weaken the economic position of its chief rival for control of wealth, the business elite.[6] In other words, resolving the tax reform situation had little to do with the needs or demands of popular organizations pressing for relief, and everything to do with competition among elite sectors of society. The Christian Democratic Party profited from the denouement to the extent that the political strength of its rivals in the intransigent business community could be defeated by the party's allies in the military. Later developments suggested that in fact the business elites were more successful in this round than the visible evidence on taxation reveals.

The Cerezo Administration at Mid-Term

Results of policy decisions in the first half of the Cerezo administration were mixed. The government's position was that the economy had shown signs of progress since 1980: the gross domestic product had grown by 2.5 percent (PCRP 1/88: 4).[7] Second, the inflation rate was only 9.6 percent for 1987, while private investment increased 14 percent. Third, exports of nontraditional products increased over 60 percent, and fourth, the unemployment rate decreased 25 percent. The Quetzal was said to be exchanging at a rate very near the official rate of Q2.50 to the dollar.[8]

The government claimed success in stabilizing inflation and exchange rates and therefore would move, in 1988, to reactivate the economy on a larger scale, using credit to assist small- and medium-size producers and to distribute funds to municipalities (8 percent of the national budget, per the constitution) (PCRP 1/88: 4). But the ratio of the value of exports to the servicing of foreign debt, which had dropped from 16.5 percent in 1970 to 11.7 percent in 1979, increased dramatically in the 1980s, to 35.8 percent in 1987 (*Momento* 2/89: tables, 5–6).

A variety of social conditions reflected the economic crisis and at the same time augured poorly for the future. The number of people employed in the industrial sector in 1987 had increased by 2.49 percent since 1985, but the 1987 figure was still 5.9 percent *less* than the figure for 1980–1981 (*Momento* 4/89: table, 5). Based on data from the Guatemalan ministry of labor, "72 percent of the population cannot meet their basic needs, compared to 50 percent in 1986" (UOG 7/8/89: 4). The agrarian problems addressed by the Reverend Andrés Girón's Pro-Land Movement (see Chapter 6) remained unsolved.[9]

Overall health and health services indicators were dismal. Infant mortality rates persisted at astronomical levels, 73.7 per thousand, a rate that disguises the even higher rate in rural areas (160 deaths per thousand births). Each of the ten principal causes of infant mortality continued to be a condition or disease preventable by policy decisions (Guatemalan Human Rights Commission—GHRC). Health care services continued to be badly skewed in favor of urban areas, especially Guatemala City. The health care situation was complicated further by repression of health care promoters, the spending policy of the health ministry (which disbursed 80 percent of its resources in Guatemala City), and the requirement that medical facilities report suspicious injuries to the military (ROG 1/88: 12).[10] Finally, youth gangs began to proliferate in Guatemala City (*On Their Own*). Social equity continued to be a major problem.[11]

In short, halfway through the Cerezo administration the economy did not have the capacity to produce capital for either major social-spending programs to reduce some of society's inequities or for the massive capital accumulation sustained development implies.[12] From the perspective of the popular organizations, the macroindicators were unsatisfactory.[13]

Economic Policy, 1987–1989

In 1986, the new Christian Democratic government had elaborated an economic development plan to stimulate growth. At the outset Guatemala relied heavily on external economic aid. From 1986 to September 1989, economic and military assistance from the United States totaled $878 million, of which about half was loans. An additional billion dollars came from international lenders in which the United States had voting power, of which less than $10 million were donations and the rest loans.[14] In 1988 and 1989, the government initiated a shift toward a neoliberal, export-driven model of economic growth, what President Cerezo referred to as the "modernization" of the economy, summarized in two economic plans, the "Plan for 500 Days," and "Guatemala 2000."[15]

The nation began 1989 with fairly dismal economic conditions around some positive signs of recovery. A precipitous drop in coffee prices, and hence state revenue, posed a new economic threat and again revealed Guatemala's dependence on international markets beyond its control. During 1989, policy decisions revealed a renewed emphasis on exports as the basis of the country's economic growth model. Although export-driven growth models are not a new alternative in Guatemalan history, the new plan emphasized nontraditional exports, defined as anything except the traditional agricultural commodities and crude oil. The inspiration for this model was the successful East Asian examples such as Taiwan and Korea (*Momento* 2/89: 10).

In June, to stimulate exports and reintegrate the country more tightly into international markets, the government passed a law creating opportunities for assembly industries (*maquila*) and new incentives for nontraditional exports; it predicted the new program would generate more than a half billion dollars in foreign exchange annually and would create some seventy thousand jobs annually. These incentives, which reduced the cost of production for exported goods, were essentially tax vacations for from two to ten years on all import taxes and tariffs, income generated from exports, and export taxes on assembled products (PCRP 6/89: 3).

The immediate results of these policies were mixed. The government projected about 4 percent growth in GDP for both 1989 and 1990, which would mark the first sustained departure "from the economic stagnation of the past decade"—no small achievement. Based on data from the first half of 1989, the projected annual growth rates for sugar, bananas, and basic grains were positive (uncorrected for population growth), but coffee and cotton projected declines. Inasmuch as coffee revenues produce about 35 percent of Guatemala's export earnings, the 4.9 percent decline in output implies a significant revenue shortfall for the government. In fact, the data suggested a 6.9 percent increase in earnings from exports, but a 7.1 increase in imports. The size of the budget deficit for 1989 was projected to be 370.7 percent of the 1988 deficit (which in turn was 138.3 percent greater than the 1987 deficit) (*Momento* 8/89: 11–12).

In August 1989, the government announced its "500-Day Program," the blueprint for Guatemalan development for the remainder of the Cerezo administration, and part of the DCG's overall master plan for Guatemalan development, "Guatemala 2000." Essentially neoliberal, the program centered on privatization and nontraditional exports, combined with a trickle-down approach to social justice.[16] Policy aims included reducing state expenditures by 10 percent, creating free-trade zones, and reviewing minimum wages and ways to control inflation.

The first concrete steps, however, were devaluation of the Quetzal to Q2.78 to the dollar and deregulation of interest rates (PCRP 9/89: 3–4).[17] The government subsequently let the Quetzal float, permitting the market to determine the actual value of the currency. The Quetzal immediately dropped in value to Q3.60 to the dollar but appeared to be averaging about Q3.25 by the end of 1989. Although this clearly meant a drop in purchasing power for the impoverished majority, the president of the Bank of Guatemala described the new policy as properly neoliberal, adding that "the stability of the Quetzal will now depend on the strength of the economy and not on subsidies that lead only to more international indebtedness" (PCRP 11/89: 5).[18]

The purchasing power of Guatemalans was further reduced by inflationary pressures. Inflation was 12.3 percent and 11.1 percent for 1987 and 1988, respectively, fairly significant in the context of currency devaluation, the lack of increases in salaries and wages, and increases in costs of basic services and consumer goods. Inflation for the period from December 1988 to June 1989 was 4.7 percent. The devaluation of the Quetzal to 2.78 to the dollar had immediate effects: the Guatemalan daily *El Gráfico* reported that consumer prices increased by 9 percent in the twenty-four hours after the devaluation announcement.[19]

The Cerezo administration had taken several concrete steps to spur economic growth and to help accumulate investment capital, but on the question of minimum wages, the government had promised only a quick review, a "rapid process of consensus-building (*concertación*)" for new salary levels (PCRP 11/89: 5). The concrete steps taken in 1989 resulted in new declines in the working sectors' quality of life.[20]

Economic performance showed some successes. In 1989, the GNP rose 4 percent (not corrected for population growth, itself about 3 percent). The three major productive sectors of the economy, agriculture, commerce, and industry, each showed positive growth rates that were lower than the 4 percent overall growth, suggesting slower growth in these major sectors. Construction, electricity production, and transportation were the most dynamic growth sectors and accounted for the overall growth rate (*Momento* 3/90: 2).

The export-driven nature of the model continued to be the official policy. But coffee prices dropped drastically in 1989 (from $130 to $70 a sack), so that although production had doubled in 1989 over 1988, "the foreign exchange generated was similar ($251 million and $288 million, respectively)." Nontraditional exports, mostly vegetables, generated $20.3 million in foreign exchange by the end of 1989, still relatively small compared to coffee. The maquila program organized in 1989, to assemble semifinished imports and then re-export them, with tax breaks, led to disappointing results in the first quarter of 1990, with only four hundred new jobs and $20.5 million output generated (ROG Sp/90: 6–7). Government deficits continued to pose a challenge for policymakers, rising 141.3 percent from 1988 to 1989, from Q284.9 million to Q687.4 million (*Momento* 3/90: 13, table).

Nontraditional exports were a major factor in the positive growth noted in 1989. Traditional exports declined in value from 1988 to 1989 by 4.5 percent, but nontraditional ones increased their performance by 77.7 percent, producing 29.8 percent of the total value of exports (PCRP 2/90: 8). As of the end of 1989, tourism had become the second largest earner of foreign exchange, producing about $150 million during the year (PCRP 2/90: 7–8).

The growth pattern was not without problems. Total foreign debt as of the end of 1988, based on data from the Bank of Guatemala, was $2.648 billion, 150 percent of the debt as of 1980 (*Momento* 2/90: 5).[21] In 1988, debt service equaled 36.5 percent of the value of exports and cost Guatemala 40 percent of the foreign exchange earned. Largely because of the decline in the value of the Quetzal, service on this debt rose from 5.6 percent of tax revenues in 1987 to 14.9 percent in 1989; and from 3.8 percent of public spending in 1987 to 10.1 percent in 1988, even with tax reform measures taken into account (*Momento* 2/90: 10).

The overall growth rate in 1989, moreover, owed much of its performance "to an influx of international loans." Although the GNP grew 4 percent in 1989, the foreign debt rose $150 million to nearly $3 billion. Inflation was 13 percent for the year. Unemployment and underemployment averaged 47 percent. "The buying power of 1989 salaries was less than one fifth of its 1980 equivalent" (GMG 5/90: 3).[22]

In addition to these macroeconomic problems, economic policies of the Cerezo administration sometimes resulted in hardship for the working poor, which meant resistance from popular organizations. In late 1989, for example, the government was considering privatizing its electricity-generating industry (Industria Nacional de Electricidad—INDE), and the proposed layoffs of some two thousand INDE workers had produced a very militant union in the utility. The economic plan also called for ending tariff barriers, which would force Guatemalan industry to compete internationally with its antiquated and inefficient equipment, forcing yet another hardship on workers who were likely to be squeezed in order to maintain competitiveness.

Floating the Quetzal in November 1989 had led to a de facto currency devaluation of 30 percent, the Quetzal falling from Q2.70 to the dollar to Q3.40. This led to higher fuel prices, which in turn led, in late 1989, to bus fares doubling and electric and water rates being raised substantially. Currency fluctuations continued in 1990. Decisions in early April resulted in the Quetzal dropping from Q3.22 to the dollar to Q4.90. Although the government described these as homegrown decisions aimed at improving the economy for the next administration, evidence suggests that international lenders were conditioning future credit on the policies (GMG 5/90: 2).[23]

Presumably responding to these conditions and other isthmus events, the presidents of Central America met in an economic summit in Antigua, Guatemala, in June. The resulting "Plan of Action" and "Declaration of Antigua" set out specific policy accords, including a timetable, to help achieve a Central American Economic Community. In the two documents the presidents "agreed to a coordinated regional approach to promote industrial and agricultural production and attract new investment." But neither document mentions either agrarian reform or new social welfare programs. In short, the presidents proposed a free-market, trickle-down approach at the regional level, an attempt to re-create and surpass the Central American Common Market in new and more difficult economic circumstances (WPost 6/20/90: 35A).[24]

U.S. Secretary of State James A. Baker appeared at the closing of the three-day economic summit at Antigua. Though the role of the United States was vague at this point, Washington apparently planned to act as coordinator of international assistance to the region. Yet at the same time, overall U.S. assistance to Central America was declining and funds were shifting to Nicaragua and Panama (NYTimes 6/19/90: 3A). The real value of U.S. participation remained unclear, except for symbolic support for the economic model endorsed by the presidents.

Fiscal and Budgetary Politics

The problematic aspects of economic growth were reflected in fiscal policy as well. The Christian Democrats had publicly embraced reduced government spending early in their administration, but in fact the budget increased by 24 percent in 1989, with a projected additional increase of 5.2 percent in 1990 (ROG Sp/90: 7).[25] Little or none of these new funds were programmed for productive capacity or social programs. In the 1990 budget the combined expenditure for the military and internal security ministries was 32 percent, and 21 percent was foreign debt service and repayment, totaling 53 percent in these types of expenditures (GMG 5/90: 5).

The 1990 budget was not approved by the National Congress, however, so the 1989 budget remained in effect, at least at the beginning of the year. This budget applied to about half of the state's activities, since municipal-level government, certain autonomous agencies, and the national university had separate budget processes (*Momento* 1/90: 2). Considerable legal confusion surrounded this event: on the one hand, Guatemalan law appeared to give the president carte blanche, since he has the authority to make adjustments in the budget when there is no formal budget approval. On the other hand, the law also says that in the absence of a budget, the previous year's budget remains in effect (*Momento* 1/90: 2–4).

In a compromise President Cerezo accepted the 1989 budget for 1990, but received authority to make internal adjustments in the budget received. The government had projected an increase, from 1989 to 1990, of Q189 million, two-thirds of which was destined for increased salaries. The government then (1) assigned all ministries the same percentage that had been proposed in the 1990 unapproved budget; (2) dropped the salary increases from the new plan of action; and (3) allowed the previously proposed cuts in two ministries to stand. According to DCG figures, these actions resulted in a budget document that actually saved Q17.7 million, which was then redistributed amongst various ministries. This meant, in effect, that there would be no salary increases for state employees affected by this measure. This, added to the impact of inflation and the decline of the Quetzal, meant a 35 percent decline in purchasing power for Guatemalans (*Momento* 1/90: 5).

Revenue projections in the budget included anticipated foreign assistance. Loans included a large increase in funds from European nations but a decline, from $80 million in 1989 to $56.5 million in 1990, from the United States. Most of this revenue went to shore up the budget in the face of declining foreign exchange, to service the debt, and to prevent further currency devaluation. Again, relatively little even of foreign aid was for productive investment or for social programs (ROG Sp/90: 7). In terms of revenue projections, 85 percent would be generated by taxes on goods and services, and only 15 percent would come from property and income taxes.[26] Very little in the total budget process suggested a policy commitment toward redistributing resources or providing opportunities for Guatemala's impoverished majority.

The overall conclusion by 1990 was mixed economic performance, in spite of reasonable economic indicators over the first six months of the year. The construction sector was a leader in generating growth in 1989, but it suffered major setbacks in 1990. Agricultural production maintained or increased production levels, especially in domestic food products, responding to scarcities caused by earlier crop failures (*Momento* 8/90: 1–3, 20). The projected rate of the government's deficit for the year, as of mid-1990, was only slightly (1.6 percent) worse than the 1989 deficit, an improvement over previous performances. The balance of payments remained negative. Coffee exports rose dramatically in volume, after the international quota system was dismantled, but the price dropped by 50 percent in 1990, showing a net gain of about 3 percent over the corresponding first semester of 1989.

Overall, traditional and nontraditional exports both showed significant growth in production and value of exports for the period. But two factors countered the positive impact of exports on general growth. First, imports soared to $715.8 million, up 33.1 percent compared to 1989's first semester. Second, there was a significant negative flow of capital, including capital flight and amortization as well as declines in foreign investment and international credit (*Momento* 8/90: 1, 5–6, 7–9, 21–table).[27]

The principal fiscal problems, as of mid-1990, included the government's lack of liquid assets; excessive liquidity in the private financial market; deepening of the negative balance of payments; the pressures of foreign debt; a general recession in economic activity; and the effects of these last two on employment levels and on price inflation (*Momento*, 8/90: 19). Thus, there was scant overall success for the neoliberal economic plan, in spite of several years of concerted and well-financed policy efforts to maintain an export-driven growth model.

Developments in 1990

Subsequent world events put greater strains on Guatemala's economy later in 1990. The Iraqi invasion of Kuwait and subsequent Gulf War led to sharply increased fuel prices for Guatemala, producing a new wave of inflation when the Cerezo government increased oil prices by 45 percent for consumers (NYTimes 11/7/90: A11; TOA 10/17/90: 8). For consumers the direct impact was obvious, but even the indirect impact, on debt and development programs, for example, suggested continuing long-term problems. As an oil producer, Guatemala, if not the majority of its citizens, stood to benefit from these increased prices, which made exploitation of the estimated twenty-six million barrels of reserves economically feasible. Output in late 1990 was four thousand barrels daily, "less than 15 percent of consumption" (TOA 10/17/90: 8).

Other developments during the year suggested shifts both in policy and in the nature of the economy. In July the world market for cardamon, a spice that is one of Guatemala's main exports, collapsed, and the government suspended all exports in order to protect the price for its producers (*Centroamérica Hoy* 7/30/90: 11). Finally, more resources were apparently turning to drug-related activities: "Guatemala now ties for fifth place in world production of opium" (ROG Sp/90: 7). In short, the government seemed less able to weather the economic storms created by international developments.

Conclusion

This overview of macroeconomic and fiscal policy reveals a mixed pattern. The Christian Democratic government was committed to economic plans to increase the export-driven nature of the economy, thereby hoping to stimulate growth. This policy style meshed nicely with the neoliberal international economic visions prevailing in the West. As a result, a good deal of international assistance flowed to Guatemala. Securing this assistance was a victory for the government and the military that supported it, inasmuch as international legitimacy as a result of elections was a goal of the military's counterinsurgency plan in the early 1980s.[28]

The combination of policy choices and international aid resulted in economic growth indicators for at least some periods of the Cerezo presidency, but growth was inconsistent. To some extent, this can be blamed on policy inefficiency and excessive state spending, the argument raised by conservative opponents of the Christian Democrats. But probably to a greater degree, the economic problems of the government resulted from international market factors over which President Cerezo had no control.

Finally, of course, policy choices were themselves limited by the reality of the domestic political scene. Although focusing here primarily on macroeconomic policy provided an incomplete picture of the relative strength of domestic political sectors, nevertheless, the social impact of the DCG's policies was apparent: inflation and other results pointed to harder times for Guatemala's citizens. The overall pattern of policy outputs suggested continuing declines in the ability of popular sectors to meet their basic needs as well as the continuing dominance of elite sectors.

Of particular concern was the impact of macroeconomic policies and programs on basic quality of life, which in Guatemala means food security, given the precarious nature of marginal economic life. In fact, the nation was faced with a continuing crisis in food security for a variety of reasons. Inflation and a declining currency made the costs of agricultural inputs for producing basic grains very problematic, causing declines in food availability. Replenishing food supplies with international donations, a sometimes necessary humanitarian gesture, also drives production downward since they increase supply without reducing the costs for domestic producers. On the consumer side, inflation and corresponding lower salaries reduced demand, as opposed to need, for food and basic grain products.

In short, macroeconomic policies aimed at improving the balance of payments and increasing foreign exchange earnings may have made sense at the macrolevel: the combinations of factors made it more rational for small producers, traditionally the source of the bulk of domestic food supply, to turn to nontraditional agricultural products. But policymakers seem to have ignored the sectoral consequences for small producers, as well as the negative impact on food security for most of the populace (*Momento* 4/90: 7–9). Both international and domestic incentives are thereby reducing the domestic food supply.

Continuing impoverishment has an impact on political participation, especially since such changes lead to increased organization by groups representing the poorest sectors of society. Since the Christian Democrats were officially committed to democracy and at least some measure of social reform, they needed to respond to these pressures.

Notes

1. The overall growth rate has declined almost every year since the early 1980s, including drops of 3.5 percent in 1982, 2.6 percent in 1983, and 1.0 percent in 1985, with a positive growth rate of .5 percent in 1984 and a zero rate of increase in 1986 (Millett: B312). Based on data from the Bank of Guatemala, from 1978 to 1988, the accumulated growth rate in the industrial sector was 4.97 percent, an average annual rate of 0.45 percent (*Momento* 4/89: table, 4).

2. A Christian Democratic analysis of the roots of this crisis states:

Guatemala has passed through a profound socio-economic crisis in the early 1980s, due to a recession in the international economy, difficulties

in obtaining external financing, a drop in private investment, capital
flight, and the breakdown of the Central American Common Market. This
crisis is structural in origin, and can be seen in the fact that the majority
of Guatemala's inhabitants do not have their basic needs met. The crisis
is intimately related to the low level of national income and its in-
equitable distribution, to a high rate of unemployment, to the inadequate
integration of the Guatemalan economy in the international economy, and
to the inadequate participation of the public sector in national development (Maldonado Ruiz: 42).

3. Accessibility to the U.S. market has become increasingly important to the
Guatemalan economy. The value of exports to the United States increased from
28.2 percent in 1970, to 29.7 percent in 1979, to 40.4 percent in 1987.
    4. These questions show that there were several key economic issues that
might have been discussed and debated in the electoral campaigns of 1984 and
1985. The absence of serious debate on nontrivial issues in those campaigns cannot be ascribed to the lack of serious problems in Guatemala.
    5. That is, owners themselves set the declared value of their property. This
time-tested approach to taxation was used in the early part of the century on rural
lands, allowing the United Fruit Company to grossly underassess its productive
lands, for example. The attempt by the Arbenz land reform program to compensate
the company for expropriations according to the values the company itself had
declared was part of the basis for the company's vendetta against the government
in the 1950s.
    6. These analyses were expressed in interviews held in Guatemala City and
in Mexico City in January 1987.
    7. This source does not explain whether this figure takes into account popu-
lation growth or if it is merely a nonadjusted measure of growth.
    8. The Quetzal (Q) is Guatemala's unit of currency. Since the end of World
War II, the Quetzal had been on par with the U.S. dollar, but after 1980 it was
impossible for Guatemala to sustain that relationship, as the currency began to
devalue on the black market. A major dimension of the social justice question in
the 1980s is the impact of devaluation policy, which makes exports feasible but
reduces quality of life domestically.
    9. A report from the Guatemalan Church in Exile claims that:

The agrarian crisis grows worse each day in economic, social and political terms. The large and medium sized farms, which represent 2.2 percent
of total farms, absorb 65 percent of cultivable land, while the remaining
97 percent have only 35 percent of the cultivable land. Officially, there
are 419,620 landless peasants, and of these 309,119 are without any permanent work. Meanwhile, 1,200,000 hectares of private land lie idle
(IGE 1988: 5).

10. ROG estimates that 90 percent of the dentists, 80 percent of the physicians, and 50 percent of the nurses are in Guatemala City, which has no more than
30 percent of the national population. See von Hoegen for an analysis of the geo-
graphic concentration of development, reflected in educational and investment
indicators. ROG's overview of health conditions in late 1987:

Even the most basic human needs of the majority of Guatemalans are not
met. An estimated three out of every four suffer from some degree of

malnutrition, and only 20 percent of the population has access to potable water or to latrines. The major causes of illness and death in the country stem from malnutrition, gastrointestinal problems, including parasites, and respiration problems, such as pneumonia. Such illnesses could be easily prevented or treated if the population was adequately nourished, immunized, and able to afford even minimal curative (as distinct from preventive) health services. There is evidence that the recent [military] violence in the country has worsened the already bad health conditions (ROG 1/88: 12).

11. According to Cockburn, overall social conditions were in serious decline in 1988:

> The staggering social poverty has been untouched by Cerezo. . . . Forty percent of all Guatemalans live in extreme poverty, with this figure reaching 83 percent in rural areas. Half of all children die before reaching the age of nine, and 81 percent [of these] die from malnutrition. Finally, half the population can't read or write and 70 percent of all deaths in Guatemala result from readily curable diseases, such as tuberculosis and pneumonia (Cockburn: 2).

12. For an overview of 1988 with similar figures but with a more positive interpretation, see PCRP 4/89: 3–4. In this source, for example, substantial price increases in basic commodities—such as electricity for consumers, up 25 percent; diesel fuel, up 38 percent; and gasoline, up 8 percent—are described as appropriate "adjustments in distorted prices for basic services." For the Economic Commission on Latin America's review of the 1988 Guatemalan economy, see "CEPAL."

13. One summary of the first two years of the Cerezo administration claims that

> popular demands have generally been ignored as the government worked to reinforce its relations with the traditional pillars of military and economic power. . . . There are few indications of a significant shift in policy to address the country's serious social and economic inequities. Government measures to promote economic growth have instead been oriented around the "trickle down" approach reminiscent of previous regimes (CAR 1/29/88: 26).

14. For a detailed listing of all foreign economic and military assistance to Guatemala during the Cerezo regime, including both loans and donations, see *Special Service* 10/89: 4–6.

15. The complete text of these two economic plans can be found in "Partidos demócrata."

16. The twin emphases of these plans in their various configurations were "to stimulate exports while not ignoring domestic needs, thereby producing a more equitable and redistributive style of development, which in turn will produce a more stable and autonomous nation" (PCRP 11/89: 5–6).

17. Until 1980, the value of the Quetzal was one U.S. dollar. In the mid-1980s, the Quetzal was pegged at Q2.50 to the dollar. Before the 1989 devaluation, the Quetzal had been devalued to Q2.70 to the dollar in 1988. At the same time as

the August 1989 devaluation to Q2.78, interest rates were freed from regulation and allowed to find their levels in the market (*Momento* 8/89: 1).

18. In spite of the government's rhetoric about its desires to pursue free-market models, the devaluation policies apparently were conditions of an Agency for International Development (USAID) loan of $75 million, designed as a short-term solution to the combination of a lack of foreign reserves and a negative balance of payments (GMG 9/89: 4).

19. GMG 9/89: 4; data on earlier years from *Momento* 3/89: 1; data from 1989 from *Momento* 8/89: 4.

20. Because of inflation even the minimum wage, often not paid, produced "less than half the cost of the daily minimum diet. . . . Eighty-two percent of rural families live in complete poverty, with insufficient income to meet their most basic needs. . . . Guatemala, along with Haiti, has the worst social indicators in all of Latin America" (IGE 1988: 5).

21. This issue of *Momento* provides a thorough and detailed breakdown of data on Guatemala's foreign debt.

22. As of early 1990, "Guatemala's foreign debt [was] 60 percent of the country's total GNP and 42 percent of export earnings" (ROG Sp/90: 7). The inflation rate for all of Guatemala, from 1988 to 1989, had been 17.9 percent (for Guatemala City, 20.2 percent) (*Momento* 3/90: 6).

23. The Quetzal is quoted at Q4.70 to the dollar in *Excelsior* 4/27/90: 2A. For measures taken to shore up the currency after the floating process failed to stop inflationary pressures, see ROG Su/90: 15.

24. For details on the Central American Economic Summit and the decision to pursue the elaboration of the Central American Economic Community, see PCRP 6/90: 26–27. For the texts of documents emanating from the Antigua summit meeting, see *Panorama Centroamericana: Temas y documentos de debate* 9/90.

25. This source ascribes this spending to DCG patronage and corruption.

26. "Guatemalan big business only contributes 7 percent of these income and property taxes" (GMG 5/90: 3–4). Tax policy has centered on sales taxes, an extremely regressive program under the circumstances (ROG Sp/90: 8).

27. For an analysis of Central America's role in international trade, see *Momento* 7/90: 2–12.

28. The Christian Democrats acknowledged from the start that democracy was still in the future, not the present. Before the 1985 elections they were sanguine in assessing the overall situation and understood that in the mid-1980s, international pressures meant that the dominant groups in Guatemala needed a purer form of "electionism." As candidate Cerezo remarked during his campaign, "They need a President who can obtain money for the country" (NYTimes 4/21/85: A8).

6

Popular Sectors During the Cerezo Administration

In his 1985 campaign for the presidency, Vinicio Cerezo had made at least vague promises on behalf of the poor, but quick and easy economic solutions were impossible once he took office. Consistent with the spirit of a democratic opening, many popular-sector groups mobilized after the inauguration with the goal of influencing government to improve the lot of the poor and working classes. Chapter 5 charted the administration's policy attempts to raise investment capital and spur growth, and this one measures its responses to demands by the popular sectors for distribution of social wealth. One measure of democracy is the relative success of those groups favoring social reform versus those who oppose reforms in favor of pursuing economic growth.

Poverty was commonplace in Guatemala during the 1980s. According to data from the United Nations Economic Commission on Latin America, the percentage of Guatemalans in poverty rose from 79 percent in 1980 to 87 percent in 1987, and median monthly wages declined significantly between 1984 and 1988 in rural areas, industry, and even government jobs.[1] As a result of these conditions, popular groups expressed their demands in marches, demonstrations, and other modes of direct participation throughout the Cerezo administration. These groups, some with long traditions and most with enduring unmet demands, immediately began to organize, or resurface, and articulate their demands. This chapter studies the activities and demands of popular sector groups in both rural and urban areas, as well as the Cerezo administration's responses to them.[2]

Popular Groups and Policy Responses

The Land Movement

> Land reform must be the issue in Guatemala. If we don't have it, we are going to continue to have blood and violence.[3]

95

The land tenure question is perhaps the key issue in Guatemalan politics, both as an historical legacy and as the basis for a decent quality of life
for a large segment of society. Increasing landlessness has been characteristic of economic growth cycles, especially on the South Coast, since at
least the beginning of agricultural modernization in that region in the
1950s, which produced both economic growth and more social injustice. In
1980, a massive strike occurred in the region, at first among sugarcane
workers but later spreading to other sectors as well.[4] Led by the Committee for Peasant Unity (Comité de Unidad Campesina—CUC), the strike
involved thousands of workers including both migrants and southern
coastal resident workers as well as both Indian and ladino workers.

At first glance, the 1980 strike appeared to have been successful: that
it happened at all in the face of terrible and oppressive working conditions
was no small achievement. Moreover, agricultural production was interrupted, and the military government raised the official daily minimum
wage from Q1.90 to Q3.20.[5] The aftermath, however, was a wave of
repression that targeted progressive clergy as well as peasant leaders.
Repression hit CUC leaders both on the South Coast and in the highland
home villages of migrant workers. After 1980, the CUC was forced under-
ground, its leaders murdered or exiled.

The strikers had won the policy response they had demanded, a new
official minimum wage, but constraints on open mass politics limited the
substantive success of the strike. The government did not enforce its
new wage policy, and in most cases the minimum wage was not paid. In
effect, the landowners got what they wanted: little economic change plus
the removal of "subversives." In the short run, the strike's victories were
Pyrrhic.

Shortly after President Cerezo's inauguration in 1986, an organized,
articulated demand for land distribution began functioning: the Pro-Land
Movement, or ANC, led by the Reverend Andrés Girón, a Catholic priest.[6]
A major catalyst in the organization of the ANC was the decision by many
landowners around 1985 to shift their land from cotton to sorghum,
because of market factors. The result was a major decrease in the demand
for rural labor at a time when rising prices and a weakening currency made
the need for work more urgent than normal. Rural unemployment in the
coastal region increased dramatically. The marginal progress gained
through earlier organizing and even a poorly enforced minimum wage law
had been reversed by the decisions of a few plantation owners. The formation of the ANC was therefore neither ideological nor demagogic, nor
even tied solely to the electoral process. It began as a social movement
reflecting both the historical context and the socioeconomic reality of the
south-coast region. Economic factors were the key ingredients in the mobilization process of the ANC (Cambranes 1986a: 213).

The first public meeting led by Reverend Girón took place in February 1986, when the priest delivered a speech to about five thousand peasants outside his parish church in south coastal Guatemala (Cambranes 1986a: 215).[7] In April and May 1986, Girón led a nonviolent march of some sixteen thousand peasants from Nueva Concepción on the south-coast agricultural plains to Guatemala City, finishing with a rally at the National Palace. During the march and at the rally, the Christian Democratic government expressed at least indirect support, inasmuch as Guatemala's first lady, Raquel Blandón de Cerezo, appeared with the marchers. By late 1986, 100,000 persons were registered members of the association (Cambranes 1986a: 10).

The ANC demands were not inconsistent with a capitalist market system. The association demanded land, but not expropriation of land being used efficiently. The land to be taken would be purchased from owners who had abandoned it or that was for sale and therefore already available. Purchase funds would be advanced by the government. The new owners, the members of ANC, would organize into cooperatives so that parcels would not become tiny *minifundios* but would remain structurally unchanged, except that they would now be owned by cooperatives. The government's loans would be repaid from the production of the cooperative.

The ANC exerted pressure through organization and public demonstrations; it was committed to the nonviolent philosophy of Dr. Martin Luther King, Jr., with whom Girón had been involved in the United States (Cambranes 1986a: 78–79). But its demands were urgent. Girón was effective in using the media, his organization, and his legitimacy as a member of the clergy. The ANC's adherents, probably because of economic desperation and the climate of fear, were very committed to both the goals and methods of the organization. The movement was nonviolent, nonconfiscatory, and capitalist, that is, within the prevailing norms of Western private property relationships, although it was politically direct and insistent, and hence disruptive.

From the beginning the private sector vociferously opposed the ANC's activities. CACIF, the coordinating organization of the private sector in Guatemala, published an open letter to President Cerezo in July 1986, characterizing the movement as demagogic (Cambranes 1986a: 237–239). The National Agricultural Union (Unión Nacional de Agroexportadores—UNAGRO), the organization of the export-agriculture sector, accused Girón of being a "self-appointed" and irresponsible agitator who was fomenting class struggle. UNAGRO again expressed its opposition to any form of agrarian reform in February 1987 (GNIB 2/87: 9). Later, it instituted criminal proceedings against Girón for allegedly inciting criminal behavior (*Boletín* 3/26/87: 5).

Early government responses to the ANC included both symbolic and substantive actions. The ANC gained its legal status as an incorporated group early in the Cerezo administration, and the government publicly expressed support for its aims and methods. The government also repeatedly insisted on respect for the law and expressed dismay and alarm when Girón allegedly made statements in early 1987 to the effect that impatient peasants might begin seizing land if government did not respond more quickly to their demands.

In response to the elite's public opposition to the ANC's demands and to Girón's style, the government continued to reject the notion of "agrarian reform."[8] Instead, it developed a market-based program of land acquisition. Abandoned land or land that owners were willing to sell would be purchased and then redistributed to peasant groups, with long-term mortgages. The first transfer of land to the ANC, in November 1986, was the Monte Llano farm in Yepocapa, consisting of about 1,450 acres, for three hundred families. The farm was purchased by the Guatemalan government for approximately $600,000.

In December 1986, the minister of agriculture announced that the government would transfer three more farms to the ANC. In January 1987, the director of INTA (National Institute for Agrarian Transformation) revealed plans to purchase five additional farms for transfer to peasant organizations. At the same time, he strongly cautioned Reverend Girón and others against using illegal methods to seize land (GNIB 12/86: 13–14). Four state-owned farms (*fincas nacionales*) were transferred to peasant cooperatives in late March in the municipality of San Pedro Jocopilas (*Boletín* 4/10/87: 6). Government land policy also included attempts to increase taxes on idle land, efforts to adjudicate ongoing land-title cases, credit and technical assistance to increase agricultural productivity, and subsidies for agricultural inputs. Expropriation continued to be rejected, because of the threat to the democratization process that would result, according to President Cerezo (*Boletín* 1/29/87: 4). By April 1987, the government was urging that new measures be taken—within constitutional limits, however—to obtain land for redistribution, and the situation was growing more tense.

Clearly, the most positive direct response to the ANC's demands was the market-based program and government-owned property transfers. The ANC received only two fincas in its first two years of work, however, and the second only after the land had already been invaded by peasants. The ANC's public position was that President Cerezo had "neither the power nor the will" to implement the plan to buy plantation land on the market and then resell it (ROG 1/88: 7). Dissatisfied with the pace of distribution, Girón increased his calls for swifter government action and apparently developed plans for the "peaceful occupation" of lands if the government's responses were not satisfactory. At the same time, he called for Congress to pass "a Law of Agrarian Reform" (GNIB 12/86: 13–14).

One result of the relative success of Reverend Girón's movement was a surge of peasant groups seeking land. Several additional groups announced marches (GNIB 12/86: 14; and *Boletín* 4/10/87: 6). Besides marches, there were land occupations by peasants and dispossession of some of the squatters. In December 1987, more than one hundred peasant organizations met and formed the National Peasant Confederation (Confederación Nacional Campesina—CNC) under the leadership of Andrés Girón. CNC "claims to represent 500,000 landless peasants" (ROG 1/88: 5). Faced with these pressures, Cerezo found himself in a difficult situation. The early success of the ANC in attracting media attention and gaining adherents worsened the political problem: the increasing spiral of demands for land led to intensifying opposition from the agricultural elite.

By mid-1988, the Catholic church hierarchy had become involved in the land issue. The Guatemalan bishops had frequently written pastoral letters attacking the country's horrid social and economic conditions, including political violence, but had never directly confronted the cause of these symptoms before the 1988 pastoral letter on land reform (ROG 1/88: 8). Referring to land tenure, they urged the power structure to "accept the idea that a change in the sinful and obsolete social structures in our country is necessary and urgent" (Guatemalan Bishops Conference: 17). The bishops further suggested that the government "legislate with a view towards an equitable distribution of the land, beginning with the vast State-owned lands" and that "insufficiently cultivated estates should be distributed to those who can make them fruitful" (GBC: 17).

UNAGRO responded that the problem of land tenure was beyond the competency of the church and assailed the bishops for creating conflict in Guatemalan society, suggesting that the pastoral letter "appeared like a proposal from the Nicaraguan clergy." UNAGRO further noted that in fact land redistribution was taking place continually under the auspices of the free market, as seen in purchases and sales of property (ROG 1/88: 11).[9]

President Cerezo's response was that landowners should acknowledge the land problem and that the bishops' letter could help bring about this recognition, but that the pastoral letter's recommendations were not necessarily solutions. In short, the president continued to oppose agrarian reform as a concept, while favoring increased efficiency of land use and improvements in peasant living conditions and access to land. He proposed to continue the market-based program and to use state-owned land for development projects (ROG 1/88: 9).

In his report to Congress in January 1988, President Cerezo announced that the government had distributed nine parcels by the end of 1987, a total distribution of 77.5 *caballerías*, benefiting over two thousand families. The first two of these had been distributed to the ANC and the third to another peasant organization led by Carlos A. Dubón. These three parcels totaled forty-one caballerías, benefiting some 1,550 families. Of the total of nine distributions, four were announced only two weeks before Cerezo's report to Congress. These four totaled only 20.5 caballerías, benefiting an additional 160 families (PCRP 1/88: 5).

While the *number* of total transfers more than doubled in the second half of 1987, the amount of land transferred had been reduced by about 50 percent and the number of benefited families was even lower. The government also announced plans to triple the number of transfers in 1988, turning over some three hundred caballerías to benefit five to six thousand families (PCRP 1/88: 6).

The data show a continuing symbolic commitment to transferring available land to peasant organizations, but realistic analysis shows a slowing down of the program's substantive impact on the quality of life of the several hundred thousand landless families seeking land. Overall, government's responses to the ANC were supportive symbolically, but the government was unsuccessful in resolving the problem. The market-based program was pragmatic but not reformist, for no policy proposals addressed any of the conditions causing land problems in the first place.

Consistent with its ideology, the Christian Democratic Party sought to respond to all sides in the land issue by acquiring enough resources to at least begin meeting demands of groups like the ANC without offending the intransigent sectors of the elite, a difficult prospect at best. The DCG's policies were assailed by the elite, which viewed any concession as support for leftists. For their part popular groups described the first year of the Cerezo administration as one in which the government refused to pursue social reform in order to avoid provoking a military coup, and hence of defrauding the people in order to protect the democratic process (*Boletín* 1/29/87: 3). Both sides responded to the government's actions with increased pressure.

Besides political pressure from various sectors, economic conditions may have doomed the DCG strategy from the outset. Given scarce public resources, for example, the necessary funds were simply not available for large-scale purchases of land on the open market to satisfy even the first wave of several thousand families, let alone the needs of approximately 400,000 landless and unemployed rural workers and their families. Moreover, not enough land was available on the market to begin to cover current needs or to meet the demands that would emerge if initial efforts at obtaining land were successful.[10] State lands could fill some of these needs, but even if inefficiently used land were included, less than half the needs of the landless sectors could be met.[11]

The Labor Movement

Guatemala's 1965 Constitution and subsequent labor code guaranteed labor the right to organize: Articles 111 through 116, for example, guaranteed a variety of rights and explicitly stated that the constitutional guarantees were to be considered "non-renounceable minimum guarantees" that could not be ignored by contracts or other agreements. The provisions affecting labor in the 1985 Constitution are generally similar to those of earlier documents,[12] although the constitution oscillates between liberal economic philosophy and conservative or corporatist political principles. It acknowledges labor's inalienable right to organize, but subject to the laws and regulations of the government (Linares Morales: 24–28). The emphasis on individual rights is consistent with the needs of property owners and the business sectors, but the precarious position of economic elites requires that the state have the legal resources to prevent any unregulated mobilization of working groups.[13]

One promising dimension of Guatemala's political *apertura* after 1985 was the opportunity for groups to reorganize. In the mid-1980s, the context affecting urban political movements was similar to the rural atmosphere, including willingness of popular sectors to take advantage of the new political opening after the 1985 election. Mainstream political parties had been as timid in adopting the political agenda of urban popular groups as they had been in the rural context. Labor faced memories of repression, ongoing legal struggles for recognition of unions and strikes, and continuing repression (GNIB 6/87: 15–16). But the problems of social injustice were extremely acute. Timidity notwithstanding, the need for improvement in the quality of life for the popular sectors was more than obvious.

Labor had been well organized and visible, at least historically, but not a major urban political force before the 1970s.[14] As rural groups, moreover, repressive violence is a key dimension in labor's history. The legacy of violence was apparent in 1985, inhibiting attempts to mobilize, the apertura notwithstanding. In spite of the obstacles, however, labor again organized to make demands, largely within prevailing political and economic structures. By 1987, several major labor federations had been organized, including:

1. The Guatemalan Confederation of Labor Unity (Confederación de Unidad Sindical Guatemalteca—CUSG), founded in 1983 during the Ríos Montt government. CUSG received funding from the National Endowment for Democracy via the AFL/CIO and its affiliate, the American Institute for Free Labor Development (AIFLD).[15]

2. The General Coordinator of Guatemalan Workers (Coordinación General de Trabajadores de Guatemala—CGTG), founded by Christian Democrats and supported by CLAT, the Latin American Workers' Confederation.
3. Guatemalan Workers Labor Unity (Unidad Sindical de Trabajadores Guatemaltecos—UNSITRAGUA), an independent organization considered to be the least-compromised federation. UNSITRAGUA was founded in 1985 by survivors of earlier federations that had been decimated by repression in the early 1980s, including the CNT and the Guatemalan Federation of Labor Associations (Federación de Asociaciones Sindicales Guatemaltecas—FASGUA) (ROG 3/88: 6–7, 13).[16]

In addition to the three main federations, there was a regional organization, the Quetzaltenango Workers Union (Unión de Trabajadores Quetzaltecos—UTQ), with sixteen affiliates, and several independent unions, including the Union of Workers of the National Electricity Industry (Sindicato de Trabajadores de la Industria Eléctrica—STINDE), which represented workers at the state-owned electric plant and was the largest single union in Guatemala (ROG 3/88: 6).

While these organizations represent a sizeable proportion of Guatemala's working class, another labor movement, solidarism, reflected the organization of labor by management. Based on cooperation between owners and labor, solidarism generally involves prohibitions against collective bargaining and strikes in exchange for company-organized but employee-funded social services.[17]

Imported from Costa Rica, solidarism was first introduced to Guatemala in 1954, after the CIA-led coup. As of mid-1987, there were 110 Guatemalan solidarist associations, consisting of forty thousand members. Associations are organized in both rural plantations and urban workplaces, including both industrial and service institutions. According to the GSU, associations exist in 38 percent of the businesses in Guatemala City, in 22 percent of those outside the capital city, and on 40 percent of the plantations (ROG 5/88: 5).

Solidarism represents the articulation of the demands of business owners, not organized labor. Since workers voluntarily renounce the right to strike, collective bargaining ceases to exist as a resource for labor and weakens labor as a movement. Solidarism represents the transformation of labor energy from social and political thinking to pure bread-and-butter issues, reducing chances for any long-range perspective on social change. Yet given the economic crisis and poverty, not to mention the repression of workers in the late 1970s and early 1980s, solidarism was a fairly rational strategy for workers to follow (ROG 5/88: 4–5). Nevertheless, economic progress for workers became a function of the owners' good will. Ironically, even this form of unionizing was opposed by major sectors of Guatemala's business elite (ROG 5/88: 15).[18] Organized labor continued to struggle in 1990 on another, more organizational front, as it sought to avoid being replaced by unions representing the solidarist labor movement (ROG Su/90: 4–5, 11).[19]

With the exception of the solidarist organizations, labor continued to federate after 1986. The Unity of Labor and Popular Action coalition (Unidad de Acción Sindical y Popular—UASP) was formed in late 1987 and early 1988, initially by UNSITRAGUA and the electrical workers' union, STINDE, but was then joined by the other two major federations, CUSG and CGTG. UASP was noteworthy first because it united disparate organizations that had differed ideologically and had been divided by political party and funding affiliations. Second, the leadership came from UNSITRAGUA, generally perceived to be the least accommodative and most activist of the labor federations (ROG 3/88: 6–7). The CUC, discussed earlier in connection with rural strikes in 1980, re-emerged publicly after years of repression, exile, and clandestine operation, to become an affiliate of UASP (ROG 3/88: 12).[20]

Labor Policies

Although legal minimum wages had increased, real wages for workers had declined overall and in every category between 1980 and 1986 (see tables 6.1 and 6.2). Real annual wages for all workers registered with the Guatemalan Institute for Social Security (IGSS) went from Q1,389 to Q1,127, a decline in purchasing power of Q262, or 19 percent, from 1980 to 1988. During the period, however, real wages for most categories of workers generally increased from 1980 to highs around 1983 (during a period of macro-level declines in the economy), and then declined abruptly in 1985 and 1986 (during a period of macro growth). The perception of decline, therefore, was even more acute than the six-year summary statistics suggest.[21]

The policy strategy of the Christian Democratic government vis-à-vis labor and management stressed collaboration and consultation, that is, concertación, with organized groups. The goal in effect was to integrate organized labor and capital into economic policymaking so as to improve economic performance and social justice while regulating social conflict. Although this suggests a major role for the state in economic decision-making, this would be countered, according to the party, by the effective pluralism of competing organizations (Maldonado Ruiz: 43–44). The government's economic plans for 1987 and 1988 included steps to increase revenues so that accumulated funds could be used for a mixture of purposes,

Table 6.1 **Minimum and Real Wages, 1980–1988**

Sector	Minimum Wage 1980	Minimum Wage 1988	Increase (Decline)
Agriculture	3.20	4.50	1.30
Mining	3.72	5.00	1.28
Industry	3.84	5.80	1.96
Services	3.63	6.66	3.03
Construction	—	16.00	—
	—	10.00	—
	—	8.00	—
Commerce	3.48	7.04	3.56
Average Wages	3.57	5.80	2.23
Real Wages			
(1980 base)	3.57	2.64	-0.93

Notes: All data in Quetzales per day; calculations based on cumulative inflation rate of 219%. Wages in Industry and Services are averages of subcategories included in those categories. Wages in Construction reflect new categories created in 1988.
Source: Based on CAR 1/29/88: 31.

Table 6.2 **Annual Real Wages, 1980–1986**

Sector	1980	1981	1982	1983	1984	1985	1986
Agriculture	619	833	844	894	773	717	611
Mining	4006	3966	4047	4193	4086	3142	1942
Industry	2108	2348	2415	2349	2479	2232	1815
Construction	1889	2308	2299	2142	1478	1277	996
Essential Services	1889	2853	1585	1948	1840	1604	1301
Commerce	2870	2788	3026	2844	2799	2590	2073
Transportation	1788	1700	1891	2430	1675	1567	1233
Services	1974	1825	1937	1898	1727	1413	1157
All Workers	1389	1636	1734	1754	1596	1377	1127

Notes: Data are average annual real wages for workers registered with the Guatemalan Institute for Social Security (IGSS). Data are in adjusted Quetzales, with 1980 as the base and an accumulated inflation of 219%. The figures for All Workers are averages for all workers registered with IGSS, not averages of the figures in the other categories.
Source: Based on IGSS data, reproduced in CAR 1/29/88: 32.

including paying for the military costs of counterinsurgency, promoting development, and supporting social programs to pay the "social wage." Specifics included a reform package with a property tax, new minimum wages, removal of price controls on basic foodstuffs, and increases in electric rates (ROG 3/88: 2). The DCG also called for the creation of new jobs, coordination of salary scales, and support for workers' organizations (Maldonado Ruiz: 44).

In December 1987, the government announced a 40 percent increase in electricity rates, ostensibly to pay the foreign debt incurred because of military corruption in building the huge hydroelectric power project at Chixoy. Opposition surfaced not only among consumer and popular groups but on the right as well, which claimed the new rates demonstrated the government's inability to manage the public sector. Even the human rights ombudsman entered the fray, claiming that increasing the rates would be tantamount to violating human rights (ROG 1/88: 11).

In January 1988, UASP led the largest demonstrations in Guatemala since 1980. As a result, the government entered into negotiations with the UASP on several ongoing issues: electricity rates, minimum wages, price controls on basic foodstuffs, legal and political validation for CUC and the Mutual Support Group (Grupo de Apoyo Mutuo—GAM)—the organization that had been demanding investigations into human rights violations since the Mejía Víctores government—and safety for returning refugees and exiles (UOG 3/88: 2–3).

After the demonstrations and negotiations, the government rescinded the rate increases, resulting in a final schedule of increases that averaged 25 percent overall and "perhaps less for low-income households" (ROG 3/88: 6–7). The government increased the minimum wage in early 1988, the first time it had been adjusted since 1980 (see Table 6.1).[22] CACIF called the agreement between the government and the UASP "socialistic" even though most of the provisions of the pact were abstract and nonspecific, awaiting later implementation to become concrete (UOG 3/88: 3). Although the pact was largely symbolic and would improve social tranquility while providing little fundamental change, CACIF interpreted it as a threat. In short, although the political arena was being more utilized by popular-sector organizations, business groups also escalated their public protests against wage and tax increases, the activities of the government's human rights ombudsman, and increases in electricity rates (CAR 1/29/88: 26–27).

Other Rural Organizations

Besides the ANC, the Reverend Girón's land movement, other organizations became active in rural areas after the 1986 election. The CUC, which had helped lead the 1980 agricultural strike against south-coast plantations, resumed functioning on behalf of rural workers. In January 1989, CUC supported another farmworkers' strike on the southern coast, demanding a daily minimum wage of Q10 ($3.70). The strike was supported by UASP, which had become the country's largest popular organization in the late 1980s.[23]

The government's initial reaction to the strike was to militarize the zone, an attempt to threaten the worker groups into submission. But in February, for the first time in Guatemalan history, face-to-face negotiations began between owners, represented by UNAGRO, and a labor representative from

UASP. Neither side trusted the government in these negotiations: UASP because the government had ignored earlier agreements and had militarized the south-coast zone, and UNAGRO because of the upcoming electoral campaign and not wanting to appear to lend support to the Christian Democrats (GMG 3/89: 9–10).

By late 1989, however, the negotiations between UASP and UNAGRO had come to naught: UNAGRO proposed wages of Q5.10 per day, an increase over the Q3.20 minimum wage won by workers in a 1980 strike but significantly less in terms of purchasing power, given the decline of the Quetzal and inflation. Ironically, even the UASP proposal for a daily minimum wage of Q8.00 was less than the 1980 wage. The two sides could not agree on this or other proposals, and the negotiations stalled. With the continually deteriorating working and living conditions on the main plantations of the South Coast, CUC called for new labor action in late 1989 (GMG 11/89: 3–4).[24]

In response to this call, in late January 1990, "some 60,000 workers at dozens of . . . plantations and sugar processing plants stopped work to demand higher salaries." The strike was organized by the CUC and other peasant groups and supported by the UASP (ROG Sp/90: 15). In public, landowners responded with a customary hard-line approach, but behind the scenes, as in 1989, there were negotiations between UNAGRO and the UASP (ROG Su/90: 11). UASP and the peasant groups demanded initially a minimum wage of Q20, the minimum required for food purchases, but later reduced their demand to Q15. UNAGRO's final offer was a daily wage of Q7.20. The negotiations were not successful in resolving the gap (*Excelsior* 4/10/91: 1A).

The Christian Democratic government became involved in the process again. Early in the year, because of the continuing recession the government announced an austerity program that raised prices, including a "30 percent increase in gasoline, 50 percent increase in propane, and similar increases in electricity and water." UASP and the CGT protested the decree, and both called for peaceful resistance. A series of demonstration marches took place in the capital in late April 1990 (*Excelsior* 4/27/90: 2A). The Council for Free Commerce (Consejo de Comercio Libre—CCL), a neoliberal organization representing elite interests, also protested these policies, arguing that they would produce social upheaval and blaming the problems on the DCG's spending policies (*Excelsior* 4/11/90: 2A).

With pressures and tensions intensified in both urban and rural areas, the government decreed a new rural minimum wage of Q10 (approximately $1.60 at the current exchange rates). UNAGRO claimed this was a campaign ploy by the faltering Christian Democrats, while UASP supported the government's resolution of the impasse, claiming a significant victory (*Excelsior* 4/10/90: 1A). Although successful by Guatemalan standards, these "victories" seemed to produce scant gains for laborers.

Other Organizations

Other organizations began to emerge during this period, at least partly in response to public policy. For example, the University of San Carlos student association (Asociación de Estudiantes Universitarios—AEU), inactive in 1984 and 1985 because of repression during previous years, began to reorganize, albeit with some difficulty and under a virtual siege mentality. The AEU participated in a march supporting labor groups in December 1987, publicly opposed increases in electricity prices, and supported dialogue between the government and the insurgent forces of the URNG (ROG 1/88: 6).

At the lowest end of the popular-sector income scale are the residents of El Mezquital, a crowded, Guatemala City slum that is a well-organized settlement, perhaps partly because of international private volunteer organizations as well as official social agencies. Because no urban services or facilities existed there, El Mezquital petitioned the government for assistance in 1987.[25] Tainted water caused the deaths of several children in 1987, whereupon residents demonstrated at the National Palace because the government had ignored their requests for piped water. In response, the government provided water and promised to buy the land the settlement had invaded, then resell it to residents with low mortgage financing, provided some of the residents resettled elsewhere (ROG 1/88: 7).

Conclusion

The extent to which national elections in 1984 and 1985 had a democratic impact on the distribution of political power has been measured in this overview of government and other elite responses to popular-sector demands. As our ultimate concern is the question of democracy and the impact of policy upon it, the public-policy decisions of the Cerezo administration reveal much about the democratic character of the regime. By the standard of the level of political participation itself, for example, the fact that organizations surfaced, made demands, and demonstrated speaks to the real quality of the procedural opening in Guatemalan politics. Given the historical context, this is no small achievement. As with the holding of honest elections, popular participation is a positive sign.

But though the system was more open for mobilization and public expression of demands, both rural and urban workers typically received little positive response to urgent wage and work-condition demands, either from business owners or the government. By the standard of judging the impact of policy on quality of life for the neediest citizens, the net impact of public policy during the Cerezo government seems to have been negative. This standard of judgment need not be overly rigid. But no improvement at all in the poor's living standards—indeed, declines instead—in spite of international assistance and a government with a reformist ideology, suggests that power in society does not lie with reformers or popular organizations demanding change.

Economically, the data show that public policy did not improve the situation in any dramatic fashion. If the success of macro-level policies aimed at economic growth seemed mixed under President Cerezo, what was consistent was the steady decline of the quality of life for most Guatemalans, in spite of repeated and well-organized demands of popular-sector groups. One study concluded that as of 1988, Q9 daily was necessary to feed a family of five a minimal diet, and Q18 daily to meet food and other basic needs. The Nutritional Institute for Central America and Panama (INCAP) calculated that as of January 1989, meeting minimal nutritional requirements for a normal family required a daily income of at least ten Quetzales,[26] but the average daily wage in 1988 was Q5.60. Although Guatemalans therefore received less per day than the hourly minimum wage in the United States (Q5.60 equaled slightly more than $2 at the 1988 exchange rate), prices for basic foods such as beans and eggs were only slightly lower than in the U.S. (ROG Sp/90: 8).

The most positive sign in the study was the wave of popular participation that occurred after 1985, political activity that indicates a strong democratic tendency among popular groups and their leaders. Observers who fear that Guatemalans may not be ready culturally for democracy may take some consolation from this pattern of behavior. On the negative side the popular groups examined represent a minority of the country's poor; for many of them organization and participation may be too costly. This chapter has looked at the successes and failures of the most well organized of Guatemala's impoverished majority; if even these relatively well-organized groups cannot influence policy, then the overall prospects for social progress, and hence for liberal democracy, are problematic.

In yet another dimension of political life, the elite minority has responded historically to increased participation by popular groups in a variety of ways, sometimes accommodating the demands of grassroots organizations but more often ignoring or repressing them. During the Cerezo administration, the government was increasingly reluctant to enter into the dialogues requested by the popular organizations. The DCG strategy of concertación between government and the popular sectors fell by the wayside.[27]

Notes

1. The figures: in rural areas, from Q80 to Q60 ($30 to $22); in industry, from Q276 to Q231 ($102 to $86); and in government jobs, from Q145 to Q129 ($54 to $48). "More than half the working population lacks a full time job, and subsists largely through the informal economy" (ROG Sp/90: 11).

2. For other descriptions and analyses of this topic, see Barry: chapter 4; and Jonas 1991: chapter 12. For comparative purposes, see Foweraker and Craig's edited volume on popular movements in Mexico, which covers roughly the same period.

3. Reverend Andrés Girón, quoted in Goudvis and Richter: 5.

4. This description of the 1980 strike is based on the Guatemalan press and on interviews. For additional details, see Frank and Wheaton: 58; and Concerned Guatemalan Scholars: 34.

5. In 1980, the Quetzal was on par with the U.S. dollar.

6. The colloquial name for the movement was the Movimiento Pro-Tierra (MPT). After the movement gained legal status, its official name became the Asociación Nacional Campesina Pro-Tierra (ANC). For the sake of consistency, I will refer to the movement using the second acronym, ANC.

7. Although the ANC became a public organization, individual members apparently sought anonymity because of the political climate of fear and intimidation. One researcher reports that all his interviews and contacts—and even his own participation as a researcher—had to be identified by pseudonyms because of "the climate of fear" (Silver: 193).

8. In his biography of the Reverend Girón, Cambranes writes:

> On August 4, 1986, President Cerezo met with the Directors of UNA-GRO in his office. In the presence of the Ministers of Defense and of Agriculture, he assured the Directors that his government would not decree any agrarian reform law (Cambranes 1986a: 232).

9. In fact, though the assertion about the market is correct technically, historically most land in Guatemala has become private property because of violent seizures (e.g., the Spanish Conquest), at times sanctioned by the state (e.g., the Liberal Reforms) and enforced by a violently repressive military apparatus throughout. Calling this a "free-market system" is cynical.

10. Given the number of those needing land and the amount of available idle land, approximately one million hectares would somehow need to be obtained from the private sector, in a nation whose new constitution prohibits taking private land for purposes of agrarian reform (Sandoval V.: 36–37).

11. As the Guatemalan Church in Exile commented:

> At the present time, the "vast State-owned lands" to which the bishops refer total 369,467 hectares, which would satisfy 12.5 percent of the landless peasants. Insufficiently cultivated lands total 1,200,000 hectares, which would benefit 41 percent of the landless (IGE 1988: 5).

12. For an interesting discussion comparing and contrasting the new 1985 Constitution with several earlier documents, on the question of labor and on other dimensions as well, see Linares Morales.

13. Linares Morales's analysis, in fact, goes further: he suggests that some constitutional provisions seem to legalize the forced, unpaid labor of Guatemalans

in civil defense patrols and in model villages/development poles, which I described earlier in more detail (Linares Morales: 24–25).

14. Historically, although labor has been active and visible, membership has been relatively low. According to figures calculated on the basis of government statistics, 1.62 percent of the economically active population were members of unions in the early 1970s, the lowest rate in Central America (López Larrave: 119). Guatemala is the most highly industrialized nation in Central America but ranks last in union membership.

15. The National Endowment for Democracy is a North American "private" foundation that receives all of its funds from the U.S. Congress, then disburses them through other foundations affiliated with either the Republican Party, the Democratic Party, the American Chamber of Commerce, or the AFL/CIO. In 1987, CUSG expected to receive $147,600 from AIFLD in 1988. "In 1986, AIFLD received $280,000 from USAID for its work in Guatemala" (ROG 3/88: 6).

16. On February 2, 1980, I witnessed the murder of two FASGUA leaders outside the organization's headquarters in Guatemala City. After the daytime assassination, the death squad calmly drove away.

17. The Guatemalan Solidarist Union (USG) defines solidarism as "a movement for achieving harmony and well-being for workers and owners through cooperation and solidarity between a business and its labor force" (quoted in ROG 5/88: 4).

18. The solidarist approach to labor organizing has been strongly endorsed by U.S. government officials, including former U.S. Ambassador Alberto Martínez Piedra (*Special Service* 11–12/87: 7–8).

19. For a more complete perspective on this struggle, including a chronicle of efforts from 1983 into 1988, to replace existing unions with solidarist associations, see *The Trade Union.*

20. In a surprising twist, Interior Minister Juan José Rodil, a Christian Democrat, responded to CUC's emergence by referring to it as one of the groups responsible for the 1980 massacre at the Spanish embassy. Rodil threatened CUC leaders with arrest and prosecution should they surface. Ironically

> police officials later refuted Rodil's accusation against CUC, saying that although the case has never been fully investigated, available evidence suggests that police agents were responsible for the fire (CAR 1/29/88: 27).

21. For construction workers, for example, the high salary of Q2,308 happened in 1981. From that point on, real annual wages declined by 57 percent through 1986, an annual average decline of over 11 percent for five years running. Yet the construction workers fared better than others. For all workers taken together, the decline after 1983 was Q627 (from Q1,754 to Q1,127), a decline of 36 percent and an average annual decline of 12 percent in purchasing power.

22. This legislation also added twelve new job classifications to the list covered by minimum wage legislation, for a total of thirty-eight regulated occupations.

23. In addition to a wage increase, workers also demanded

> three daily meals, work tools, medical service for the farmworkers and controls on the exact weight of the harvested product, given past fraudulent practices by the owners (GMG 2/89: 6).

24. Workers also demanded three meals a day, free tools, and medicines when needed, adequate transportation to work locations, living space with water and electric light, an end to ethnic and age discrimination, and an end to overnight collection, by owners, of crops harvested but not turned in by harvesters. Usually working seven days a week but receiving pay only for six, they also demanded payment for the seventh day.

25. El Mezquital was settled by a land invasion, or squatter settlement, in 1983, when Guatemala City was flooded by a wave of refugees fleeing military violence in rural areas. It symbolizes the unanticipated costs of rural counterinsurgency. For a description of more recent activities in this settlement, see Jensen.

26. *Momento* 8/90: 5. These figures pre-date the currency devaluations that occurred in 1989 and early 1990.

27. According to one report:

In virtually all of the recent conflicts, the government has imposed policy without prior consultation with the affected groups. Dialogue has only taken place after a period of confrontation and has come to be seen more as a concession than a policy (CAR 1/29/88: 27).

7

Human Rights During the Cerezo Administration

Between 1980 and 1984, Guatemala failed to meet minimal standards of respect for human rights. Indeed, the country ranked among the world's worst violators of human rights during that period.[1] The military's intervention in political life between 1982 and 1985 promised not only to reestablish security and law and order but civil politics as well. In the eyes of many observers, the 1985 election marked the beginning of a new era in Guatemalan politics: the military promised to return to its barracks, and Vinicio Cerezo, a man committed to protecting basic human rights, who had himself survived attempted assassinations and had seen many colleagues in the Christian Democratic Party murdered by death squads, assumed the presidency.

Liberal-representative democracy requires more than a prescribed set of institutional arrangements centering on elections and political parties. The principal additional requirement is effective political participation. Effective citizen participation ultimately means successfully influencing public policy. In this chapter, however, effective citizen participation means only the opportunity to participate politically without serious recriminations or sanctions, a condition taken for granted by most citizens in the United States, for example. In Guatemala, where a participant's safety cannot be taken for granted, this means a study of the human rights environment. Without a reasonable opportunity to participate effectively, democracy can hardly be said to exist in any society. A favorable human rights atmosphere is a prerequisite for popular groups to influence public policy.

This chapter focuses on the ideology of the Christian Democrats and their programmatic approach to the most basic of political rights in a liberal democracy—the opportunity to participate without incurring a threat to one's life—and also on the quality of the human rights environment during President Cerezo's tenure.

113

Guatemalan Christian Democracy

Since at least the 1960s, the Christian Democrats have been perceived by their right-wing opponents as dangerous reformers at best and crypto-communists at worst. Yet from the left, the party has been considered merely a reformist organization representing a conservative middle class and offering inappropriate solutions to problems requiring more profound changes. The DCG generally fared poorly in the decades before 1984. The 1965 Constitution initially outlawed parties like the DCG because of their foreign connections and "exotic ideology." The party's candidate in 1974, General Ríos Montt, probably won that election but was prevented from taking office by another faction of the military.

Over the years the DCG has often lost its more progressive members, usually because the party leadership was choosing a more cautious approach at a given moment. As a result, with time the party has become more conservative in its reformism and has survived probably because of this pragmatism. Nonetheless, during the Lucas García regime (1978–1982), especially after 1980, dozens of party activists were assassinated, including both national- and municipal-level leaders, and several attempts were made to assassinate Vinicio Cerezo. After the systemic crisis of 1982 and the subsequent military coups and elections, the party opportunistically took advantage of the situation, further reducing its reformism in order to gain legitimacy with the ruling military hierarchy.

The Christian Democrats describe themselves as a "third way," an alternative to both the materialism of the socialist left and the intransigence and immorality of the capitalist right.[2] Christian Democracy's epistemology is idealist, not materialist, in contrast with Marxists, and its idealistic concepts include "the dignity of the individual," "the primacy of the common good," and "the perfectibility of society" (Soberanis Reyes: 5). The social basis for action is community; it is neither social class, as it is for Marxists, nor the individual pursuing wealth in an atmosphere of formal civic and economic equality, as it is for classic liberals.

Communities begin with families and continue conceptually up to the international community. For Christian Democrats development occurs within these structures, in which "solidarity" produces on the one hand respect for individuals and their dignity, and on the other cooperation that can lead to progress (Soberanis Reyes: 5). The economic program provides for a regulated market, but the state should have a much more restricted role than that envisioned by social democrats, for example, for whom the state is the principal regulator and guide for the whole economy.[3] This approach in effect restricts the government to a reactive role. Marxist analysts frequently assail such a role for government in capitalist societies, inasmuch as the "social inequalities" and the "external forces" Christian

Democrats seek to regulate have often been transformed into real political power before the state can react to prevent the negative social consequences implied.

For Christian Democrats the social model is pluralist. There can and will be many communities in any society, each with different values and goals. Faced with this, the strategy is not to homogenize society by eliminating the differences, nor even to conceptually reduce the differences to simpler questions of social class, and relationships to production factors. In fact, the tendency is to celebrate these differences as symbolizing human dignity, and the strategy is to control the potential negative effects of social heterogeneity by promoting solidarity among the various groups. The goal is solidarity in upper-level communities (nations), which will allow for steady progress toward the common good even when there are differences at the lower levels.

Christian Democrats distinguish their approach from social democracy, which is also pluralist but which sees the working class as the predominant group. Although they acknowledge that workers are the majority, Christian Democrats do not see the workers as a single class but as several communities. From the perspective of class models, using communities as the basic analytical unit undermines class unity and analysis. Ideologically, it also means that Christian Democrats are not necessarily pro labor, but rather, pro common good, which means equal participation for any community, including the wealthy.

Christian Democrats favor participatory democracy, but within a structure of groups. "Groups" include political parties as well as organizations such as "cooperatives, neighborhood organizations, community organizations, labor unions, etc." (Soberanis Reyes: 7). The political vehicle for achieving this participation is a style of dialogue called concertación. The Christian Democratic strategy of concertación is the pursuit of social consensus through dialogue, based on assumptions of good faith.

The role of the political party in government is therefore a dual one. First, Christian Democrats see their role as one of facilitating and coordinating the process of concertación. Second, the major tactical activity is strengthening the organization of communities at all levels of society, so that each has a real basis for participating in the process of pluralistic dialogue (Soberanis Reyes: 8). The cardinal sin in politics is refusal to enter into dialogue with these assumptions. In short, confrontations between the Christian Democratic government and other social or political groups is not the result of ideological or policy differences with these groups, but a result of unwillingness on their part to dialogue (Cerezo 1987: 49–50).

In this, Christian Democrats again contrast their approach with that of social democracy as well as Marxist and classic liberal approaches. To Christian Democrats, social democrats overemphasize the participation of political parties within representative government structures and hence place too much weight on the party itself, as the vehicle, and on workers as a class (Soberanis Reyes: 7). Liberalism stresses the politics of wealth organized into pressure groups, proscribing meaningful participation by weaker groups. Marxist approaches emphasize resolution of the class struggle in favor of the working class; Christian Democrats assume this will be violent and fear it may represent neither the common good nor adequate respect for individual dignity or pluralism in society (Soberanis Reyes: 48).

Although the 1984 and 1985 election campaigns perhaps had no serious-issue content, the DCG does hold to a program encompassing major changes. The party is reformist and seeks to implement meaningful reforms at the earliest opportunity, within its strategy of respect for pluralist differences and participatory dialogue. The Christian Democrats promised to begin building a solid basis for future democracy. Besides influencing public policy, political participation affects the ability of others to participate. Guided by the DCG's criteria on dialogue and participation, a review of human rights conditions during the Cerezo administration is germane to the study of the quality of procedural democracy in Guatemala.

Human Rights—1986 to 1989

The history of Guatemalan human rights reveals a portrait as grim as that of any nation of the Western Hemisphere. Besides the history of atrocities since the 1950s, the immediate legacy inherited by the Cerezo government was dark and bitter: estimates are that over four hundred villages and hamlets were eradicated and several thousand people killed during the counterinsurgency campaign of the early 1980s.[4]

The Christian Democrats' ideology and their victimization in the past make human rights a key question in the democratization of Guatemala's political system. Shortly after coming to office, after a period of public debate, the Cerezo administration began its tenure by refusing to overturn a military decree from the Mejía dictatorship that established an amnesty for individuals who had violated human rights; these included insurgents and also government security forces. Members of the military were exempted from future prosecution for past human rights violations.[5]

The official attitude, in other words, was to let bygones be bygones. Alternatively, the Christian Democrats pledged to improve the future climate for human rights, including creating institutions to investigate violations that might occur after January 1986. As a beginning the party created a new ministry of development and sought to establish development councils, with specific individuals as "promoters of development," in every municipality. The party presented this as evidence of its good faith in attempting to improve human rights, calling the poverty and marginalization of the population a "social debt, the satisfaction of which constitutes the first objective of our government" (Cabrera Hidalgo: 61).

Within a more traditional definition of human rights, the government took several steps. First, in keeping with provisions in the Constitution of 1985, the government created the office of human rights ombudsman. It also established a presidential commission to investigate human rights violations, set up a fund to assist widows and orphans, signed the Inter-American Convention to Prevent Torture, and created programs to repatriate and relocate refugees. As evidence of the overall success of their efforts, the party cited the return of many exiled intellectuals and professionals (Cabrera Hidalgo: 59–60).

The success of the Christian Democratic program is disputed by many observers. In general, human rights violations were at lower levels overall than in earlier regimes, but violations continued—and continued not to be investigated. Meanwhile, the position of human rights ombudsman remained unfilled for some time and was severely underfunded. Gonzalo Menéndez, the first ombudsman, was criticized by the right because of his attention to demands of the GAM, the Mutual Support Group organized by relatives of persons who had disappeared; they continued to demand information from the authorities. Moreover, Menéndez was attacked for his willingness to investigate any human rights issues, for example, the existence of clandestine cemeteries. At one point, Menéndez accused the DCG of attempting to prevent foreign delegations from consulting with him, to "prevent the outside world from learning the truth about the situation inside Guatemala" (VM 5/88: 9).[6]

After a relatively quiet year in 1986, political violence showed a dramatic upsurge in 1987 and 1988. In terms of assassinations and kidnappings, the statistics for the period are disputed. In general, the U.S. embassy and the Christian Democrats saw an improving situation. Other observers saw patterns largely unchanged from the period after the Ríos Montt coup, when Guatemala saw an abrupt decline in total levels of urban repressive violence. In spite of the decline, the number of violent deaths still reached several hundred each year during the Cerezo administration.[7] The U.S. State Department's report for 1987 differs markedly from most other international observers. The United States claimed that "political killings declined significantly for the fifth consecutive year" and reported only eighty-eight "politically motivated killings" in 1987, compared to 131 in 1986.[8] By comparison, data from the Guatemalan press showed there were 1,021 such cases in 1987 (GNIB 1/1/88: 8).

References to specific events provide a clearer perspective. In late 1987, a small group of exiled leaders of popular organizations returned openly to Guatemala from Mexico, to test the level of freedom of expression. They were allowed to hold press conferences and meet with local groups, but they were threatened by the right. President Cerezo characterized the group as espousing "radical positions." The exiles responded that all of their activities were conducted within the law. The group left after one week because of fears for their safety (Cáceres: 13).[9]

The Christian Democrats saw an improved situation. In his report to the Guatemalan Congress in January 1988, President Cerezo described his government's progress on civil liberties and human rights:

> For the first time in years, . . . Guatemalans can express themselves without restriction through political groups, unions, or individually, on any measure or area in which they feel the government is affecting their interests. Freedom of the press is exercised with no restrictions, and basic human rights are respected by the government and strengthened by judicial institutions established and regulated by a Constitution (PCRP 1/88: 3).

In contrast, in mid-1988, approximately halfway through President Cerezo's term, the Guatemalan Human Rights Commission asserted that the government had

> neglected its responsibilities vis-à-vis the facts, [and had] assumed an attitude of passive tolerance, covering up political violence committed by the government's army, various police units, and the clandestine apparatus for repression that is controlled by the high military commanders (VM 5/88: 9).

By late 1988, domestic criticism included an indictment from Edmundo Vásquez, president of the Guatemalan Supreme Court: "The situation in Guatemala is in a state of collapse in terms of human rights, meaningless legislation and demagogy."[10]

Clearly, the situation regarding human rights was in dispute throughout the first half of President Cerezo's regime.[11] The country began 1989 already under attack by several major, international organizations because of the human rights climate (GMG 2/89: 5–6; *Special Service* 2/89). Yet the Christian Democrats' position remained optimistic and quite positive: according to President Cerezo, Guatemala enjoyed "a climate of total respect for human rights as well as other individual rights" (in *El Gráfico*, quoted in GMG 2/89: 2).

The apparent contradictions in these views are partly because the Christian Democratic government has tended to use legal and constitutional provisions as the basis for their position, whereas other observers point to the statistics of actual violations. As evidence of consolidating the democratization process and protecting human rights, for example, Cerezo cited the creation of the office of the human rights ombudsman, new judicial procedures, laws protecting the rights of labor to organize, the practice of dialogue (concertación) between government and organized interest groups, including labor, legal registration of several new labor organizations, and the law establishing development councils in Guatemala's municipalities (GMG 2/89: 2).

These legal provisions were the basis of the government's position in its first major international test in early 1989, the Geneva meeting of the United Nations Commission on Human Rights. In Geneva human rights advocates urged, and the government opposed, that Guatemala be listed among nations in which "grave and systematic" violations of human rights have occurred. Although Guatemala was discussed under this agenda item (#8), as well as under other agenda items on ethnic questions (#10) and the need for a United Nations expert advisor (#21), the commission agreed that Guatemala was subject only to the last item and assigned an expert advisor with expanded responsibilities (GMG 4/89: 4).

Although human rights advocates saw the extensive and acrimonious debate in Geneva as evidence of serious problems in Guatemala, the government saw the outcome as a political victory, inasmuch as Guatemala avoided the most serious rulings from the commission (PCRP 3/89: 3). In addition to criticisms from human rights activists, however, the conservative press attacked the government's position as well, although partisan political reasons may partly explain this criticism. *Prensa Libre*, for example, editorialized that

> the truth is that in this country—among other things—disappearances, assassinations and anonymous notes threatening the lives of citizens of different political tendencies continue, not to mention the blacklists that are in the hands of the national security branches (quoted in GMG 4/89: 4–5).

Despite the government's diplomatic victory in Geneva and its formal-legal provisions supporting human rights, the combination of the farm-workers' strike on the South Coast in January, a major teacher's strike from May to August, and the open participation of opposition groups in the National Dialogue process (see Chapter 8) led to a dramatic increase in human rights violations in the second half of 1989. As in 1988, the surge of violence closely followed an attempted military coup in May 1989.

In addition to threats and violence toward popular organizations, other groups suffered repression. In August bombs exploded at the offices of GAM and of Peace Brigades International, a group providing "witnesses" for threatened individuals. Among the most serious atrocities were renewed attacks on the university community. Beginning in August at least a dozen student leaders disappeared or were murdered during several incursions onto university campuses in Guatemala City and Quetzaltenango. Other student activists quickly fled into exile.[12]

In September 1989, the renewed violence prompted the U.S. State Department to issue a traveler's advisory for Guatemala, a reluctant acknowledgment that high levels of political violence existed even in areas frequented by tourists (PCRP 9/89: 5). At about the same time, GAM announced its plans to sue the government for human rights violations in a case to be brought to the Inter-American Human Rights Court. GAM placed responsibility for the atrocities it has experienced—murder and the disappearance of many of its leaders—on the security forces (PCRP 11/ 89: 6).

The government had argued at the beginning of 1989 that the situation in Guatemala was much improved over the conditions inherited by the government in 1986, since the violation of human rights was no longer a state policy. During the course of the year, in the face of mounting evidence implicating public security forces, the government continued to insist that it was not guilty of human rights violations but was totally committed to protecting and improving the human rights situation in Guatemala, and that extremists of the left and the right, and/or "common criminals," were responsible for the atrocities that did occur (PCRP 10/89: 4).

Complicating the picture, two UN observers offered conflicting assessments after visiting Guatemala. Héctor Gros Espiell, the observer on Guatemalan human rights under agenda item 21, reported in November that the climate of human rights had not in fact declined in past months, in spite of terrorist actions by extremist factions, and that there was no official policy of repression in Guatemala, as had been the case in the past (PCRP 11/89: 6). Another UN observer, however, reported that:

> In a country where part of the population doesn't know at night whether it will live to see the light of day, where families have no safety, one could say the situation is of grave concern (GMG 10/89: 4).

Although Guatemala had emerged relatively unscathed from the early 1989 Geneva meeting of the Commission on Human Rights, by late 1989, the government suffered a diplomatic defeat in the United Nations. In spite of President Cerezo's speech to the General Assembly in September and Ambassador Villagrán's vigorous defense of the government's human rights performance, Guatemala was denied a seat on the UN Social and Economic Council. The debate included widespread condemnation of the Guatemalan government from the European community (GMG 12/89: 3–5).

Human Rights—1990

Guatemala's dominant elites have long perceived genuine democratization as a significant threat to their interests. Their consistent response to political participation by popular groups or reformist political parties has been political violence aimed at deterring such participation. These dynamics reemerged in 1990, in systematic violations of human rights.

As in earlier years, observations about human rights showed extreme contrasts. The government's position at the beginning of the year was that the human rights climate had significantly improved, although more was needed to eliminate terrorism of both the right and left.[13] On the other hand, Catholic bishops meeting in Quetzaltenango in January asserted that "human rights, such as the right to dignity and equality, do not exist" (quoted in Lovell 1990). During 1990, the same pattern from the past emerged with, if anything, intensified levels of human rights violations, concurrent with the election campaign and the dialogue process.[14]

The Judicial Process

A key pillar of the Cerezo administration's approach to human rights has been its insistence on improving the quality of the judicial process in order to strengthen investigations of human rights violations. But as of late 1989, the only convictions ever obtained for human rights violations were those of six members of the Guatemalan National Police arrested for kidnapping and killing two agronomists in 1987. As evidence of the deteriorating human rights climate in 1990, these six were released after an appellate court overturned the convictions. Since they were based on evidence produced after the United States funded a technical assistance project to increase Guatemala's capacity to collect evidence in crimes, the key factors seemed less a question of technical competence and more those of the political will of judges and the overall atmosphere created by state terrorism (NFAW 8/90).

In fact, the United States has sponsored several programs to improve human rights by increasing the technical competence of judicial institutions, including programs supported and/or administered by the U.S. Agency for International Development, the Latin American Institute for Crime Prevention and the Treatment of Offenders, and the Center for Criminal Justice of Harvard University's Law School. But none of these projects aim at arresting or prosecuting those guilty of violations. Political barriers seem to prevent even increases in technical capability from having a positive impact on the human rights climate.[15]

Perhaps the best illustration lies in the activities of the office of the human rights ombudsman, a position created early in the Cerezo administration to show its support for human rights. The first ombudsman, Gonzalo Menéndez de la Riva, had resigned in October 1989, and was replaced by Ramiro de León Carpio. Early in 1990, de León publicly decried the existence of clandestine prisons in Guatemala, but no investigation followed. Later in the year, the ombudsman "claimed that 163 extrajudicial executions were carried out in the first six months of 1990, with the 'majority (of the victims) suffering bullet wounds, torture, knifing, or incineration'" (quoted in TOA 10/31/90: 3).

Without gainsaying the symbolic import of these revelations, the office of the ombudsman did little else to improve the human rights climate, and the question of technical capacity versus political will is again salient. Although initially underfunded when it was created in 1986, and understandably cautious at that time, by 1990 the ombudsman office had a staff of 150 persons. In addition to other programs, West German assistance was being used to increase the forensic capability of the office, so that it could collect its own evidence on human rights violations, reducing dependence on the police. Still, "not a single member of Guatemala's security forces has been jailed in connection with more than 100,000 political killings over the past three decades" (*Excelsior* 3/25/90: 2A; MHerald 9/15/90: 19A).

Geneva

Again in 1990, the question of the nation's human rights climate was the subject of intense debate at the Geneva meeting of the Human Rights Commission. Both the government and its critics were able to point to "victory" in this process, for although the report to the commission by Héctor Gros Espiell, the UN's special observer for Guatemala, asserted that "the government has neither the power nor the authority necessary to guarantee the exercise of human rights," Gros Espiell essentially reinforced the Christian Democratic perspective as well:

> There have continued to be increasing levels of violations of civil and political rights of citizens, especially assassinations and disappearances. Apparently, these have not resulted from any official policy nor from any governmental order, but from decisions taken by other power sectors and from the persistent climate of violence, factors that have escaped effective government control.[16]

The Geneva meeting, as before, suggested cautious approval of the government's activities while offering continued assistance to improve the human rights climate—by calling, for example, for more effective educational programs to create proper cultural appreciation for human rights and democracy. An additional report was requested for 1991, with an observer again assigned.[17]

Popular and Middle-Class Groups

In both urban and rural areas, human rights violations, as in past years, reflected attempts of popular and middle-class organizations to participate openly in the political process. For labor, 1990 was a difficult year, marked by some successes (see Chapter 8) but also by increasing repression and a weakening of the political party system and electoral institutions as potential allies in its struggle. Nonetheless, the prospect of organized worker success led to intensified repression directed against both working-class groups and middle-class professionals perceived as their allies. Dozens of labor activists were murdered or forced into exile in 1989 and in the first half of 1990.[18]

Professionals, too, paid a heavy price. Religious workers, social scientists, and journalists were all singled out for repression. An American nun, Diana Ortiz, was abducted and tortured, then allowed to escape when her captors realized she was a U.S. citizen. In September, Myrna Mack, a leading Guatemalan anthropologist, was murdered as she left her research institute in downtown Guatemala City (Manz).[19] Byron Barrera, president of the Association of Guatemalan Journalists, who had come back during the political opening implied by the return to constitutional democracy after 1984, and whose newspaper, *La Epoca*, had been destroyed in the wave of terrorism following the attempted military coup of May 1989, was wounded in a car-bomb explosion that killed his wife (Rodríguez; Tenneriello 11/11/90).

Human Rights Activists

Human rights activists, including members of GAM and the Runujel Junam Council of Ethnic Unity (Consejo de Comunidades Etnicas Runujel Junam—CERJ)[20] also found themselves targeted. CERJ was created in 1988 to demand enforcement of the constitutional provision (Article 34) that service in civil patrols (PACS) be voluntary. PACs were first established as part of the Army's counterinsurgency efforts in the Indian highland regions in the early 1980s; at the time, all Indian males were obliged to serve tours of duty on a regular basis. In spite of Article 34, "hundreds of thousands of Indian men continue to serve as involuntary, unpaid labor at the service of the Army." CERJ dedicated itself to informing Indian communities that service was voluntary and to defending Indians who ran afoul of military and civil authorities who refused to abide by the constitutional provisions. CERJ acted, in essence, as a "rural legal aid office" (Americas Watch 1989: 2).

The government's reaction to CERJ has been mixed. Some sectors, such as the human rights ombudsman and a few members of Congress, have been sympathetic. But President Cerezo and the military high command on occasion have evaded CERJ's demands or have resorted to legalities, for example, restating the contents of Article 34 and publicly insisting that service is already voluntary. At least once, the government went so far as to discredit CERJ publicly.[21]

But the most serious response has been repression. The more prominent leaders of these organizations were sometimes able to move more freely because of international attention focused on their activities. CERJ founder Amílcar Méndez was awarded the Robert F. Kennedy Memorial Human Rights Award in November 1990. But less prominent members were eliminated: several CERJ leaders and members were threatened during 1989. In spite of the U.S. State Department's recall of Ambassador Stroock in March 1990, a signal of Washington's displeasure with the level of violence in Guatemala, GAM continued to be harassed. At least five associates of CERJ were murdered and five others disappeared.[22]

> Just a few months after becoming visible, the organization finds itself battling as much for its own survival and the physical safety of its members as for the cause it originally undertook (Americas Watch 1989: 1).

Children

One particularly distressing aspect of the human rights atmosphere is a series of barbaric incidents involving homeless children living on the streets of Guatemala City. With the city's population swelling because of economic conditions and rural violence and economic opportunity waning even in the capital, the increase in the number of street children in Guatemala has been noteworthy; cautious estimates placed some five thousand children aged five to eighteen in this category at the time (TOA 9/5/90: 4; Zinner).

In early 1990, the Guatemalan police apparently began to engage in a "dirty war" against these children: "at least 45 children . . . died between January and June this year by strangulation, bullets through the head, or other means." Social service workers, even lawyers, who attempted to investigate allegations of police involvement received death threats. And Amnesty International "issued a report signaling alarm at 'escalating' abuses including extrajudicial executions against the city's . . . street children" (TOA 9/5/90: 4).[23] Ironically, Guatemala was among the earliest signers of the 1989 United Nations International Convention of Children's Rights (PCRP 3/90: 4).

Conclusion

This examination of the human rights atmosphere during the Cerezo administration provides further evidence that the position of dominant groups in Guatemalan politics basically remains intact. President Cerezo's government continued to present as positive a face as possible given these developments, frequently citing its support at the Geneva meeting of the UN Human Rights Commission. The Guatemalan government generally decried human rights violations and insisted that these were the actions of nongovernmental actors of both extremes, left and right. The DCG therefore saw the solution to the human rights dilemma in the increasing consolidation of the democratic regime, as well as continuing economic development and eradication of extremists seeking to sabotage the system.[24]

The government's analysis notwithstanding, by the end of 1990, human rights conditions continued to decline steadily, as evidenced since shortly after Cerezo took office in 1986. Critics noted a historical pattern recurring: small victories by popular groups followed by repression of their leaders. This pattern was similar to the events of 1979 and 1980 that marked the beginning of Guatemala's worst period of violence to date. Placing this record in the context of the programmatic ideology of the Christian Democratic Party adds an element of irony, if not tragedy.

Regardless of the president's and party's level of sincerity, the data suggest that power does not favor social reform or political participation free of recrimination. This in turn creates apprehension concerning the future of democratic development in Guatemala. The human rights evidence from the Cerezo period suggests that new political institutions are counterreformist as well as counterinsurgent and, except for electoral procedures themselves, antidemocratic.[25]

Access to the public-policy process, the opportunity to participate politically, is a key procedural component of any democratic system, but it does not necessarily guarantee substantial influence. But guaranteed access is clearly a necessary component of any democracy: no system can be called such if it cannot ensure its citizens the opportunity to participate openly. Without this, even the purity of balloting procedures becomes insignificant.

Notes

1. Using careful data collection and a systematic comparison, Poe ranks Guatemala as easily the most serious abuser of human rights in the hemisphere during this period. In a world sample, based on conditions as of 1982, Guatemala ranks second only to Afghanistan.

2. The following description of the DCG's ideology is based on Soberanis Reyes and on conversations with party leaders between 1980 and 1987.

3. In Christian Democracy, the state intervenes

like a set of valves, depending on the needs of society, always with the
fundamental goal of the common good, [and] intervening . . . [in a] sub-
sidiary role, when the laws of the market are altered by social inequalities
or by external forces beyond the local economy (Soberanis Reyes: 6).

4. Writing in 1987, DCG leader Alfonso Cabrera emphasized this inheritance:
"From 1978 to 1981, Guatemala reached the highest levels of politically related
assassinations ever recorded in world history in countries not at war" (Cabrera
Hidalgo: 60). Cabrera's second date is 1981, although the years between 1980 and
1984 include the worst repression in Guatemalan history to date in rural areas. By
ignoring this violence, Cabrera was either redefining human rights violations to not
include generalized warfare, or selectively remaining silent about the practices of
the military faction in power since the 1982 change of government, or both.

5. In the period after 1983, when the civil defense patrols had become well
established in rural areas, they were sometimes used in forced warfare, with PAC
members of one village forced to commit atrocities in other villages. During the
Cerezo period Defense Minister Gramajo

announced, without taking into account [Guatemala's] judicial institutions, that the members of PACs would be included in a new amnesty,
decreed as part of the Central American Peace Accords (Esquipulas II)
(VM 5/88: 9).

6. For a more detailed discussion of this office and its activities, see WOLA
1989b: 42–46.

7. For 1987, see CAR 1/29/88: 28–29. Overall, a careful, regular source for
these data is GNIB. For a point of view reflecting the views of the Christian Democratic Party, see PCRP. As an example of differing perspectives, one report claims
that: "December 1987, signaled the highest rate of violence in Guatemala since
President Cerezo took office in January, 1986" (GNIB 12/1/87: 1). But at the same
time, President Cerezo's position was that "violence has diminished in Guatemala"
and that the violence that has taken place is "common crime" (quoted in GNIB
12/1/87: 1).

8. With this claim, based on a comparison of 1987 data with 1986 data, the
State Department in effect asserted that there were continual declines in this type
of human rights violations since 1982. This claim appears to contradict evidence of
violence against civilians during the counterinsurgency campaign after 1982. Earlier, during the Lucas García regime, the State Department downplayed human
rights violations, although after the coup of 1982, government violence *before* that
coup was acknowledged. The State Department routinely denied that there were
serious violations under Ríos until after he was deposed by Mejía Víctores in 1983.
Given this pattern of revisionism, observers should be skeptical of State Department claims about Guatemala after 1983, especially in view of the contrasting
reports by most other international observers of Guatemalan human rights.

9. The Army participated indirectly in this incident when it issued a press
statement, entitled "The Army Obeys the Law," in which it announced: "We will
continue fighting the radicals," a puzzling position, since there was no law defin-
ing what is meant by "radicals" nor was there any law that claims that being radical is a crime (Cáceres: 13).

10. *Excelsior* 12/12/88, quoted in VM 5/88: 11. Even the conservative Guatemalan daily, *Prensa Libre,* described Guatemala as "one of the places on the face of the earth where the spirit of the Universal Declaration on Human Rights has been the most brutally and consistently violated" (although it may have done so for partisan political reasons rather than because of a moral commitment to human rights) (10/11/88, quoted in VM 5/88: 2).

11. Another summary of the situation after the first half of the Cerezo regime:

> Meanwhile, human rights violations continue at rates similar to those prevailing in the years of military rule. . . . The situation in the countryside is just as bad as it was under military rule (Cockburn: 2).

12. For more details on the threats and terrorist actions aimed at participants in the National Dialogue, see PCRP 8/89: 3; and 9/89: 3–4. For more details on the violence directed against the popular sectors, see UOG 7/89: 1–2; *Centroamérica Hoy* 10/8/89: 13–14. For details of killings and disappearances of students in late 1989, see GMG 10/89: 2–3; and NFAW 10/89: 2–3. The 1989 attacks on USAC student leaders were only the most recent in a long series that includes several earlier atrocities during the Cerezo administration; for details of atrocities in 1986–1988, see NFAW 10/89: 10–12. For other descriptions of recent violence, see McConahay: 8; WPost 9/29/89: A1, A50; Tenneriello 1989; and Jonas 1989.

13. For a complete exposition of this position, see "Derechos humanos." As in earlier years, the DCG approach was to lump together both the left and the right as terrorists seeking to destabilize the government and the economy, and, as such, "allies" against the government. See PCRP 1/90: 5–6; and 2/90: 5–6.

14. For a table summarizing human rights violations in the first ten months of 1990, which totaled over 1,700, see GMG 11/90: 7. Many sources describe human rights conditions in Guatemala. Among them, see especially WOLA 1990. GMG 8/90: 1–6 reports several examples of President Cerezo publicly denying any human rights violations in Guatemala. Also see LATimes 4/14/90: 1; *Excelsior* 5/9/90: 2A and 8/28/90: 2A; NYTimes 6/28/90: 3A; and NFAW 8/90.

15. WOLA 1990: 5. For a good summary of the legal and judicial procedures for investigating and prosecuting crime in Guatemala, see pages 9–22.

16. The first passage is quoted in ROG Sp/90: 4, the second in Gros Espiell. For more details of the Geneva meeting, see GMG 3/90: 4–6.

17. For the Christian Democratic interpretation, see Gros Espiell; and PCRP 3/90: 4. For an opposing point of view, see ROG Su/90: 15.

18. For details of human rights violations against labor, see ROG Su/90; *Excelsior* 1/31/90: 2A and 8/17/90: 2A. For a detailed example of one case, see ROG Fa/90: 2–3.

19. For details on human rights violations, including the incident involving Diana Ortiz, see AAS 3/25/90: 1C.

20. The words *Runujel Junam* mean "everyone is equal" in Quiché, one of Guatemala's twenty-two Indian languages (Americas Watch 1989: 1).

21. For details and illustrations, see Americas Watch 1989: 37–40.

22. N&A 6/26/90; Tenneriello 1990 reports that at least eleven members of CERJ have been killed or have disappeared since the group formed in 1988. Also see MHerald 11/22/90: 20B. For a detailed look at one village's victimization in a community that resisted illegal forced induction into civil patrols, see ROG Su/90: 6–8.

23. For other descriptions of this tragic situation, see SFChronicle 8/22/90: 2; NYTimes 10/14/90: 3; and Zinner.

24. For the best example of this position, see "Derechos humanos." The challenge for Christian Democrats, in this view, is

> to consolidate the democratization process and to foment authentic economic development, in order to reduce the gap between the minority that possesses so much wealth and the majority that has few opportunities to meet its minimum basic needs ("Derechos humanos": 63).

25. There is little evidence, for example, that judicial procedures were used to prosecute human rights violators: "As striking as the death rate is the impunity with which the killers operate" (LATimes 4/14/90: 1).

8
Power and Participation: The Late Cerezo Administration

It could be argued that, in 1986, no civilian president could have accomplished much upon taking office in Guatemala and that some time would have to pass before the lasting impact of democratic civilian rule could be perceived. By focusing on events in the last two years of the Cerezo administration in this chapter and the first two years of the Serrano Administration (Chapter 9), we give the protagonists maximum opportunity to establish the democratic credentials of their governments.

Complementing earlier analyses of public policy and the quality of participation, this chapter studies the relative strength of military and civilian political forces—in the final analysis the most salient question about Guatemalan politics and a major issue in democratic politics in general. Three topics are covered: (1) the activities of the armed forces themselves during the Cerezo administration, especially in the later years; (2) the process of national dialogue between revolutionary insurgents and the government of Guatemala; and (3) the national elections of 1990. In addition, these basic questions are asked about the Guatemalan political process: who seems to control that process, who sets the agenda, and who has the veto power?

The Military During the Cerezo Administration

Since at least the late 1800s, the Army has been a national institution with both the coercive power to achieve its goals and the willingness to use its power. In more recent times the armed forces have penetrated the economy and encroached upon the state, dominating it in political, economic, and administrative arenas, and legalizing their activities in rewritten constitutions. Military dominance is not totalitarian, however, and varies historically under certain economic and political conditions. Especially in periods of economic decline, conflicts emerge among elite groups, and military groups sometimes become involved in these conflicts: the unity of the officer corps has often been an issue affecting military dominance. At times, factionalism within the armed forces has meant the possibility of civilian ascendancy with no meaningful threat to military domination.

After the Ríos Montt coup of 1982, and especially after the Mejía Víctores coup of 1983, the military focused on reestablishing its traditional hierarchy while creating a civilian regime with elections. All factions of the armed forces supported the basic counterinsurgency plan adopted in 1981–1982, but not all accepted the idea of a civilian regime, with the party politics and moderate reforms that it might imply. During the Cerezo presidency, therefore, the military was split into two factions: "reformist counterinsurgents and non-reformist counterinsurgents" (GNIB 6/87: 8). In this context, the armed forces continued their active role during the Cerezo administration in three policy areas: counterinsurgency activities, domestic political matters (including attempted military coups), and foreign and regional policy.

Military Counterinsurgency

The counterinsurgency campaign of the early 1980s, discussed earlier, has been labeled genocidal in its intensity and viciousness. International public attention shifted from military violence by 1984, however: the military in effect declared victory over the insurgents, and the press began emphasizing upcoming elections for the Constituent Assembly. Counterinsurgency continued after the 1985 elections, in the model villages and civil defense patrols in some areas and as active warfare in zones either not pacified earlier or left for later for tactical reasons.

The "voluntary" (per the 1985 Constitution) PACs continued to be a salient feature of Guatemalan life. In 1985, an estimated one million men were in civil defense patrols, and the Army reported a total membership of 700,000 as of late 1987. Increased military offensives meant increases in forced PAC membership as well, as in the forced reorganization of PACs in Santiago Atitlán in 1987, for example. General Héctor Gramajo, the minister of defense, stated in 1987 that 1988 would see voluntary civil defense patrols in Guatemala City and Amatitlán, just south of the national capital. Even President Cerezo said that "at most, one third of all PAC members serve voluntarily" (GNIB 12/1/87: 12).

The Army publicized its military operations in late 1986 and 1987, but later was much less open about them, sensitive perhaps to international public opinion. It announced a major offensive for late 1987, for example, to finish the insurgency once and for all, but this offensive continued until at least March 1988. Although it was supported by air attacks and caused major damage, it all took place in an atmosphere of silence. The policy decision was not to stop military activities but to stop publicizing them. In 1988, the Army embarked on a military offensive in the northern Department of Petén, again in relative silence.[1]

The Military and Domestic Politics

In May 1988, dissatisfaction with the conduct of counterinsurgency warfare and factionalization in the armed forces contributed to an attempted military coup, one of "numerous coup plots against [Cerezo] in recent months" (N&A 4/21/88: 1). The coup was the combined work of a clandestine officer group called the Officers of the Mountains and rightist civilian politicians, including two former presidential candidates (WRH 6/22/88: 1, 6). The Mountain Officers generally were junior military officers fighting the insurgency in the field; they first appeared publicly in late 1987 to protest the informal meetings in Madrid between the government and URNG and the dissolution of two leading counterinsurgency brigades after the failure of the "final offensive against the insurgency" in late 1987 (which continued into 1988). The group also complained it was undersupplied in the war against the guerrillas. Finally, concern about military casualties may also have been part of the conspirators' agenda.[2]

The civilians involved in the coup attempt included Gustavo Anzueto Vielman, the 1982 CAN presidential candidate; Mario David García, CAN's 1985 candidate; and Mario Castejón, leader of the Nationalist Party (Partido Nacionalista—PN), who apparently would have been named president had the coup succeeded (*Centroamérica Hoy* 6/9/88: 13), as well as several right-wing newspaper columnists (N&A 6/2/88: 2–3). The putsch failed in the formal sense, because Minister of Defense Gramajo threw his support behind the government; it was thwarted by the military's high command, not by the president (N&A 6/2/88: 1–2).

General Gramajo called the defeat of the coup a victory for democracy, although it was his action as military chief that defeated it. But the coup was in fact an antidemocratic event that forced the government to accommodate the wishes of the right. The failure of the coup meant that the faction of the Army supporting civilian government was stronger than other factions, not that democracy had survived a military attack. Prospects for procedural democracy were weakened by their success. Nevertheless, as of early 1989, President Cerezo continued to speak confidently of his government's capacity to rule.[3]

As a political event and a "demand" on the system, the aborted 1988 coup was quite successful.[4] First, it crystallized and brought to the surface the factionalization within the Army and the civilian elites, pressure apparently due to Cerezo's tolerance of a more open political system than the right was willing to tolerate. The public perception of dissent from the right led to an abrupt change in the political atmosphere, which saw increased stridency after that date. Second, the coup succeeded in forcing President Cerezo to acknowledge and attend to certain military demands; for example, he appropriated funds for six helicopters that the Mountain Officers needed for the counterinsurgency (WRH 6/22/88: 1).

Third, right-wing terrorism increased: the office of Mexicana, the airline that had flown four exiled opposition leaders into Guatemala for the National Dialogue (see below), was bombed. TASS, the Soviet news agency, and Prensa Latina closed their offices because the government could not guarantee the lives of the correspondents after their residences and offices were bombed.[5] Activist clergy and the Nicaraguan ambassador received death threats (WRH 6/22/88: 1, 6), and the downtown office of *La Epoca*, a newspaper that had emerged as a result of the political opening, was firebombed (*Centroamérica Hoy* 6/9/88: 13).

Fourth, the Christian Democratic government felt compelled to adopt a hard line against public disorder, apparently to satisfy the rightists in the Army and the civilian elite. Shortly after the coup attempt, police violently attacked Lunafil workers, whose strike had been tolerated for several months before the May 11 coup (UOG 6/88: 1).[6] The political climate did not yet precisely duplicate but certainly reflected the intense violence of the Lucas García regime.

A second coup attempt in May 1989 occurred two days before the first anniversary of the one in 1988. Again led by younger military officers, it followed much the same pattern and resulted in many similar outcomes. It did not overthrow the government or remove Defense Minister Héctor Gramajo, the attempted coup's purported target. But like the "unsuccessful" one in 1988, this attack aimed to reduce the political sphere of influence of popular organizations.[7]

This second confrontation between factions of the Army was likewise not a failure for the *golpistas*. Indeed, subsequent developments suggest that the attempted coup may have been a staged event designed to strengthen the military's hand in general. First, the wave of violence that followed it indicated a growing consensus within the Army, as in the early 1980s, that popular organizations would not be allowed to threaten military dominance and that a hard-line response to competing organizations was appropriate.[8]

Second, there was increasing agreement in Washington that more aid be sent to the supposedly moderate faction of the Guatemalan Army, led by Minister of Defense Gramajo, in order to protect democracy against the antidemocratic golpistas. General Gramajo's visit there in late 1989 helped solidify this version of Guatemalan reality. In retrospect, it is clear that the attempted coup was not aimed at removing Cerezo but was designed to influence U.S. policy. Just as Guatemalan generals once used anticommunism as a lever to secure aid automatically, they now appeared to use anti-democratic threats as their pretext, and they were willing to use groups from either the left or the right, whichever elicited the desired response in Washington.

Although evidence suggests factionalization in the Guatemalan Army,[9] the underlying consensus is more important in understanding politics there. Conflict within the Army is not about whether the military should control society but over what steps should be taken to ensure that control and dominance (Schirmer 1989a: 13).[10] Although no legal or constitutional steps were taken to implement more direct control, the wave of violence after May 1989 clearly reflects the "central sophistry of national security doctrine, . . . that one must wage war in order to prevent war" (Schirmer 1989b: 479).

While the question of factionalization versus consensus is still not answered with total clarity, either possibility threatened democracy. Factionalization meant attempted coups and confrontations among factions, which weakened the new regime's institutional strength. But consensus could cement the national security doctrine approach to Guatemalan politics, one with little room for democracy. In late 1989, the tide seemed to turn in favor of the golpista faction, which was committed to a total-war response to popular organizations (ROG 10/89: 4).

The Military and Foreign Policy

One obstacle to military dominance in recent times has been the periodic lack of access to foreign resources needed to maintain military supremacy. Just as the Guatemalan economy is export oriented and derives its profits from foreign sales of commodities, the armed forces depend on foreign sources of technology, and sometimes cash, to counter possible threats from other organized groups in society. When domestic political and economic events threaten the military's access to these foreign resources, Army leaders have taken steps to reestablish both its military and financial supply lines.

The principal foreign policy issues during the Cerezo administration's later stages were its rapprochement with the U.S. government and the continuing erosion of President Cerezo's policy of active neutrality regarding Central American regional questions. These issues were a question of civil-military relations, in effect, as they touched on traditional nationalist themes in the armed forces as well as ideological concerns of right-wing officers. These two aspects of Guatemalan foreign policy were not unrelated, as evidenced by both increases in U.S economic and military assistance and in other policies of the Cerezo regime.[11]

The DCG policy of active neutrality toward Nicaragua and U.S. policy in the region seemed defeated at even the symbolic level by 1989. Increasing evidence pointed to closer links between the U.S. and Guatemalan governments than neutrality would allow. Published documents suggested a quid pro quo with the United States existing since 1986, by which Guatemala would support the Nicaraguan contras in exchange for increased U.S. aid (GMG 5/89: 5). In February and early March 1989, President Cerezo's visit to Washington resulted in more assistance, including military aid (PCRP 3/89: 4). Between 1986 and 1990, the military aid totaled approximately $30 million; nonmilitary developmental aid, including the August 1989 grant of nearly $70 million to counter the negative balance of payments, totaled approximately $700 million, 90 percent of which was grants (PCRP 9/89: 8).[12]

Military assistance from the United States in 1989 totaled $9.5 million.[13] It also donated $3.4 million to improve the justice system, and USAID donated $30 million to strengthen the basic level of primary education in Guatemala (PCRP 7/89: 4–5). American assistance totaled about $150 million for 1989, placing Guatemala in tenth place worldwide for American assistance (*Weekly Briefs* 8/28/89: 1). For fiscal year 1990/91, the Bush administration requested a total of $157.5 million, including $9.5 million in direct military aid (foreign military sales—FMS—and international military education and training—IMET); $87 million in economic support funds—ESF (often characterized as indirect military assistance); $35 million of development aid; and $36 million in Title I and Title II food aid (LUOG 4/89: 2).

In addition to this financial commitment, use of U.S. military troops increased in 1989, including direct combat support activities with the Army.[14] In 1987, the U.S. government, through its Drug Enforcement Agency, had become involved in the warfare, through aerial spraying over large areas where, perhaps coincidentally, insurgents were considered most active. According to the U.S. embassy, aerial spraying was entirely and totally aimed at eliminating drug cultivation (interview at the U.S. embassy in Guatemala, 1987).

U.S. officials continued to justify the military aid in terms of gaining leverage with the Guatemalan armed forces, even though increasing amounts of support had prevented neither two major coup attempts in 1988 and 1989 nor increasing human rights violations during the Cerezo administration (Tenneriello 1989; GMG 3/89: 6). Nor did the Christian Democratic policy of active neutrality in the region prevent Guatemala's direct military assistance to El Salvador in late 1989, apparently including soldiers transported in a U.S. Air Force plane (GMG 12/89: 2–3).

In sum, in the active prosecution of the war in rural Guatemala and the overall balance of power between civilian authorities and the military hierarchy, the pattern was much more similar than dissimilar to earlier periods, in spite of contextual elements that affected some fine points in that relationship. Though the scale of military violence was reduced from the extraordinary levels of the early 1980s, the armed forces continued to dominate in many regions and to establish involuntary PACs and development poles, in spite of the return to civilian rule and a constitutional regime. The military had not reduced its counterinsurgency options, as demonstrated by major military offensives in selected rural areas, including the far northern regions of Huehuetenango and El Quiché provinces and the area around Santiago Atitlán in Sololá.[15] Yet the military was beginning to feel popular pressure, largely because of the National Dialogue process.

National Dialogue: The Main Event

Stage 1: Opening Round

The Central American Peace Accords (the Arias Peace Plan) included provisions for dialogue between insurgents and governments in those nations with civil conflict. In late 1987, to open up a possible dialogue with the government, a group of exiled leaders of Guatemalan popular organizations openly returned from Mexico, testing the level of freedom of expression. As discussed in Chapter 7, the group left after one week because of fears for their safety. Subsequently, the URNG formally requested dialogue with the government in December 1987.[16]

The URNG saw dialogue as part of a series of political decisions to resolve the nation's main social problems, its human rights violations, and the military's continuing dominance of society.[17] Without dialogue as the first step to peace, civil strife would not end: "without democracy, the political struggle will worsen, the polarization of forces will continue, and the war will have to continue" (Monsanto: 4).

The government responded conditionally with the requirement that the guerrillas lay down their arms prior to any meetings; it refused to recognize an armed group within the state other than the official security forces, which it would be doing if it entered into formal dialogue with the URNG. The Army's position was that the constitution permitted only state security forces and no others, and that the Arias Peace Plan specified dialogue only after "armed groups lay down their arms."[18]

Meetings between government and URNG representatives were held in Madrid in 1988, in the presence of observers from the Guatemalan Army. Guatemalan compliance with this dimension of the Peace Plan was symbolic, however, and the meetings were quickly discontinued. According to

Cerezo, the decision to suspend further contacts was made by the president, not the Army.[19]

Stage 2: National Dialogue

The process continued nonetheless, after a hiatus of several months. The government authorized establishing a structure to be called the National Dialogue, organized as a nongovernmental entity under the aegis of the National Reconciliation Commission (Comisión Nacional de Reconciliación—CNR). The president of the CNR, which had been created as part of the Central American Peace Plan, was the Most Reverend Rodolfo Quezada Toruño, bishop of Quetzaltenango. The National Dialogue was to be inaugurated (and terminated at some undetermined point in the future) with a plenary session of its participants, but the bulk of the dialogue would take place in fifteen working commissions, which were to deal with substantive economic, social, and political issues. Agrarian reform issues were conspicuously absent from the agenda. Each participating sector was expected to send delegates to the working commissions with which it was concerned (see Table 8.1).

The inaugural plenary session of the National Dialogue took place on March 1, 1989, in the National Theater in Guatemala City, after several weeks of delays. President Cerezo did not attend. The event was boycotted by the Army and by major sectors of the right, including UNAGRO, CACIF, and two right-wing political parties, the MLN and the PID (ROG 4/89: 4).[20]

Although the traditional right simply chose not to participate, participation by the left was more complicated. The URNG was denied permission to participate, but Bishop Quezada agreed to read URNG documents into the record. RUOG, the exiled opposition group, did participate but with reduced participatory rights: voice but no vote until the final session of the Dialogue. Representatives of RUOG, who had been harassed in the 1987 visit to Guatemala (see Chapter 7), were allowed to move about freely, albeit in a generally deteriorating atmosphere.[21] The major domestic popular representative was UASP, the umbrella organization of several popular groups representing urban and rural workers, human rights activists, ethnic organizations, and academic groups.

After the ceremonial opening of the National Dialogue, however, accomplishments were slow in coming. By late April, none of the working commissions were functioning, and several of the participating groups had not appointed their representatives to the commissions. The first working committee to begin discussions focused on democratization and political issues. The ultimate success of the Dialogue was called into question by early debates about whether to discuss continuing human rights violations

Table 8.1 National Dialogue Participants, 1988

A. Sectors participating as full delegations:
    1. The government
    2. Political parties
    3. The press
    4. The churches
    5. Refugees
    6. The cooperatives
    7. Unity of Popular and Labor Action (UASP)
    8. The Council of Labor Unity
    9. The Guatemalan Human Rights Commission (CDGH)
    10. The University Student Association (AEU)
    11. The Worker/Owner Solidarity Movement
    12. The Federation of Small Businessmen and Producers
    13. Education Federations
    14. National University of San Carlos (USAC)

B. Sectors participating as "Special Guests":
    15. United Representation of the Guatemalan Opposition (RUOG)
    16. Democratic Forum of Guatemalan Exiles (FDEG)

C. Excluded from participating by government decision:
    17. Guatemalan National Revolutionary Unity (URNG)

D. Voluntarily choosing not to participate:
    18. Coordinating Committee of Agricultural, Industrial, Commercial, and Financial
        Associations (CACIF)
    19. National Liberation Movement (MLN)
    20. Institutional Democratic Party (PID)

Source: GMG 3/89: 8.

against participating delegations; refusal to discuss this topic reduced the effectiveness of participation by the labor groups being threatened (GMG 5/89: 6).

A second working commission, on human rights, presented its conclusions to the CNR for discussion in the plenary sessions to be held at the end of 1989. Attempting to build national consensus, this committee recommended "the abolition of the paramilitary Civil Defense Patrols and Development Poles," as well as "assistance to women widowed by the political violence, and the resolution of the problem of land which belongs to the more than forty thousand Guatemalan refugees in Mexico" (GMG 11/89: 6).

Because of the controversial nature of such recommendations and the early publicity garnered by opponents of the regime, participants from popular sectors and opposition groups began to receive numerous death threats, especially after the attempted military coup in May 1989. By late 1989, the National Dialogue had lost much of its momentum because of the threats and because of "the murder in August of a man representing refugees in the Dialogue" (Tenneriello 1989).[22] By the end of 1989, the National Dialogue process showed few signs of viability.

Stage 3: 1990—The Main Event

During 1990, as a follow-up to the failed National Dialogue, the CNR agreed to meet with the URNG leadership to set up a series of meetings outside of Guatemala.[23] Several factors combined to support this new dialogue process in 1990, including the persistent strength of the insurgency,[24] widespread disgust with continuing paramilitary violence and military atrocities, and the recognized negative impact of an ongoing civil war on international legitimacy and economic development.

The first meeting was held in Oslo, Norway, in March 1990, and included observers from the Guatemalan government and the Army. The participants successfully set up a timetable for several proposed meetings between URNG and various sectors of the political and economic communities, to culminate with a meeting between URNG and the government, including the Army.[25] Meeting outside of Guatemala throughout 1990, the dialogue continued to build momentum and capture the imagination of the Guatemalan public.

The first of the post-Oslo meetings was held in May 1990 in Spain between URNG and representatives of nine political parties. The meeting was successful, at least to the extent of keeping the dialogue process alive and establishing rapport between the URNG and even some of the extreme right. As part of the agreement reached in Spain, the URNG agreed not to sabotage the election process in 1990, and the political parties agreed to help get the URNG legalized as a political force so that they could participate in a new constituent assembly process, originally proposed for 1991 (ROG Fa/90: 10).[26]

The second of the dialogue meetings was held in August in Ottawa, Canada, between URNG and representatives of the business sector. Debates over participation in this meeting underscored the nature of political divisions within the business elite, which was divided over the need to dialogue with the insurgency versus an intransigent position of staying the current course of counterinsurgency. The CACIF, perhaps the country's most powerful business interest group, favored the dialogue and the meeting, but agro-exporters in the UNAGRO did not. The president of the National Association of Coffee Producers (Asociación Nacional de Caficultores—ANACAFE) did urge dialogue with the URNG (ROG Fa/90: 10; *Centroamérica Hoy* 7/30/90: 11).

Not only the list of participants but the outcomes of the Ottawa meeting clearly reflected the difficulties facing any proposed solutions to Guatemala's social and economic problems. Though cordiality was maintained, the substantive differences between the business community and the insurgency remained clear: CACIF proposed peace within "the existing political system," while URNG proposed to "overcome the historical causes of the conflict and the circumstances that make it continue to be necessary." As a result the major positive outcomes of the meeting were symbolic: as the final document showed, each side "put forth its ideological position," and "the parties demonstrated mutual respect" (GMG 9/90: 1–4).

In spite of these serious substantive differences, the dialogue process continued, with an October meeting in Ecuador between the URNG and Guatemalan religious leaders (GMG 10/90: 1–4). The final meetings in 1990 took place in Mexico, also in October. In the first, at Metepec, the URNG met with representatives of the popular sectors, including labor, student, human rights, and refugee organizations. The second meeting, several days later at Atlixco, included a diverse group of business leaders, professionals, university officials, and members of the popular sectors not at the Metepec meeting. As with all earlier ones (after Oslo), no delegate from the Guatemalan government attended these meetings, which lasted five days. They resulted in urgent requests for continued dialogue among the insurgents, the armed forces, and the government. CNR's president, Bishop Quezada, agreed to try to set up the next round of talks.[27]

Throughout 1990, the National Dialogue process succeeded in publicly committing several sectors of society to the idea of negotiating with the insurgency leadership, a process that gradually created more pressure on the Army. General Héctor Gramajo, minister of defense at the beginning of 1990, seemed willing at least to tolerate the process for a while, as witnessed by the presence of military observers at the Oslo meeting in March. But he was replaced in May by General Juan Leonel Bolaños, widely perceived as representing a harder line on counterinsurgency and the military's role in political life.

Indeed, General Bolaños stated by the August meeting in Ottawa that the Army would negotiate with the URNG only after the insurgency had disarmed itself. The impasse was quite explicit, since URNG Commander Pablo Monsanto stated that the URNG would lay down arms only if "conditions for true democracy and peace exist in Guatemala" (ROG Fa/90: 10; Rodríguez; and *Centroamérica Hoy* 7/30/90: 11). Moreover, as had happened during the dialogue efforts in 1989, the successes of these meetings were accompanied by an increase in repression against popular sectors, to the extent that the URNG claimed to be reconsidering its agreement to reduce its armed activities (ROG Fa/90: 10–11).

Before the two meetings held in Mexico in October, moreover, the Army took the extraordinary step of meeting with the popular-sector delegates to those meetings, threatening them with reprisals if there was "agreement with the insurgency on too many points." U.S. Ambassador

Stroock also met with the delegates to express his opposition to any accords that would favor "demilitarizing Guatemalan society." After the meetings the Army cautioned the CNR and Bishop Quezada not to push for dialogue independent of the government's timetable and conditions for dialogue (GMG 11/90: 2–3, 5). For its part, the URNG announced it was not willing to continue dialogue with the Cerezo government but was anxious to talk with the new president after the inauguration in January 1991 (TOA 11/28/90: 4).

Dialogue and Pressure on the Armed Forces

As late as December 1989, the Cerezo administration had successfully kept dialogue with the URNG off the public agenda at the regional level, even though dialogue was an explicit part of the Central American Peace Accords. At the summit meeting of isthmus presidents in Costa Rica in December 1989, for example, the Guatemalan government signed documents legitimating its approaches to civil war. Guatemala pledged to respect human rights, but the summit did not condemn human rights violations in the region, though it condemned insurgent revolutionary organizations. The presidents called for dialogue in Nicaragua and El Salvador but did not mention dialogue or negotiation in Guatemala (*Centroamérica Hoy* 4/1/90: 3–4).

By mid-1990, however, public pressure on the Army was becoming a factor. The dialogue meetings had caught the national imagination. Moreover, an official representative from the United Nations attended these meetings; although Francesc Vendrell acted as a personal represenative of the UN Secretary General rather than as an official emissary, his presence nevertheless lent international legitimacy to the dialogue process. Army officials had attended the original meeting in Oslo and agreed that the ultimate goal of the process was to hold meetings between URNG and the military, but new Minister of Defense Bolaños refused to participate. Luis Gordillo, a retired colonel who was a junta member early in the Ríos Montt government and subsequent founder of a minor political party, did participate as a representative of opposition political parties in the National Dialogue structure. Though it may have been illusory to see Gordillo as a liaison with the Army (a URNG claim), observers nevertheless saw the dialogue process as a "moral force" acting on the Army (CSMonitor 10/29/90: 6).

The pressure grew in part because of both the URNG positions and the changing international climate. The URNG stated that an end to the insurgency would come only with the creation of a truly democratic political structure. To be realized, this would require a constituent assembly to implement four basic changes:

(1) Change the counterinsurgency nature of the Guatemalan state. (2) ... change the role which the current Constitution attributes to the army, which is designed for repressing the people. (3) Recognize the right to private property, but not in absolute terms, because property must have a basically social function. (4) Special respect for the human, political, and all other rights of the Indians of Guatemala (Oramas León).

With the insurgents no longer insisting on a revolutionary change in property relations or an overturn of the political-economic system, "fundamental incompatibility" with the domestic elite no longer existed (Padilla: 10) except for the Army, increasingly isolated in its intransigence as 1990 progressed. More Guatemalans apparently came to regard the insurgency not as a cause but a symptom of basic social problems, taking the position that even a voluntary demobilization by the URNG as part of a new political structure would not end the war if basic social conditions remained unchanged. Increasingly, the military was being perceived as part of the problem, not the solution. In this context, Guatemala held its national elections.

National Elections: The Sideshow

The first round of the 1990 national elections took place on November 11, and the run-off between the top two finishers on January 6, 1991. At stake were the presidency as well as most of Guatemala's elective positions.[28] Besides the presidency, 116 deputies were elected to the National Congress (eighty-seven from Guatemala's twenty-two departments and the Central District—Guatemala City—and twenty-nine on national slates).[29] Municipal-level elections were held in three hundred localities, and voters elected twenty deputies to the new Central American Parliament (PCRP 5/90: 3; "Guatemala: Elecciones": 23, 27). There were 4.4 million people eligible to register to vote (i.e., eighteen years or older), of whom 3.2 million were registered. Approximately 50 percent of younger Guatemalans (ages 18 to 30) did not register. Guatemala City accounted for almost 20 percent of those registered voters, but overall, 65 percent of those registered lived in rural areas.

The Campaign

The political parties continued to be weak organizations in terms of mass mobilization. Only 5.8 percent of the registered voters listed themselves as affiliated with a political party, and of these, 49 percent identified themselves as members of the DCG ("Guatemala: Elecciones": 29), the party generally considered to have the best grassroots organization. Parties typically reflect narrow or personalistic interests.[30] These two factors suggest that campaigns would stress personal image issues rather than programmatic platforms reflecting coherent approaches on nontrivial issues, even in a campaign with thirteen candidates—later twelve, for the candidacy of General Efraín Ríos Montt was declared invalid late in the campaign (see tables 8.2 and 8.3).

The governing Christian Democrats began the campaign in an optimistic tone, in spite of a divisive primary campaign during 1989, but their campaign shifted through at least three phases. Unlike many other parties in Guatemala, the DCG professes a clear ideological position that it refers to regularly in speeches and statements. Yet their candidates did not take clear positions during the early stages of the campaign. In the middle stages of the campaign, Reverend Andrés Girón, the activist priest who had mobilized thousands of landless peasants in 1988 and 1989, left the priesthood and announced his support for the DCG (MHerald 3/15/90: 27A). Luis Zurita, president of the Social Democratic Party (PSD), expressed his support for the DCG's candidate, Alfonso Cabrera.

During this stage the United States began to criticize the DCG heavily. Perhaps coincidentally, the party embraced populist campaign positions, adopted an anti-U.S. stand, and invited Daniel Ortega, the Sandinista president of Nicaragua, to visit Guatemala (*Excelsior* 8/18/90: 37A). But the DCG campaign suffered from persistent accusations of fraud and corruption aimed at the president and the party hierarchy, including accusations of drug trafficking. Failing badly in the polls, the party's problems were compounded in the final stage of the campaign with the sudden, serious illness of its candidate.[31]

The lack of programmatic content was noteworthy in the campaign of the supposedly left-of-center Democratic Socialist Party. Mario Solórzano, its leader and its presidential candidate in 1985, was a candidate for deputy in the National Congress in 1990. The PSD's presidential candidate was a dissident Christian Democrat, René de León Schlotter, who helped found the DCG but who split with the party after the nomination of Cabrera to form an alliance with the PSD (ROG Sp/90: 3). The PSD claimed to be the only party with any significant role for women in the election, but it generally offered no specific policy proposals on any serious issue. The coalition's vice-presidential candidate was Aracely Conde de Paiz, the only woman running for national-level office. The PSD campaign was generally an exercise in image building, with frequent accusations about other parties' campaign spending. The most positive aspects were the attempts to increase voting turnout and encourage women to participate more fully in the electoral process ("La victoria").

With even the Social Democrats running a Christian Democrat, the party spectrum was less programmatic and more narrowly right-of-center than it had been even in 1985,[32] so that although the right seemed factionalized,

Table 8.2 Registered Parties and Candidates, 1990 Elections

Party	Presidential Candidate (Running Mate)
Alianza NO-VENTA (FRG, PID, FUN) (candidacy later ruled invalid)	General Efraín Ríos Montt (Harris Whitbeck)
Union of the National Center (UCN)	Jorge Carpio Nicolle (Manuel Ayau)
Party of National Advancement (PAN)	Alvaro Arzú (Fraterno Vila)
Christian Democratic Party (DCG)	Alfonso Cabrera Hidalgo (Marco Antonio Villamar Contreras)
National Liberation Movement (MLN and FAN)	Colonel Luis Ernesto Sosa Avila (David Eskenasy Cruz)
Social Democratic Party (PSD) and Popular Alliance-5 (AP-5)	René de León Schlotter (Aracely Conde de Paiz)
Movement of Solidarity Action (MAS)	Jorge Serrano Elías (Gustavo Adolfo Espina)
Emerging Movement for Harmony (MEC)	General Benedicto Lucas García (Héctor A. Guerra Pedroza)
Revolutionary Party (PR)	José Angel Lee Duarte (Carlos Gallardo Flores)
Democratic Party (PD)	Jorge Reyna Castillo (Carlos Torres)
United Front of the Revolution (FUR)	Leonel Hernández González (Raúl Montenegro)
Democratic Party of National Cooperation (PDCN)	José Fernández González (Adolfo Putzeys)
National Renovation Party (PNR)	Fernando Leal Estévez (Kurt Miller)

Note: Parties listed in approximate order of popularity in September 1990, per "Who's Who."
Sources: "Who's Who"; GMG 9/90: 6 and 10/90: 6; and "Guatemala: Elecciones": 22.

given the large number of parties and candidates, "[o]n the left, repression has prevented any party from emerging from [the] array of popular organizations that struggle to survive."[33] Repression and violence indeed were part of the electoral campaign, which became quite violent by the end of July (*Excelsior* 7/28/90: 2A). In the final accounting, "at least nine local candidates and party activists died violently during the campaign" (TOA 11/28/90: 4).[34]

General Efraín Ríos Montt

Perhaps the most interesting development during the election was the presidential campaign of retired General Efraín Ríos Montt, nominated by the Guatemalan Republican Front (Frente Republicano Guatemalteco—FRG), a coalition created for the occasion, which included the PID, long identified as a vehicle for the Army's more violent and corrupt elements, and a

Table 8.3 Parties and Ideological Tendencies, 1990 Elections

Ideology	Party
Extreme right	Movimiento de Liberación Nacional—MLN (National Liberation Movement)
Extreme right	Partido Institucional Democrático—PID (Institutional Democratic Party)
Extreme right	Frente de Unidad Nacional—FUN (National Unity Front)
Extreme right	Frente de Avance Nacional—FAN (National Advancement Front)
Extreme right	Frente Republicano Guatemalteco—FRG (Guatemalan Republican Front)
Extreme right	Partido Reformador Guatemalteco—PREG (Guatemalan Reformist Party)
Conservative right	Partido Nacional Renovador—PNR (National Renovation Party)
Conservative right	Movimiento Emergente de Concordancia—MEC (Emerging Consensus Movement)
Conservative right	Unidad Nacionalista Organizada—UNO (Organized Nationalist Unity)
Conservative right	Partido Democrático—PD (Democratic Party)
Conservative right	Movimiento de Acción Solidaria—MAS (Solidarity Action Movement)
Neoliberal right	Partido de Avanzada Nacional—PAN (Party of National Advancement)
Neoliberal right	Unión del Centro Nacional—UCN (Union of the National Center)
Neoliberal right	Central Auténtica Nacional—CAN (Authentic National Center)
Neoliberal right	Partido Democrático de Cooperación Nacional—PDCN (Democratic Party of National Cooperation)
Christian democracy	Democracia Cristiana Guatemalteca—DCG (Guatemalan Christian Democracy)
Social christian	Alianza Popular Cinco—AP-5 (Popular Alliance-Five)
Social democracy	Partido Revolucionario—PR (Revolutionary Party)
Social democracy	Partido Socialista Democrático—PSD (Democratic Socialist Party)
Social democracy	Frente Unido de la Revolución—FUR (United Front of the Revolution)

Notes: Parties listed by approximate ideological line, from right to left, as measured by formal party documents, not necessarily by political behavior. The PREG did not participate in the 1990 elections.

Source: Based on "Guatemala: Elecciones": 34.

smaller party, the National Front for Unity (Frente de Unidad Nacional—FUN). Ríos's vice-presidential candidate, Harris Whitbeck, was a businessman with close ties to the United States and a former U.S. Marine. The Ríos campaign stressed the need to take tough action in response to crime and corruption, themes echoing his style of government in 1982 and 1983. On civilian rule, for example, his position was that civilians had allowed the country to be dirtied again: "We eliminated the garbage once and we can do it again" (MHerald 7/4/90: 12A).

The uniqueness of the Ríos campaign lay in the constitutional questions it forced the country's institutions to resolve. The Constitution of 1985 clearly excludes from the presidency any individual who became chief of state as a result of a military coup d'état, as Ríos did in 1982. But Ríos claimed that "it is a human right to elect and be elected" and sought to have his candidacy recognized by state authorities (TOA 9/5/90: 4).

Reactions were varied. Popular organizations were concerned that a Ríos victory would mean renewed devastation of their organizations, as had happened in the mid-1980s. Ríos reportedly received major campaign financing from a former minister of the interior widely known for human rights violations during the Lucas García regime that was ousted by Ríos Montt's coup in 1982.[35] The Catholic church opposed Ríos, a Protestant fundamentalist, as well (NYTimes 10/17/90: A15). In the U.S. a spokesman for the State Department was neutral: "'Ríos Montt's got somewhat of a bum rap.'"[36] A representative of U.S. television evangelist Pat Robertson called Ríos "'a valued and respected friend'" (MHerald 7/4/90: 12A).

Ríos Montt was denied a place on the ballot by election officials when he tried to register as a candidate in August. He appealed but his appeals were rejected in turn by the Supreme Electoral Tribunal, the Guatemalan Supreme Court, and finally, the Court of Constitutionality. The ruling also extended to the coalition's candidates for the Central American Parliament, since these were national-level contests and the candidacies had been linked to the Ríos-Whitbeck tandem from the beginning of the registration and appeals processes (NYTimes 10/21/90: 20).[37]

Throughout the campaign, while Ríos Montt was being declared ineligible, then appealing each decision to a higher authority, his candidacy gained in overall popularity. In a mid-October poll, for example, he was the leading candidate, receiving 33 percent, while Jorge Carpio of the UCN received 21 percent, Alvaro Arzú of the PAN 13 percent, Jorge Serrano of the MAS 11 percent, and the Christian Democrats less than 11 percent. In the same poll, when asked what they would do if Ríos were not allowed to run, respondents most often supported Ríos Montt's associate in the early and mid-1980s, Jorge Serrano (TOA 10/31/90: 3).

As a result of the court rulings on Ríos Montt, Guatemala approached the campaign's final weeks without the most popular candidate (although he never garnered more than one-third of the support in any poll). All candidates were generally disliked, perhaps because of "the sameness of their platforms and the violence-choked political debate" (WPost 11/11/90: 26). The atmosphere of fear was attributable both to possible threats from Ríos Montt supporters as well as the general climate of human rights violations and political violence. Apathy about the presidential race was high in Indian communities because "none of the candidates will do anything for us."[38]

As of August, the campaign was described as "tainted by violence and mudslinging between the candidates" (*Excelsior* 8/18/90: 37A). None of the major candidates pledged "significant tax and land reform." None pledged "to purge the army of extremist elements" (TOA 10/31/90: 3). By election time in November, the campaign was described as "not programs addressing the country's problems, but smear campaigns and a scramble for the 'winning' image."[39] At least half the electorate expressed themselves in polls as voting for none of the listed candidates or as undecided (ROG Fa/90: 9). Finally,

> during the campaign, none of the main candidates has addressed Guatemala's fundamental problems, such as the army's autonomy, a poverty rate of more than 80 percent and the most skewed distribution of land and wealth in Latin America. To discuss such topics, analysts agree, is to invite violence and assassination (WPost 11/11/90: 26).

Though the campaign essentially was devoid of serious policy issues, there nonetheless was a concomitant rise in political violence as the election approached (*Centroamérica Hoy* 8/22/90). Even Christian Democratic associates saw the campaign as devoid of programmatic content and characterized by character assassination and dirty politics. This, plus the high number of candidacies, the climate of violence, the Ríos Montt situation, the sudden illness of the DCG's candidate just weeks before the election, and the precipitous economic decline in the first half of 1990, all combined to create an atmosphere of uncertainty and skepticism in the voting public ("Guatemala: Elecciones": 45). In sum, the campaign generally reflected few or no firm positions on nontrivial issues, especially on topics reflecting ongoing civil-military relations or social justice questions.[40]

Election Results

In spite of the potential for violence and instability and in spite of calls for boycotts by some of Ríos Montt's supporters and also the URNG leadership, by most accounts the election itself was held in an atmosphere of "absolute tranquility," with over four hundred international observers, all of whom reported the process to be free and honest ("Guatemala:

Elecciones": 50). Results from the Supreme Electoral Tribunal showed that 43.9 percent of the registered voters did not vote and that 9.1 percent of the votes cast were invalid, which means 48.5 percent of the registered voters cast valid votes. Turnout was 53 percent, "disappointingly low by Guatemalan standards" (TOA 11/14/90: 2). Jorge Carpio Nicolle (UCN) and Jorge Serrano Elías (MAS) each received about 25 percent of the vote, thereby becoming candidates for the run-off election on January 6, 1991 ("Guatemala: Elecciones": 50–51). (See Table 8.4.)

In other elections the UCN was the biggest winner in the National Congress, the Central American Parliament elections, and in municipal elections (see Table 8.5). Nonetheless, Carpio's party remained a minority in Congress, with only forty-one of the 116 seats. The remaining seats were mainly distributed among four other parties, and three others gained at least one seat. The Christian Democrats, who had polled only about 6 percent before the election, received 17 percent on election day and remained a major player in the Congress (NYTimes 11/13/90: A11). Regionally, the DCG received most of its support in four departments of the western highlands, all with Indian majorities, suggesting that the party remained the only voice in Congress not representing the far right (PCRP 11/90: 6).

In municipal elections the UCN won 132 mayoralties in the three hundred contested localities, while the Christian Democrats were second with eighty-six victories. In Guatemala City the winning candidate for the mayoralty, with 33.6 percent, was Oscar Berger of the PAN, a party presenting itself as a group of technocrats and business people with no ties to the traditional party structures. The PAN also won the majority of congressional seats from the national capital and carried the presidential vote in Guatemala City as well. Overall, the UCN and the DCG together won over 72 percent of the country's municipal elections, but the PAN, with four victories (of its sixteen overall victories) in metropolitan Guatemala City, held the municipalities in which more than one-third of the national population reside (PCRP 11/90: 4–6).[41]

Second Round: The Run-off

The campaign for the presidential run-off election began in earnest immediately after the first round, pitting Jorge Carpio Nicolle of the UCN against Jorge Serrano Elías of the MAS. Within days of the first round, Serrano was endorsed by several right-wing parties, including the PID, the PNR, the Republican Party, the extreme right-wing MLN, and the MEC. Serrano also was endorsed by one of the losing candidates for mayor of Guatemala City, Oscar Clemente Marroquín (PCRP 11/90: 4–5). Carpio Nicolle apparently hoped to appear the more moderate of the two by

Table 8.4   Presidential Election, First-Round Results, 1990

Party	Candidate	Votes	%
1. UCN	Jorge Carpio Nicolle	399,777	25.72
2. MAS	Jorge Serrano Elías	375,165	24.14
3. DCG	Alfonso Cabrera Hidalgo	271,933	17.50
4. PAN	Alvaro Arzú Irigoyen	268,796	17.29
5. MLN-FAN	Luis Ernesto Sosa Avila	74,825	4.81
6. PSD-AP5	René de León Schlotter	55,819	3.59
7. PR	José Angel Lee Duarte	33,429	2.15
8. PDCN	José Fernández González	32,325	2.08
9. MEC	Benedicto Lucas García	16,894	1.09
10. PNR	Fernando Leal Estévez	11,052	0.71
11. FUR	Leonel Hernández González	7,957	0.51
12. PD	Jorge Reyna Castillo	6,341	0.41

Note: Total valid votes cast: 1,554,313; nullified ballots: 164,267; blank ballots: 90,221; total ballots cast: 1,808,801; total that did not vote: 1,401,476; total registered voters: 3,204,955.
Source: "Guatemala: Elecciones": 53. Reprinted with permission.

Table 8.5   Congressional and Municipal Election Results, 1990

Party	Congress Seats	PARLACEN Seats	Municipal Victories
1. UCN	41	6	132
2. MAS	18	5	13
3. DCG	27	4	86
4. PAN	12	4	16
5. MLN-FAN	4	1	10
6. PSD-AP5	1	0	9
7. PR	1	0	4
8. PDCN	0	0	1
9. MEC	0	0	0
10. PNR	0	0	2
11. FUR	0	0	0
12. PD	0	0	1
13. FRG[a]	0	—	16
14. PID-FUN-FRG[a]	12	—	2
15. Civic Com.[b]	—	—	8
TOTALS	116	20	300

Notes: [a] These parties did not participate at the presidential level because their candidate, Efraín Ríos Montt, was ruled ineligible. [b] Civic Committees are nonpartisan coalitions formed for municipal-level elections. "Congress Seats" refers to the Guatemalan National Congress; "PARLACEN Seats" are Guatemala's seats in the Central American Parliament.
Source: "Guatemala: Elecciones": 54. Reprinted with permission.

picking up support from the DCG (LATimes 11/13/90: 9A). Carpio already had enlisted the support of the CUSG, a major, centrist, labor federation (PCRP 11/90: 6). Both candidates were described as moderate conservatives by most press observers.[42] Yet the far-right credentials of both candidates seem to belie this observation. Carpio's running mate, for example, was Manuel Ayau, who earlier in the campaign had been the MLN's presidential candidate. One of Carpio's public supporters was Carlos Acevedo, alleged to have been a participant in the attempted military coup of May 1989 (NYTimes 11/11/90: 9). Serrano Elías had been an important functionary during the repressive Ríos Montt regime and had profited from his association with the Ríos campaign throughout 1990. Indeed, Serrano averred that he had entered the campaign in case his "mentor," General Ríos Montt, were to be disqualified (NYTimes 1/8/91: A3). Because of this association, Serrano was installed as the early favorite in the run-off even though he had finished a close second in the first round. A poll after the first round showed Serrano with 67 percent of the vote (Colina).

As in the first-round campaign, Carpio and Serrano offered little to choose between in terms of issues and campaign positions (TOA 11/28/90: 4). As mentioned above, both were identified as wealthy conservatives, although supporters of their economic plans saw both as champions of the free market. One observer noted: "Neither candidate has proposed fundamental changes in what is one of the most unbalanced economic systems in Central America—one that has left more than half the country underemployed or unemployed" (LATimes 11/13/90: 9A).[43]

If in terms of economic policy there was little choice between the two candidates, that was not the case on religious issues, a politically sensitive aspect of Guatemalan life since at least the late 1970s, when catechists and progressive Catholic clergy were victimized by military repression, and especially because of Ríos Montt's born-again, messianic style while he was head of state in the 1980s. With Carpio Nicolle a Catholic and Serrano Elías a Protestant evangelical, the religious dimension became a central issue in the campaign. Serrano profited from his association with General Ríos Montt in this sense as well. At least one observer thought Serrano had a clear advantage in this situation, in spite of Carpio's access to greater campaign funding, because of the ability to mobilize small evangelical groups all over the country—the "Fujimori effect" (TOA 11/28/90: 4).[44]

The early and consistent response of the Catholic church hierarchy during the run-off campaign was to ask its faithful to ignore the candidates' religious affiliation and concentrate on other issues. Though the church might well have pointed out that Carpio's economic platform was at odds with its frequent messages about social justice, in fact the bishops explicitly focused on the national dialogue process, asking voters to support candidates who would participate in dialogue aimed at ending the civil war (*Excelsior* 12/3/90: 2A).

In fact, both candidates pledged to continue the dialogue structure process. Serrano was perceived as more willing to dialogue, since he had been an active member of the National Dialogue structure in 1989, and had participated in the 1990 meeting in Spain. Serrano announced his willingness to dialogue informally before the January 6 run-off election. Some suspected that this was a campaign ploy, however—an opportunistic attempt to take advantage of widespread popular support for the dialogue process, given Serrano's active role during the rural violence of the Ríos Montt administration (TOA 11/28/90: 4).

On January 6, 1991, consistent with poll predictions, voters elected Jorge Serrano Elías to the presidency for a five-year term beginning January 13, 1991; he received a majority of some 67 percent. Serrano thereby became the first Protestant to be elected president of a predominantly Roman Catholic, Latin American country (NYTimes 1/8/91: A3).

Elections, Dialogue, and the Military Reconsidered

National elections took up much of Guatemala's coverage in the international press in 1990. Though honest in terms of legal provisions and ballot counting, these elections nonetheless reflected the process designed to protect the dominant position of the Army and conservative elites. Conservative observers were correct in pointing out that the big loser in the election was the left: no candidates offered solutions for social problems other than neoliberal economics, and violence aimed at popular sectors was a characteristic of the campaign atmosphere (Thomas).[45]

The combination of violence and a campaign largely devoid of progressive solutions to nontrivial social and economic problems led to a discrediting of the traditional parties and electoral processes. Large numbers of voters expressed discontent with both the party in office, the Christian Democrats, and with the chief opposition party for five years, the Union of the National Center, whose candidate Carpio Nicolle was swamped in the run-off election in January 1991. Noting this discontent, some observers attributed voter apathy and disgust to a general historical disdain for democracy in Guatemala. Combining this with the popularity of the election campaign waged by General Efraín Ríos Montt before he was ruled ineligible, some reached the conclusion that "Guatemalans seem to be willing to trade away freedom for security" (NYTimes 11/12/90: A7).

In the Guatemalan context, however, to argue that popular support for General Ríos Montt during the campaign meant a general desire for authoritarian rule ignores many important dimensions.[46] It is fallacious to conclude that distaste for the traditional parties and military hierarchy equals distaste for democracy. Such reasoning ignores the significance of the activities of the country's popular organizations and of the National Dialogue process. In 1990, responding to their history and taking advantage of the opportunity, even if limited, directly provided by elections, Guatemalans voted to sweep out the traditional parties and elected the candidate least involved in a conventional party, Jorge Serrano Elías. And they voted for candidates who at least apparently supported the National Dialogue, a process fraught with antimilitary implications. The history of nonrepresentation by parties and the brutality of the military provides ample evidence of voter rationality.

While the honesty of vote counting during the 1990 elections has not been questioned, other components of the process are more complicated to evaluate, especially the climate of violence and the absence of serious choices beyond the right and the center right. The lack of direct or even indirect popular influence on public policy between 1985 and 1990 had reduced the public's faith in elections (or at least in the reformism of the Christian Democrats) by 1990. Finally, a good deal of political energy was devoted to the National Dialogue process during 1989 and 1990, causing elections to seem less relevant to the national situation.

Although several parties were competing for office and clear differences were apparent among the parties, the underlying and consistent characteristic displayed was extreme timidity in terms of major reform, if not outright opposition to even evolutionary change in the direction of social justice. Electoral pluralism was real in an organizational sense, but the scope of the substantive political possibilities meant that this election, like others in the past, offered relatively little to the popular sectors. Interpreting these elections as watersheds of democratic transitions, therefore, is to miss essential aspects of the overall political context.

For example, electoral results have implications for the role of the armed forces. In the 1984 and 1985 elections the best interpretation of voting behavior was that it was a repudiation of the military's role in society (Rosada Granados 1985). In 1990, a similar interpretation is reasonable. Both winners in the first round "succeeded as businessmen before turning to politics, lack ties to the country's political past and owe no power debts to the military" (Thomas). Moreover, the eventual victory of Jorge Serrano is significant because of his links to General Ríos Montt: Ríos has been at odds with the ruling military hierarchy since 1974, when he won the presidential election but was prevented from taking office by a military clique that subsequently sent him to Spain as ambassador. In 1982, the coup d'état that installed him in power overturned the traditional military hierarchy, and in 1990, his campaign was opposed by the military establishment. To some extent a vote for Serrano was a vote against the military.

Conclusion

Historically, the Army's management of society has involved political structures that would not threaten its continuing dominant position. In the mid-1980s, it was powerful enough even to include relatively open, honest elections as part of its strategy, the electoral process being not an end in itself but part of a coherent and, under the circumstances, rational plan. The structures of liberal democracy since 1984 are part of this process, at least in the eyes of the military's dominant faction.

To some degree, military control over politics was threatened by several factors during the Cerezo administration—though not by Cerezo and the Christian Democrats themselves—including internal factionalizing. More important, the National Dialogue process not only mobilized public opinion but even brought elite establishment groups into discussions with the guerrilla insurgency's leadership. Ironically, although elections involved many more participants, the major political questions facing Guatemala and its transition to democracy were debated in the National Dialogue process, the main event, and not in the elections, the sideshow. But even the electoral process, in spite of its contextual flaws, reflected pressure exerted on the military as well as elite actors within traditional political parties.

Although the 1990 election may have been less than a perfect democratic instrument, the opportunity had opened to debate society's key issues as a result of the crisis of the early 1980s and the military's rebuilding of constitutional government. Taking advantage of this opening, popular organizations pushed Guatemala toward democracy from 1985 on, although at great personal cost, as discussed earlier. But it is in the participation of popular organizations and in the more recent National Dialogue process that signs of a true transition to democracy are seen, not in the electoral process. Indeed, because of successes in those arenas in 1990, there is room for cautious optimism about the possibilities for democracy, almost in spite of the electoral process.

In 1990, Guatemalans energetically pursued the National Dialogue process, perceiving it and not the election campaign as the means to domestic peace because it focused on the fundamental issue of reducing the military's power. The dialogue process held out the best prospect for democratizing society, and even pointed to the possibility of creating a constitutional process to focus on social concerns rather than to legitimize military control of society.[47] A major issue for the 1990s is how far the National Dialogue process can go to meld disparate social sectors into a pressure group capable of forcing a diminished role for the military.

At the same time, the political conditions for increased repression also threaten, if history is any guide. Cautious optimism about pressure on the military must be tempered by the overall weight of accumulated data on Guatemalan politics, which point toward continuing military domination. Factions within the Army, for example, generally differ only on the tactics to follow: consensus continues on the goal of maintaining institutional dominance and economic opportunity for military officers.[48] If institutional democracy along with repression cannot achieve that goal, then the constitutional order may crumble, limiting opportunity for political action. In the long run, however, the question of the military's dominant position is still the major obstacle to any major movement toward democracy.[49]

The weight of the evidence here and from earlier chapters is that Guatemala continues to be dominated by a single institution, its armed forces, in spite of the occasional exceptions that mean this dominance is not total. The two key poles of power, the military and the civilian state, appear to have essentially the same relationship they have had since 1954, if not earlier, even though the government has assumed a different constitutional form since 1984.

Notes

1. The Army

built a wall of silence around the disastrous effects of the military campaign waged against the rural civilian population, during which they have killed noncombatant civilians and destroyed crops, houses and domestic animals ("The Actors": 8).

2. According to the URNG leadership, the Army suffered 2,720 casualties, including both dead and wounded, between January 1986 and May 1988 (VM 6/88: 2, 7).

3. "Of course the army has a role in this country, but it isn't running the government the way it used to. . . . The society is steadily becoming less militarized, and that can only happen if the army leaders have confidence in the government. We're building that confidence" (quoted in Kinzer 1989: 50).

4. The aftermath of the attempted coup of May 11, 1988, is best understood in a framework of political influence, or interest group politics. Unable to increase their influence through elections in 1982, 1984, 1985, and the municipal elections of 1988, the parties of the right resorted to putschist tactics. Like popular organizations, right-wing organizations often use unconventional modes of participation in order to influence ruling groups, especially when government institutions are unresponsive to their demands. Whereas for the left this means public demonstrations based on their major resource—the numbers they can mobilize—for the right this means rumors of coups, plotting, and attempted coups, based on their major resource—access to weapons and, on occasion, dissident military factions.

5. The day after the correspondents had left Guatemala, President Cerezo announced their "temporary expulsion" (WRH 6/22/88: 1, 6).

6. Attempts to modernize the police have been a prominent part of the Christian Democratic agenda, ostensibly to increase respect for human rights and to decrease incidence of common crime, especially in Guatemala City, where roving street gangs had become a fairly serious social problem by the mid-1980s. In 1987, Spain promised patrol cars and motorcycles, a forensic laboratory, and weapons (GNIB 6/87: 10). Mayor Andrew Young had tentatively accepted an invitation to

have the Atlanta, Georgia, police help train Guatemalan police, but he reversed that decision in 1988, after a major public campaign was mounted in the U.S. against aiding the Guatemalan police. See also *Special Service* 2/88: 6.

7. This coup was described as

a way of achieving political concessions through military means that can not be achieved through political means. In effect, political spaces are reduced, the Cerezo administration comes under tighter military control, and repression increases (ROG 5/89: 9).

8. For a similar analysis, see N&A 10/26/89: 1–2; and Schirmer 1989b: 478–479.

9. For a fascinating account of the ideological position of the Officers of the Mountains, see Schirmer 1989a. Among the opinions expressed by the officers Professor Schirmer interviewed are these: the Christian Democrats are communists, many members of the civilian government are drug traffickers, the leading economic actors have sold out to foreign interests, the military high command is corrupt, and the minister of defense, Héctor Gramajo, is a "communist without balls."

10. Writing before the attempted May 1989 coup, for example, Schirmer noted that the Guatemalan Army's approach to the doctrine of national security, as well as its nervousness over the possible replication of the civil war situation in El Salvador, could lead to a "preemptive state of siege" (Schirmer 1989b: 479).

11. In this text I have concentrated on domestic politics in Guatemala. For a more complete discussion of the foreign policy issues facing President Cerezo, see Barry: chapter 5; and Jonas 1991: chapter 13.

12. Amidst these grants the United States was conspicuous in its absence from the list of Western democracies that had contributed funds needed to hold the National Dialogue in 1989, discussed later in this chapter. Guatemala received $132,000 from European nations and Canada for this process but nothing from the United States (PCRP 9/89: 8).

13. The aid figures for the period were: "In 1987, Guatemala received nearly $5.5 million in military aid, and $177.3 in economic aid," and in the first three months of 1988 Guatemala had "been allocated $80 million in Economic Support Funds [ESF]" (N&A 4/21/88: 3).

14. For details see GMG 3/89: 6–7, 4/89, 5–6, and 5/89: 4, in which the URNG asserts evidence of "at least 37 cases of US military presence in Guatemala" in the preceding six months. Also see WPost 8/18/89: 26.

15. For details of these particular actions, see newsletters of the Guatemalan Church in Exile (Iglesia Guatemalteca en Exilio—IGE) and timely issues of UOG and VM.

16. This section on the National Dialogue is based on several issues of PCRP, ROG, UOG, GMG, and other newsletters and interviews.

17. The insurgency's position was that the militarized regime imposed in 1954 was still in place despite the 1985 elections: "What we have in Guatemala today is a government whose purpose is to cover up this regime. But in reality the structures and components of this regime continue to exist" (Monsanto: 3).

18. The Army's position was that it was "not possible for one thousand armed terrorists to set conditions for a country with eight million inhabitants who have opted for democracy" (*El Gráfico* 12/30/87, quoted in GNIB 12/1/87: 9).

19. "The army is not in charge of political dialogue. The government and the president have that responsibility" (*Special Service* 3/88: 8).

20. For more details on the National Dialogue as institutional structure, see UOG 5/89: 1–2; and PCRP 3/89: 5.

21. One RUOG delegate commented:

We, as exiles who were persecuted in the past, are now privileged by the fact that we can go back and move with more freedom than people who normally live in Guatemala have at this time (quoted in ROG 4/89: 5).

22. For more details on threats aimed at participants, see GMG 4/89: 2–3; and NFAW 7/89: 7–8.

23. For good discussions about the background for the 1990 round of dialogue between URNG and various Guatemalan actors, see ROG Fa/90: 10–11; CSMonitor 9/26/90: 5; and N&A 26/6/90.

24. The military and the DCG held two positions on this: that the guerrillas had ceased to be a serious military force, and that because democracy had existed since Cerezo's inauguration, the need to continue fighting the government was over (PCRP 4/90: 6–7).

25. For a more thorough discussion of the Oslo agreement, see N&A 6/26/90; GMG 4/90: 2–3; and, for the DCG view, PCRP 4/90: 6–7.

26. For more details on the meeting in Spain, see PCRP 6/90: 5–6; and GMG 6/90: 1–5; for the URNG reaction see the interview with URNG Commander Pablo Monsanto in Oramas León.

27. For more details of the October dialogue meeting at Metepec (Puebla), Mexico, see GMG 11/90: 1–5; and Rodriguez.

28. This section is based on several sources, including various issues of PCRP and ROG, in addition to the text references. The most comprehensive source of the election's formal-legal provisions and other basic information is "Guatemala: Elecciones Generales." This source and PCRP's analysis, in general, are upbeat and supportive of the Christian Democrats. For more critical overviews with a good deal of basic information about the electoral process, see "Elections in Guatemala 1990–91"; "Who's Who"; and N&A 6/26/90.

29. Between 1986 and 1990, Congress had legislated an increase in its size, from 100 to 116, because of increased population in some of Guatemala's departments. One seat was added for each increase of 80,000 people over the 1985 figures.

30. A *New York Times* analyst commented:

Guatemalan politicians and Western diplomats say the plethora of political parties remain little more than a collection of tiny factions and established interest groups, usually under a caudillo, or a strongman. Instead of battling for their party's nomination, politicians often shop for a suitable party (NYTimes 10/11/90: A11).

The same source also quotes Alvaro Arzú, former mayor of Guatemala City and the PAN presidential candidate: "'There's no real difference between any of us.'"

31. For accusations of corruption within the DCG administration, including accusations against its candidate Cabrera, see *Excelsior* 3/16/90: 2A. For details of Cabrera's illness, see "Guatemala: Elecciones": 45.

32. For a similar analysis, see ROG Su/90: 3.

33. "The Social Democratic Party, which is Guatemala's only left of center party, is on the verge of extinction" (ROG Fa/90: 2). And: "The political system remained closed to the left. The 12 presidential candidates who ran in November's first round ranged from the right to the extreme right" (NYTimes 1/8/91: A3).

34. For details on violence directed against the Mutual Support Group (GAM), the human rights organization, see *Excelsior* 25/7/90: 9. See NYTimes 10/9/90, for another source that details political violence directed against candidates but which ascribes violence to local-level rivalries.

35. The Guatemalan paper *Siglo XXI* claimed that Donaldo Alvarez Ruíz, minister of the interior under Lucas García, had contributed $50,000 to the Ríos campaign (*Excelsior* 7/18/90: 2A).

36. This statement echoes the famous comment by President Reagan in early 1983, when under Ríos Montt the most vicious wave of state terrorism in Guatemalan history was underway in rural regions.

37. For other summaries of the Ríos Montt candidacy and its rejection by legal authorities, see "Guatemala: Elecciones": 40–43; TOA 9/5/90: 4 and 10/31/90: 3.

38. MHerald 9/30/90: 22A, quoting a local Indian leader. This is not an anti-democratic or anti-voting stance, however: "In the last presidential elections, fewer than half of the town's voters went to the polls. Votes in the town's mayoral race far surpassed the number cast for presidential candidates." It is perhaps in this spirit that a long-time North American resident of Guatemala commented, perhaps with tongue in cheek, that Guatemalans "will not vote for someone stupid enough to want to be President" (personal communication, April 1991).

39. To review the positions of several candidates on issues of primary importance to the Maya communities, see Esquít Choy, ed., which documents both statements of the candidates as well as questions and answers by a panel of Mayan scholars and activists.

40. Candidates "announced ambitious programs to stabilize the foundering economy. But they have not dared to do more than hint at plans for demilitarization, agrarian reform, population control or land redistribution" (NYTimes 11/11/90: A9).

41. Mayoralty candidates included: (1) Oscar Clemente Marroquín Godoy, a newspaper publisher, nominated by a civic committee, UNIDAD, who had finished second in the 1985 municipal election; (2) Rafael Escobar Donis, who resigned his position as president of the National Bank for Housing in order to run for mayor; (3) Oscar Berger of the PAN, the party that won the mayoralty in 1985 with Alvaro Arzú, its presidential candidate in 1990; (4) Pedro Asturias of the UCN; and (5) three minor candidates, Oscar Rafael Prem, Enrique Montano Vela, and the perennial (and perennially unsuccessful) candidate, José María Ruíz Furlán, a Catholic priest (PCRP 4/90: 3).

42. In addition to general sources listed earlier, this section on the run-off campaign is based on TOA 11/14/90: 2; NYTimes 11/13/90: A11; PCRP 11/90: 3, 6; and LATimes 11/13/90: 9A.

43. This sameness was comforting from the conservative side of the spectrum. Manuel Ayau, Carpio's vice-presidential running mate, was praised because his "commitment to and support for free-market philosophy throughout Central America is legendary." And were Serrano to win the run-off, the same observer saw no problem, for "it is unlikely that his commitments to free-market economic policy changes will be any less dramatic that those of Mr. Carpio's" (Thomas). Thomas, dean of the Francisco Marroquín University in Guatemala City, notes that Ayau has been praised by Nobel laureate Milton Friedman for his economic philosophy of free-market capitalism.

44. President Fujimori's electoral victory in Peru, earlier in 1990, is sometimes attributed to the role of evangelical grassroots' groups.

45. For this source, the "left" means the Christian Democrats as well as the Marxists, who are lumped together as "statists." Thomas notes that the victory, however, belongs to the "new right," not the old right of violence and military ruination. The "new right" is

> a young and educated private sector committed to the principles of an open society and understanding of the market economy as a tool for progress. They know that dynamic growth and foreign investment are no more than fantasies as long as unstable rules, shaky currency and confiscatory taxation are in place. Hard work in a free society can overcome poverty (Thomas).

46. This argument was clearly presented in several articles by Lindsey Gruson of the *New York Times.* In addition to articles cited earlier, see 10/9/90, 10/11/90, and 11/12/90.

47. For similar arguments, see "Elections in Guatemala."

48. "High-ranking members of the national armed forces are a stubborn, repugnant breed who still see communism behind legitimate demands for a country as rich in resources as Guatemala to avail these resources more equitably" (Lovell 1990).

49. For a comparative analysis of the question of the military-civilian relationship in five South American countries, see Zagorski.

9

The Serrano Presidency, 1991–1992

At the time of Jorge Serrano's inauguration in January 1991, Guatemala was beset by such major problems as chronic poverty, massive unemployment, an uncertain pattern of economic growth, a military struggle between the URNG insurgency and the Army, human rights violations, and pressure from the Mayan communities to acknowledge their national identity. The domestic social situation showed marked continuity from the Cerezo period, but international events produced a different macropolitical climate. The Cold War was ending very quickly. The Sandinista party lost an election in Nicaragua, relinquishing its hold on the presidency. El Salvador was involved in serious negotiations to end its civil war, with the United Nations as a major participant. Some semblance of peace and normalcy seemed to be returning to the region.

Inside Guatemala, "normal" political activity was beginning to be less acceptable. The continuing civil war had put all other issues on hold, but by 1991, the war was seen as a drain on resources and a burden on economic development. Civilian government had alienated the popular sectors and remained weak because of its continuing reliance on the military. The social and political intransigence of the right and of some factions of the Army was beginning to appear less a bulwark against communism and more a part of the problem. The politics of the Cerezo administration, which papered over major social problems to avoid a military coup, had produced widespread cynicism about political parties and civilian government. In short, President Serrano had more opportunity to deliver, but more pressure to do so as well.

Serrano himself brought strengths and weaknesses to the presidency. Having worked closely with the military during the Ríos Montt and Mejía Víctores periods in the early and mid-1980s, he was on the whole an acceptable candidate to the military establishment. As a conservative, Serrano

159

could be expected to make relatively few moves toward serious social reform. This same quality might earn initial support from elites, but it made him quite suspect in the popular sectors. His born-again evangelism made Serrano less palatable to the Catholic church.

As his term began, Serrano expressed four goals: social and economic justice; an end to the guerrilla war; the "end [to] military and government-sponsored human rights abuses; and [an] improvement in the democratic system." His program included a plan to tax landowners and proposals to alter the makeup of the military high command, a particularly hard-line group of officers at the time of Serrano's inauguration (LATimes 9/24/91: 2H).

In the economic sphere, Serrano inherited from the Christian Democrats the model of relying on nontraditional exports, with few, if any, discontinuities. In 1990, traditional exports totaled $600 million and nontraditional exports $300 million, while apparel was the second most valuable export to the U.S., second only to coffee (ROG Wi/91: 8–9). Social conditions were also continuous: most of the population of 9.2 million was mired in poverty.[1] Politically, Serrano began with a model similar to Cerezo's, based on concertación and an organized *pacto social*, designed to maximize communication among organized groups, including the popular ones.

This chapter focuses on the first two years of Serrano's presidency. Bringing the analysis to the end of 1992 means data on Guatemala's transition has been provided for a full decade, from the time of the Ríos Montt coup in 1982 through the beginning of 1993. As before, we study the quality of political participation through an overview of selected issue areas facing the president: demands of the popular sectors, policy responses of the government, and some of the social outcomes, including human rights and other key indicators of democratic transitions. The principal questions remain the same: does the quality of political participation indicate development of a democratic political process? Does public policy and its social impact reveal movement toward a democratic society and social justice?

Economic Issues and the Popular Sectors

Tax Policy

Tax reform has been a major issue in Guatemala since at least the 1960s. In 1991, as part of the conditions for a proposed agreement with the World Bank, the country again faced the question, as the bank pressed for tax modernization.[2] The tax reform plan included extending the IVA, Guatemala's value added tax; changing income tax brackets for moderate- and upper-income citizens; and tax simplification for businesses. The extension of the IVA, essentially a sales tax, could be seen as hurting the lower-income sectors. With the current income-tax-bracket percentages ranging from 4 to 30 percent, the proposed reform meant a decrease in income tax for the wealthiest Guatemalans but a squeeze on middle-income groups. Finally, the business tax reforms involved a flat tax rate, which would mean increases for the smaller businesses and decreases for the largest, as compared to the current tax structure (ROG Sp/92: 10–11).

The popular-sector groups opposed the IVA reforms. By eliminating all product and service exemptions, the reform would mean increases in prices for food and medicines, among the products previously excluded from the IVA. CACIF neither condemned nor endorsed the plan, stating firmly its opposition in principle to any diversion of capital to the state. CACIF saw the reforms as perhaps a necessary response to the World Bank, but not necessarily a good idea for Guatemala (ROG Sp/92: 10–11).

The tax modernization plan was originally proposed in Congress in August 1991. Two major opposition parties, the Christian Democrats and the Union of the National Center (UCN), publicly opposed the plan. With his own party, the Solidarist Action Movement (MAS), holding only eighteen seats in Congress, Serrano was unable to force the issue in 1991, and Congress simply postponed dealing with the question. Nevertheless, in early 1992 the reforms were approved. The three reforms of the Fiscal Modernization Program aimed to increase government revenue by nearly $200 million, a 19 percent increase in annual revenues (PCRP 7/92: 4–5).[3]

Passage of the tax package met the World Bank requirements but did not resolve the problem of how to invest increased revenues for more social progress. With little bureaucratic infrastructure in place to implement social programs, the government was not equipped to do so for social reform packages. Moreover, the generally regressive nature of these tax reforms would produce more need for social programs, not less (PCRP 7/92: 4–5).

Housing, for example, continued to a problem area for society, if not a target of public policy. The government's own statistics showed a housing deficit of 650,000 units in 1986 (in the capital it was 350,000) and, in 1991, of 840,000 units. The genesis of this increase was a combination of the 1976 earthquake, people fleeing violence in rural areas, and lack of government action. As of mid-1992, the Serrano government had spent no funds to resolve the housing dilemma. One result was land invasions: some six thousand families invaded lands in various places in Guatemala City in early 1992, including over three thousand families in one settlement on the south side of the city. In late March police invaded this settlement and destroyed it, leaving fifteen thousand people homeless (ROG Su/92: 8–9, 14).

The Maquila *Question*

The maquila sector illustrates the basic dynamics of Guatemalan politics very well. The maquila is a strategy for economic development, a deliberate decision to "permit exploitation of its cheap, abundant labor force in exchange for foreign currency, employment, and hoped-for long term industrialization" (Petersen: 5).[4] This is potentially an excellent strategy because it is a labor-intensive model that could reconcile an export-driven model with social justice. The maquila strategy can generate growth in internal aggregate demand, precisely what is needed for sustained development and social democracy. The maquila sector is the fastest growing sector in the economy: as of 1991, at least forty-five thousand workers, mostly women, were producing clothing, primarily for the United States. The exported products were a major portion of Guatemala's nontraditional exports (ROG Wi/91: 8).

Because no labor unions were functioning in the maquila sector, this resulted in poor work conditions, lack of security for workers, and extremely low wages. Both organized labor and workers in general found themselves in dire straits in 1991 and 1992. Besides high levels of unemployment and underemployment, workers were faced with high inflation rates in the late 1980s and 1990, which led to a decline in purchasing power of about 80 percent since 1980 (IPS 10/31/92).

At the level of individual workers and unions, labor was caught in a bind. Workers could legally bring complaints against employers, but there were far too few labor courts to hear the complaints and far too many cases, hence a huge backlog. Moreover, procedures allow owners to appeal rulings, delaying final action for years, even if they lost an initial judgment. Finally, workers feared dismissal if they filed a complaint; since roughly two were unemployed for each person working, the incentives were against filing complaints.[5]

These conditions led to international pressure on the government in 1992, with a renewed campaign in the United States to convince the U.S. Trade Office to review Guatemala's labor conditions.[6] The review could have led to a reassessment of Guatemala's preferential trade status in the Caribbean Basin Initiative, which in turn would be a major blow to the apparel industry, by far the largest component of the maquila sector and heavily dependent on exporting to the United States. This campaign became a major concern for Guatemala.

In 1991, the Trade Office rejected the review requests because Serrano promised to reform the labor code, hire inspectors, and raise the minimum wage. The U.S. position was that Guatemala was making substantial progress. But as of early 1992, the labor code had not been reformed, no new inspectors were hired, and the minimum wage was still insufficient, when it was paid at all. Reports circulated of formal requests for labor union certification sitting in the president's office for two years, in spite of constitutional provisions supporting labor. Moreover, the State Department's human rights report on Guatemala noted that twenty union leaders received death threats in 1991 and had to flee the country, and that forty-five thousand Guatemalan children between ages six and fifteen were employed illegally, meaning, among other things, that they were not receiving social benefits mandated by law (WPost 8/1/92: 18A).

Throughout 1992, a coalition of international groups and popular organizations supported the campaign to have conditions investigated by the Trade Office. Business leaders adopted two tactics in response: first, they claimed to be aware of some abuses but said they were doing their best to correct them in order to avoid losing the jobs put at risk by the petitions calling for investigations.[7] The second tactic was to label the labor unions communist organizations (IPS 10/18/92).

Reforms in working conditions were proposed in Congress and were fought by CACIF (IPS 10/22/92). Nevertheless, in late 1992, the National Congress did pass changes in the labor code, including stiffer fines for employers who violate the code and new protection for women. The reform was "a product of U.S. pressure," according to Christian Democratic congresswoman, Catalina Reyes Soberanis. In the popular sectors many leaders approved the measure, but only as a first step, while others saw it as more propaganda, because conditions will depend on future government policy actions (CSMonitor 12/14/92: 8).

The maquila sector's growth, as well as its place in the political arena, illustrate many of the major structural issues facing the nation. To make the economic strategy successful beyond the short term requires government investment in infrastructure, including education and health. Without this, the maquila sector will quickly exhaust the human resources now available. The short-run results may be acceptable to new profiteers, but long-term development will not materialize. This public investment is lacking, however; the lack of social infrastructure programs condemns even the government's own program to failure. The resulting situation leaves Guatemala's majority with little improvement, if any, in the overall quality of life, in spite of the employment generated in the short run.[8]

Consistent with that hypothesis, actual conditions have not reflected significant progress for workers, in spite of growth in the maquila area. UASP estimated that 75 percent of the people working in this period were not receiving the minimum wage guaranteed by law.[9] Some firms were not registering their employees with the national health service, as required by law, and worse, some of these firms deducted the cost of health insurance from employee wages anyway. In 1991, according to the ministry of labor, wages went up 90 to 150 percent, but purchasing power declined by 28 percent because of inflation (IPS 10/31/92). One result of these dynamics was a large May Day labor parade, with fifty thousand participants, the largest since the 1980 parade, during which dozens of participants were murdered or disappeared (GMG 3/92: 6). In short, as these few illustrations suggest, labor issues remained explosive in late 1992.

Rural Land Issues

In rural areas access to land remains the primary issue. The imminent return of possibly thousands of refugees from Mexico increased pressure on land during this period. One example will illustrate most of the common dynamics. In early 1992, some two thousand peasants invaded and seized a farm in San Jorge la Laguna, on Lake Atitlán, that had been taken from the Maya during the Liberal Reforms in the 1870s. Since the farm lies between the village and the lake, access to the lake via the land has been a necessary part of San Jorge's life. But the current owners announced plans to build a tourist resort on the property, ending public access and transit rights. This prompted the invasion and seizure of the farm by the community, on the basis of their historical right to it, which predates the "legal" claim of the current owners. The government response to this action was to evict the community violently, with sixty-seven arrests, dozens of injuries, and two individuals killed.[10]

Environmental Issues

Environmental problems and policy responses—in this case concerning oil production—also illustrate the dynamics of domestic versus international economic needs. Exploration and drilling for oil began in the Petén region in the mid- to late 1970s. Activity has been sporadic, reflecting international markets as well as security problems caused by the guerrilla insurgency. New leases were being developed in 1991 and 1992. It is clear that the oil industry causes ecological problems in the Petén, and the oil leases are located within the legally protected Biosphere Reserves. The oil industry employs few people, but the jobs are perceived as good ones and land pressures are strong in the highlands. Every new oil well means building a road, and this brings migrants flooding into the region to burn the rain forest and plant corn—an escalating, indirect impact of the oil industry. But Guatemala needs oil: oil imports currently equal 10 percent of all imports (CSMonitor 4/29/92: 8).

Faced with these demographic, economic, and ecological realities, the government has been able to do relatively little: laws and government programs to preserve biospheres and other environmental measures fail because the state is weak ("it's the Wild West"), a corrupt military permits exploitation, immigrants flood into the area, and the poor are unlikely to preserve a resource if they are starving and unemployed (CSMonitor 4/29/92: 10). Reports indicate that toxic waste, including nuclear waste, is being dumped in the Petén region of Guatemala. This is of course illegal, but one report, attributed to the chair of the Guatemalan congressional committee on the environment, was that "money has proved powerful" (IPS 8/13/92).

On the positive side, Guatemala entered its first environment-for-debt swap in 1992: Conservation International gave the government U.S. bonds to cancel $1.3 million of its foreign debt—Guatemala's total debt is estimated at over $3 billion[11]—in exchange for title to land in the Mayan Biosphere Reserve in the Petén. The government agreed to finance and administer a biosphere preservation project in the area with the interest from the bonds (IPS 5/30/92). There were also several "eco-tourism" projects in the rainforest area.[12]

Foreign Policy

Most of the issues facing Guatemala have international as well as domestic implications. Two areas more international in scope were the Belize question and the ambitious foreign campaign waged by Serrano to attract aid and investment to the country. Both had political and economic implications.

On the question of Belize, Guatemala's long-standing position has been that Belize is legally an integral part of its national territory, and this has caused conflict with Mexico and Great Britain at various times. The Belize question typically has been a nationalistic rallying cry in Guatemalan politics. Treading where few Guatemalan leaders have dared to step, Serrano recognized Belize as an independent state in September 1991 (*Excelsior* 9/7/91: 2A), a calculated risk aimed at improving prospects for international foreign assistance and trade access to Caribbean markets. In the agreement Belize agreed to accept maritime boundaries giving Guatemala guaranteed shipping access to the Caribbean. Belize further guaranteed to build a road to a deep-water port in Belize, again ensuring Guatemalan access. In turn, Guatemala agreed to accept the existing territorial boundaries of Belize (IPS 11/16/92).

An immediate storm of nationalistic protest erupted in Guatemala. A formal complaint was initiated, claiming that Serrano's actions had violated the constitution and that he should therefore be impeached. Serrano insisted that recognizing existing boundaries was not the same as giving up Guatemala's claim to Belize, which is forbidden by the constitution (IPS 11/16/92).[13] In November 1992, more than a year later, the Constitutional Tribunal ruled in Serrano's favor, by a vote of four to three. Under the constitution Serrano's action still needed approval from the National

Congress and from a popular plebiscite (IPS 11/16/92); Congress ratified Serrano's recognition of Belize's sovereignty in November 1992 (SFChronicle 11/26/92: 16A).

Before the Belize announcement Serrano had undertaken an extensive international agenda. He visited Honduras, Venezuela, and Colombia to secure financial support and enter into trade agreements, and in August 1991, Guatemala joined the Movement of the Non-Aligned Countries as an observer (PCRP 9/91: 7–9). The initial move to recognize Belize can be seen as a successful item on this international agenda, since it resulted in vocal support from the governments of Honduras, El Salvador, Mexico, and the United States, and from the European Economic Community (IPS 11/16/92).

In late 1991, on a visit to the United States, Serrano met with President Bush and congressional leaders and made formal appearances at both the Organization of American States and the United Nations. The United States called the visit a working visit rather than a state visit, thus reducing the prestige of the encounter, a move based on U.S. dissatisfaction with human rights conditions in Guatemala. Nevertheless, at the substantive level Serrano was successful. President Bush accepted Guatemala into the Initiative for the Americas programs, increasing trade relations. Guatemala also obtained $50 million in emergency stabilization funds (ESF) from the U.S. and a new $431 million line of credit from the Inter-American Development Bank (PCRP 10/91: 7; ROG Wi/91: 10).

In February 1992, Serrano received a formal visit from Mexican president Carlos Salinas de Gortari. This meeting committed the two nations to increasing their international commercial ties as well as to other bilateral agreements on communications and health (PCRP 3/92: 7). An official visit by the president of El Salvador, Alfredo Cristiani, in March 1992, produced an agreement to establish a free-trade area, a step toward increased economic integration of the isthmus (PCRP 4/92: 4). The legitimacy produced through these successful visits was increasingly counterbalanced, however, especially in the United States and Europe, by the human rights situation, the impunity of the military, and eventually, the lack of substantial progress in negotiations with the guerrilla insurgency.

Summary

Economically and politically, 1991 and 1992 were mixed years for both the government and the popular sectors. Economically, the government clearly enjoyed some success: inflation was held to 8 percent for 1991, compared to 60 percent in 1990, and the Quetzal was stabilized at five to the U.S. dollar, compared to the frequent fluctuations that characterized the second half of the Cerezo administration. As Serrano reported in his

State of the Union address in 1992, the deficit in spending had been reduced, foreign reserves increased, and foreign debt reduced. In spite of this cooling down in the economy, the GDP rose by 3.2 percent (ROG Sp/92: 10–11, 14).[14] The government's analysis was that because 1991 produced stability in the economy, 1992 would reflect more genuine progress. The Central Bank of Guatemala predicted a 4.5 percent growth rate in 1992 (*Excelsior* 12/20/91: 2A and 1/2/92: 2A).

The government outlook was not universally accepted. CACIF, for example, appreciated the stabilization of the economy but noted that exports were down in 1991 while imports were up, suggesting a problem with the deficit.[15] The church expressed its opposition to the government's economic analysis by stressing that the economic growth was not benefiting the nation's poor (*Excelsior* 1/2/92: 2A).

The Christian Democratic Party, now in the opposition and holding a major bloc of seats in the National Congress, had remained silent for several months after Serrano's inauguration. But after public protests over electricity rate increases, the DCG ended the honeymoon, claiming that the government lacked any coherent economic policy plan. To the DCG Serrano was living off the democratic infrastructure created during Cerezo's term (PCRP 7/91: 11). In the Christian Democrats' view some stabilization of the national economy in 1991 could be attributed not to Serrano's efforts but to the legacy of policies pursued by President Cerezo late in his term (PCRP 1/92: 4–5). Finally, the DCG accused Serrano of doing nothing to continue developing democratic institutions, seeing this inaction as the cause of a definite decline of those institutions (PCRP 7/91: iii).

The popular sectors were critical and pessimistic. The UASP criticized the extension of the IVA tax, predicting a downturn in the economy as a result of higher prices, lower sales, and more unemployment. UASP predicted more actions by popular organizations to express their demands in 1992, and voiced its concern that an increase in popular participation might lead to a wave of repression directed at popular-sector leaders (*Excelsior* 12/27/91: 2A). According to the CUSG labor federation, the government had enacted no public policies to improve the purchasing power of the internal market, and hence no growth had occurred in this area of the economy (*Excelsior* 1/2/92: 2A).

Socioeconomic data seemed to bear out the pessimistic view. A United Nations' ECLA (CEPAL) study claimed that the percentage living in poverty rose from 83 to 87 percent in 1991 (ROG Sp/92: 11). A study produced by UNICEF and the UN Development Program, submitted as a report to the Guatemalan Congress, noted a continuing breakdown in social services, including health and education services, as well as continuing poverty: 86 percent of all families fell below the poverty line.[16] UNICEF reported approximately 700,000 people living in fairly new slum settlements in and around Guatemala City, and five thousand street children living in the capital (*Excelsior* 2/29/92: 2A). By mid-1992, economic and social conditions were still abominable, including a malnutrition rate alleged to be worse than Haiti's (*Excelsior* 6/20/92: 2A).

In sum, progress in macroeconomic conditions meant little in terms of socioeconomic progress in the early years of the Serrano administration. Indeed, growth may have imperiled already poor conditions. Popular-opinion polls reacted accordingly: Serrano's approval rating fell from 71 percent in January 1991 to 36 percent by October (ROG Wi/91: 10); and from 51 percent in December 1991 to 31 percent in late June 1992 (*Excelsior* 6/20/92: 2A). Even the conservative National Advancement Party (Partido de Avanzada Naciónal—PAN), supporters of the government, demanded more social reform to prevent a "social explosion" (*Excelsior* 6/20/92: iv–2).

These developments and the trends in Serrano's approval ratings are symptomatic of what may be the literally impossible tasks facing constitutional democracies like Guatemala, beset by difficult international economic conditions and unrelenting political pressures from both the established elite, including the military, and the popular sectors.

Peace Negotiations

The National Dialogue process (see Chapter 8), not the 1990 electoral campaign, was the "main event" at that time. In fact, President Serrano owed his electoral victory at least in part to his commitment to securing a negotiated end to the civil war, as well as to the perception that he would be able to fulfill that commitment because of his earlier participation in military governments between 1982 and 1985. Negotiating an end to the war was also important economically, and—at least to the government—ending it was a prerequisite to improving the human rights climate.[17]

Under Cerezo, General Héctor Gramajo, minister of defense, was identified with a modernizing tendency within the Army. Coup attempts in the late 1980s reflected the restlessness of a more hard-line attitude in military circles. With Gramajo out of the country near the end of Cerezo's term, changes in the military hierarchy suggested that it was swinging toward a more hard-line position, even as the nation headed in the direction of negotiations.[18] After his election Serrano moved military people who supported the negotiations into key positions, appointing General José García Samoyoa as minister of defense to replace General Mendoza and General Jorge Perussina as new military chief of staff, replacing General Godoy. Both were relatively moderate and had participated in the peace talks (MHerald 12/8/91: 27A).

Two major sets of talks took place between the government and the URNG in 1991, centering on the question of democratization in Guatemala.[19] Under the leadership of the official mediator, Bishop Quezada of the National Reconciliation Committee, the first set of talks, between April and July 1991, culminated in the Querétaro Accords and established an agenda for future talks. The Querétaro Accords on Democratization were signed in Mexico on July 25, 1991, committing both sides to a set of general principles concerning the preeminence of civilian rule, an endorsement of constitutional government as a necessary component of democracy, and unconditional respect for human rights.[20]

The document, however, did not include details for implementing any of these principles not already in place, nor did it propose a concrete timetable for doing so. The accords were a symbolic, though perhaps necessary, document, not a concrete step toward democracy. On the one hand, the government merely acknowledged what it insisted was already the case in Guatemala: for example, the realities of constitutional government, civilian ascendancy over the Army, and respect for human rights. The government gained international legitimacy, and Serrano began to deliver on a campaign promise.

For the URNG a bilateral accord recognized their existence as a formal part of the Guatemalan political process, and they in turn agreed to work within the current constitutional framework, a change from earlier, more revolutionary positions (ROG Fa/91: 3). The URNG was describing itself, in effect, as a constitutional, liberal-democrat movement, accepting the fundamental structure of the regime while acting as an armed pressure group.

The success in the Querétaro round was followed by failure; in September–October 1991 a second set of talks focusing on human rights resulted in a vague endorsement of human rights but failed to reach agreement about possible concrete steps or their timing. Implementation of the Querétaro Accords had been left for after a cease-fire, but for the URNG the timing on human rights was more critical. The URNG wanted implementation immediately, but the government insisted that human rights could be guaranteed only after a permanent cease-fire. The participants could agree only to meet again in January, with Bishop Quezada agreeing to meet with each side separately until then. But the January meetings in Mexico produced no agreement, and in the highlands armed confrontations began to increase (*Excelsior* 12/7/91: 2A and 1/28/92: 2A).

Issue positions seemed polarized at this point.[21] The URNG saw immediate human rights protection as a sine qua non for continuing negotiations, and they insisted on investigation of past violations, the dismantling of the civil defense patrols, and an end to impunity for violators of human rights. The URNG proposed a truth commission under UN supervision, akin to the model in El Salvador's negotiations process (ROG

Sp/92: 4–5). The government position at this point was its "Plan for Total Peace," which to the URNG appeared to be a demand for unconditional surrender. This plan implied that the military was strong enough, relative to the civilian government, to prevent serious negotiations.

The PAC issue exemplifies many of the difficult positions to be resolved in the negotiation process. Originally created after the Ríos Montt coup in 1982, PACs have remained a salient feature of rural life in the Indian highlands ever since. The Constitution of 1985 makes participation in the PACs voluntary for all citizens, but numerous investigations have shown that patrols are compulsory in many localities and that they sometimes violate human rights.[22] Although PACs may have had reason to exist in the early and mid-1980s, if, as the Army says, in 1992 there were only eight hundred ill-trained combatants in the URNG, PACs seemed less necessary. Yet in spite of the human rights complaints and changing conditions in conflict zones, PACs were as widespread in 1992 as in earlier years, apparently part of a continuing, low-level campaign of "cleansing" in the highlands.[23] The question of the PACs continued to reverberate in the public arena into late 1992.

Besides the principals, the URNG and the government, other groups raised issues relevant to the negotiation process. The business group CACIF asserted that no aspects of the Salvadoran peace plan would be acceptable in Guatemala (ROG Sp/92: 4–5). Popular-sector groups, including the church and Mayan groups, feared that URNG and the government were negotiating a secret agreement that would exclude them. The Mayan groups specifically requested the right to participate as separate entities when the negotiations discussed indigenous rights (CSMonitor 11/26/91: 4). These groups essentially wanted to restructure the negotiations' process to resemble the National Dialogue process described in Chapter 8 (*Excelsior* 12/7/91: 2A).

Negotiations in 1992

Progress in 1991 had been met by impediments in 1992, however. Serrano had some success in convincing the Army to support the negotiation process, but each positive step became a new obstacle as lines hardened. By late 1991, he had encountered serious military opposition, perhaps because the process was raising issues that greatly concerned the military, where the extreme, hard-line group, Officers of the Mountains, began to issue position statements opposing the negotiation process. Besides the example from El Salvador's process—which showed what might happen in Guatemala—evidence of military involvement in high-level corruption and drug trafficking made the possibility of genuine civilian control threatening to sectors of the Army.[24]

Moreover, the military's hard-line position assumed that victory over the insurgency had already occurred, not because the Army had eradicated the URNG but because the collapse of the Soviet Union and the Nicaraguan Sandinistas meant the URNG would wither away from lack of the international support that fueled it (ROG Sp/92: 2–5,14).[25] Business elites were willing to tolerate the negotiations' process to placate international public opinion but were loath to accept any reforms that would affect them (ROG Sp/92: 4).

As of spring 1992, fundamental disagreements still existed over not only the previous questions but on the URNG demand that an independent "truth and justice commission" be created to investigate past human rights violations (ROG Sp/92: 14). In spite of the apparent collapse of the process in early 1992, negotiators could point to the government's agreement to "end forced recruitment, the elimination of paramilitary groups 'if there are any,' protection for human rights monitors, and compensation for the victims of human rights violations" (ROG Sp/92: 14). Moreover, the United Nations was accepted as the future monitor when final accords are reached.

Bishop Quezada attempted to initiate new talks by his continuing efforts to meet privately with each side. But a wave of bombings of government and other buildings took place in April and May 1992. Although first indications were that the URNG might be reopening an urban front in its insurgency, evidence quickly pointed to the right (*Excelsior* 4/16/92: 2A).[26] The goal of the violence was to destabilize the government to such an extent that, first, Serrano would back down on social reform and negotiations, and, second, the popular sectors would stop making the kinds of demands seen in 1991. This terror campaign was clearly an antidemocratic form of political participation.

Increased public and international pressure was applied to the government to bring peace to Guatemala, especially in view of the successful negotiations in El Salvador, but the military's opposition to the process hardened as well. To resolve the impasse, Bishop Quezada offered a proposal on the human rights issue, calling for respect for human rights, voluntary civil defense patrols with no human rights violations by them, and a domestic truth commission called the Commission for Peace and Reconciliation to investigate past human rights abuses. The commission would include the ombudsman, Ramiro de León, a representative of the public universities, and an observer from the United Nations (*Excelsior* 6/19/92: 2A).

The government tried public pressure on the URNG to resume negotiations in early summer as the nation awaited responses to Bishop Quezada's proposals on human rights. It proposed meeting every two weeks without fail until the peace accords were signed (*Excelsior* 7/4/92:

2A). Meanwhile, Bishop Quezada threatened to resign as mediator, announcing he would not participate again until a human rights agreement between the government and the URNG was forged. UN observer Francesc Vendrell also left the process, at the request of the government (*Excelsior* 7/8/92: 2A).

Part of the public pressure in favor of these kinds of proposals included a coalition of groups seeking to participate in the negotiations, which represented the church and the popular sectors. The Civilian Sector Coordinating Committee (Comité Coordinador del Sector Civil—CCSC) brought together over one hundred organizations from Catholic and Protestant churches, organized labor, the Mayan sectors, human rights organizations, and others. Against this evidence of democratic participation from society was arrayed a newly intransigent military and an anti-reformist economic elite trying to hold fast (LAP 6/18/92: 6).

In this difficult atmosphere negotiations resumed. In response to Serrano's call for a broader agenda,[27] the URNG offered new proposals: first, full representation for the Mayans "at all levels of society"; and, second, a package of economic reforms centered on developing an internal market within a social-democracy model that acknowledged private property as the basis for development. Guatemala's two major parties, the UCN and the DCG, both endorsed the plan (*Tico Times* 5/29/92: 5).

Some progress occurred in mid-1992. Mexico City meetings produced a partial agreement on human rights. Focusing on the thorny issue of the PACs, both sides agreed to two points. First, the Army agreed not to arm any civil defense patrol unless there were a specific military threat: if there were no guerrilla attacks, then there would be no armed PACS. Second, the human rights ombudsman was given (1) the right to investigate existing PACs for evidence of forced recruitment or human rights violations, and (2) the power to bring charges. The URNG position saw two major weaknesses in this proposal: first, the military could still organize and arm PACs, and, second, the accord would not be implemented until a total agreement on human rights occurred (NYTimes 8/9/92: 7).

By late 1992, signs of progress were in evidence as well as ominous obstacles. Both sides agreed to create the "Commission on the Past" to investigate past human rights violations and assess the extent of civilian suffering during the guerrilla war, without necessarily assigning responsibility for violations. To be chaired by the human rights ombudsman, the full composition of the commission, however, was still in dispute.[28]

The Refugee Question

Perhaps the most positive area was the question of repatriation of Guatemalan refugees in Mexico. During the counterinsurgency campaign in the early 1980s, thousands of highland Indians had fled to Mexico, but few refugees had come back during the Cerezo administration in spite of government attempts to have them return. In 1991, at least forty-three thousand Guatemalan refugees were in Mexico in camps near the border under the supervision of the UN High Commission for Refugees. Both the UN and Mexico had long agreed that refugees could return to Guatemala on a voluntary basis and would not be forced out of Mexico. In 1989, the Permanent Commissions (Comisiones Permanentes—CCPP), the representatives of the refugees in the camps, had announced that the refugees wished to return but only as a collective group, with international witnesses and other guarantees from the government. Discussions continued in 1991, but few persons returned.[29]

Anxious to go back and feeling some pressure from Mexico to leave the camps, the refugees formulated a tentative plan to repatriate some thirty thousand people between 1992 and 1995. In late 1991, the government recognized the CCPP as the legitimate representatives of the refugees in Mexico, agreed in principle to a collective return, but did not agree with the refugees' requests for guarantees. Key issues of timing and procedure remained unresolved in early 1992, not to mention several substantive issues that included land and freedom of movement. The CCPP continued to demand an end to the civil defense patrols, for example, and conditioned the refugees' return on continuing success in the negotiations between URNG and the government (*Excelsior* 2/28/92: 2A).

Serrano signed a six-point accord creating guarantees for the refugees in mid-1992, but it set no timetable for the massive influx of refugees the agreement was supposed to engender (*Excelsior* 10/9/92: 2A). Perhaps to test the waters, an initial group of fifty-three people came back in August 1992. They were met at the border by the Guatemalan vice-president, Gustavo Espina, and by representatives of the government's Special Commission for Attention to Refugees (Comisión Especial para Atención a los Refugiados—CEAR). By then, the government had agreed to the six conditions demanded in Mexico by the CCPP.[30]

With the negotiations resolved, at least in principle, a larger group of five thousand refugees organized to return in late 1992, even though "the conditions are not propitious" (IPS 9/4/92). As the time came closer, in spite of the agreements between CEAR and the CCPP, the government began to ask for delays and tried to impose conditions on routes refugees would take and on how many people could travel together (IPS 11/21/92). This seemed to contradict the government's own agreement and illustrates the style of the policy process on many issues. Refugees did make a widely publicized return in early 1993.[31]

Meanwhile, in spite of the refugee agreements, or perhaps because of them, the military escalated its own campaign in mountainous areas inhabited by internal refugees, the so-called Communities of People in Resistance (Comunidades del Pueblo en Resistencia—CPR).[32] In a revealing announcement Defense Minister José García Samoyoa asserted in December that captured URNG documents indicated the CPRs were an arm of the guerrillas and that the issue of returning refugees was being manipulated by the URNG (IPS 12/19/92). Elsewhere, combat between the URNG and the military intensified at the end of 1992, with land mines being used in Huehuetenango department (*Excelsior* 12/20/92: 2A).

In spite of occasional steps forward, then, the government's negotiation strategy at the end of 1992 seemed to be a military victory over the URNG, accomplished by escalating counterinsurgency warfare, as in the early 1980s, in areas still considered conflict zones. At the same time, the government was anxious to maintain the negotiations process in place, partly for public opinion reasons and partly to provide the URNG with an acceptable forum for its effective surrender. For example, Serrano proposed that the URNG simply stop fighting and become a political party.

Consequently, progress was agonizingly slow compared to El Salvador, for several reasons. First, the Army was less dependent on Washington in particular and on international sources in general. Second, the URNG had far fewer combatants than the FMLN in El Salvador, which meant the military could consider itself victorious and avoid concessions. Third, the URNG had less popular support than the FMLN. As of late 1992, Bishop Quezada was continuing his shuttle diplomacy with little success. In early 1993, President Serrano was blaming the URNG for the stalemate, and the level of warfare between the insurgents and the military intensified (NYTimes 1/16/93: 5; *Excelsior* 1/2/93: 1, Mundial section).

Human Rights

The Cerezo administration ended with higher rates of human rights violations than when it began, leaving plenty of room for improvement when President Serrano was inaugurated. But conditions generally worsened in 1991 and 1992, and overall, statistics on human rights violations show no improvement, varying only in the waves and lulls that occurred during these two years.[33] For example, a wave of violence in mid-1991 targeted leaders of progressive popular organizations, leaving some twenty people dead.[34] For the first eight months of 1991, 548 people were killed and 114 kidnapped (LATimes 9/19/91: 1A). The Mutual Assistance Group (GAM) reported that 730 people were assassinated and one hundred had disappeared in the first eight months of 1991 (*Excelsior* 10/15/91: 2A). The Catholic church reported that human rights violations in 1991 were worse than in 1990, with over a thousand serious violations in the first ten months of the year, over half of these extrajudicial killings—a rate of two per day. Typical of many government responses to such claims, Vice-President Gustavo Espina denied these figures, and Serrano called the report speculative and rejected its conclusions (*Excelsior* 12/2/91: 2A). The archbishop immediately insisted that the report was accurate (GMG 1/92: 7).[35]

The church's human rights office reported 399 assassinations in the first six months of 1992 (*Excelsior* 7/21/92: 2A). The Guatemalan Human Rights Commission, a private organization, reported 427 summary executions in 1992, sixty-two disappearances (including fifteen children), 102 cases of torture, and 253 attempted murders. In order to increase international pressure, the commission presented its report to the United Nations (IPS 12/5/92). Throughout the period, there was a constant pattern of threats against church and popular leaders and the press (*Excelsior* 9/1/91: 2A).

Yet one of the positive steps in the human rights situation was the vocal protests of the human rights ombudsman, Ramiro de León Carpio. For example, de León reported data on forced recruitment into the Army, documenting 267 cases in 1992, compared to 234 in the last six months of 1991. He assailed the government as well, noting that both state and non-state human rights violators continued to act with impunity (IPS 8/16/92). When releasing figures on human rights violations for 1991, he placed part of the blame on the URNG but cited the state and the security forces as well. He was critical of the government, specifically because of the persistent state of impunity for recent human rights violations, while remaining critical of violence by the left (*Excelsior* 1/29/92: 2A). And he asserted that Serrano's attention to human rights was at the level of speeches only and that total impunity still prevailed (*Excelsior* 11/15/91: 2A).

In addition to denying the accuracy of human rights statistics, the government's main response was to place the blame for them on lack of progress in negotiations to end the civil war.[36] Yet here too, by acknowledging that human rights violations are a serious problem, the president did take a step forward in the human rights situation (LATimes 9/19/91: 1A).

In Guatemala's favor, the UN Human Rights Commission in Geneva refused to condemn the country as in previous years, in spite of the continuing violations and impunity and the lack of investigations: Guatemala was not listed under agenda item 12, which would have meant a UN Special Rapporteur's investigation (IPS 3/29/92). Support for adding Guatemala to the list came from Canada and the European Community but was opposed by most of Latin America.[37] The committee compromised and decided to send an "expert" with advisory powers only. As had been the case during the Cerezo years, the human rights situation was not condemned outright by the United Nations because the government had taken enough symbolic steps in the right direction.[38] Nevertheless, with the UN observer in place, international pressure increased on the government. Later in 1992, pressure came from the Organization of American States as well, when a delegation from the OAS Human Rights Commission urged speedier action on the human rights portion of the negotiations between government and the guerrillas (IPS 11/9/92).

The OAS was also involved in the case of CERJ, the indigenous human rights group organized against compulsory military service. CERJ continued to be harassed by "unknown assailants" in 1991 and 1992. After the murder of one of its human rights monitors, however, a survivor identified an assailant and warrants were issued, but the government failed to arrest the accused assassin. CERJ appealed to the OAS Inter-American Court of Human Rights, which issued a nonbinding "injunction" against the government of Guatemala, requiring the president to protect CERJ members (CSMonitor 8/6/91: 5). Subsequently, CERJ's founder, Amílcar Méndez, who had received the Robert Kennedy Human Rights Center award and the Carter Human Rights Award, was arrested for allegedly distributing explosives (IPS 11/28/92).

Impunity and "Demonstration Justice"?[39]

In addition to high levels of violations, a second aspect of the human rights situation is the question of impunity: the lack of investigations or punishment of violators. Impunity means that the apparatus of human rights violations remains intact, in spite of the human rights ombudsman's efforts. As a result, the quality of political participation by progressive citizens remained problematic. This can be seen best in four notable individual cases that became public during 1991 and 1992, for if even in these notorious cases little is accomplished in uncovering and punishing human rights violators, one must assume that still less is possible in cases involving ordinary people.

In the first case, the government announced the arrest in August 1991 of a high-ranking naval commander and several other military personnel, in connection with death-squad activities allegedly involving smuggling. Swift public reaction praising the action came from the president, the human rights ombudsman, the archbishop, and the president of the National Congress, who stated that these arrests showed "that impunity is nearing an end" (*Excelsior* 8/17/91: 2A). The fact that the naval commander's group was involved in smuggling rather than in more direct political activities appeared to make it easier to arrest and prosecute. Yet the commander was released within weeks of the incident, and the rest of the group subsequently were found not guilty by a military court (CSMonitor 11/5/91: 4; *Excelsior* 8/13/92: 2A).

Three other cases illustrate the reluctant functioning of the judicial system; all drew international attention: the murders of Myrna Mack and William Devine and the kidnapping and torture of Diana Ortiz, an American nun. In each of these cases, investigations were undertaken because family members or close associates, strongly assisted by international pressure, were able to convince the Guatemalan government to look into the crimes. In all three cases, clear evidence seemed to implicate state security forces, yet little has happened, even when show trials were held, to bring criminals to justice.

In the case of Myrna Mack Chang, an internationally respected Guatemalan anthropologist, José Miguel Mérida, the police chief in charge of investigating her 1990 assassination, had previously made a formal accusation regarding her murder and had discovered that her accused assassin had been an employee of G-2, the intelligence section of the Army. He had further discovered that "high-ranking military officers were behind the 1990 stabbing death." But Mérida was assassinated outside national police headquarters in downtown Guatemala City in mid-1991 (*Excelsior* 8/5/91: 2A). His murder illustrates the lack of control President Serrano had over the military and police apparatus. Myrna Mack's accused murderer was subsequently arrested in Los Angeles (*Excelsior* 12/4/91: 2A).[40]

In the case of William Devine, an American living in Guatemala, his murder led to a temporary suspension of U.S. military aid, a strong message to the armed forces and the government. In September 1991, an army colonel, Guillermo Portillo Gómez, was ordered to stand trial along with ten soldiers for the crime (MHerald 9/4/91: 7A). Five soldiers were found guilty and sentenced to thirty years, but the officer who ordered the killing was found not guilty (SFChronicle 9/30/92: 10).[41] Subsequently, three of the group being held were released (CSMonitor 11/5/91: 4).

Diana Ortiz, an American nun who was kidnapped and tortured in 1989, returned to Guatemala in 1992 for the first time since her abduction. Guatemalan prosecutors had frequently claimed they wanted to investigate the case but could not because of Ortiz's silence. Ortiz gave testimony before a judge, providing evidence so that the investigation could proceed with her cooperation. After Ortiz's testimony, however, the prosecutors claimed that her evidence was relatively worthless because of the delays. Moreover, because she had now made her charges inside the country, the Army threatened to prosecute her for defaming the military.[42]

That any of these cases even could be investigated is a step forward in the human rights climate, but the results are still quite meager. And though courageous Guatemalans press for investigations, it is clear that the government responds to international pressure in these cases, not to its citizens' desires.

Street Children

Less well known than the victims just discussed, abandoned children living on the streets of Guatemala City continued to be a serious problem, not only as an indicator of socioeconomic decay but as victims of human rights abuses. Between March 1990 and October 1991, twelve street children were murdered, with the police implicated in many, perhaps most, of the beatings. In one incident in late 1991, seven street children were severely beaten (*Excelsior* 11/15/91: 2A).

Covenant House of New York has established programs in Guatemala City to aid street children, including a legal aid office that has pressured the government to investigate human rights abuses against children. In one case four policemen were successfully prosecuted for the murder of a thirteen-year-old boy. After the convictions, however, the sentences were overturned by a higher court. The Covenant House legal aid office was attacked by machine-gun fire in July 1991, and in August the government ordered the office closed, allegedly for interfering in the attorney general's efforts to protect children (AAS 9/8/91: 7A). The pattern of lengthy, reluctant investigations, light or no sentences, and subsequent attacks on persons pushing for human rights investigations is an all-too-familiar one. By late 1992, ninety-two cases of child brutality were still unresolved (ROG Wi/92: 6–7).

In sum, then, not much had improved in the human rights atmosphere by 1992. Public statements by President Serrano and some of his appointees were important symbolically but did little to reduce the levels of impunity and hence to improve the quality of political participation. Far more progress came from the efforts of the Catholic church, the human rights ombudsman, the peace negotiation process as a whole, and the efforts of popular organizations, sometimes allied with international groups that supported their efforts. Again, even in terms of procedural democracy, the improvements originated largely from outside the establishment, and the government, especially the military, bent only slightly—and reluctantly at that.

The Maya Question: The Nobel Committee's Answer

The quincentennial of Columbus's arrival in the Western Hemisphere was not cause for celebration among the Mayan communities of Guatemala. From their perspective the historical relationship was established in the Spanish Conquest, or invasion, as the Maya call it, and current politics is more of the same struggle. In the early 1980s, when the Maya sought to recover some of what they lost in the conquest, most of their leaders were killed, and massive repression smothered their efforts.[43]

Out of that process different tendencies emerged in the Mayan community. While many Maya remain integrated into popular-sector movements as well as the URNG insurgency, others have formed a Pro-Mayan movement, seeking to recover traditional social structures in order to rebuild their communities. From this perspective the indigenous are conquered nations, not ethnic minorities. The movement sees the need for at least semisovereign arrangements with the state, and it regards maintaining at least a separate identity from popular-sector and URNG movements as a necessary component of its approach. The nationalists fear that integration will mean sacrificing Mayan values to more Western, alien traditions, and they fear that non-Indian popular and revolutionary sectors of the left may have political agendas not necessarily consistent with their own.

Indigenous groups throughout the hemisphere began to organize pan-hemispheric meetings, and the second "Encounter of the Continental Campaign of 500 Years of Indigenous and Popular Resistance" was held in Quetzaltenango (Xela), Guatemala, in October 1991. The Encounter occasioned a large mobilization by the Mayan communities, perhaps taking advantage of the international attention to act more freely than they might have otherwise. The event also revealed conflict within the indigenous communities between the two perspectives described above. Among the participants was Rigoberta Menchú, who had been nominated for the Nobel Peace Prize. In spite of her international acclaim and involvement with non-Indian movement groups, or perhaps partly because of these factors, the Pro-Mayan representatives expressed some concern over Menchú's presence and participation.[44]

Tensions among the groups manifested in a variety of ways. Some nationalistic Maya resented the presence of Indians involved in the integrated political movements.[45] In early 1992, other Indian groups demanded separate participation in the peace negotiation process, and they, along with other popular-sector groups, were allowed to submit demands and be consulted after February 1992. Later in 1992, a group of Mayans filed a lawsuit for Q1 million against the URNG for pain and suffering, stolen crops, and kidnapping (MHerald 6/17/92: 14A).

The Nobel Peace Prize

Rigoberta Menchú's nomination for the Nobel Peace Prize was a major issue in Guatemala in 1992. From Uspantán, in Quiché province, Menchú's life was not atypical of her region: she and her family had worked as seasonal laborers on coffee plantations, and she had been a maid in Guatemala City, where she learned Spanish. Active as a community leader, her father was a victim of the Spanish embassy massacre, and Menchú lost almost all her family in subsequent repression in the early 1980s. She fled the country at that time and spent the decade organizing support for Indian communities from her base in Mexico.[46] She became very popular in Guatemala, at least among the popular sectors, as demonstrated during visits for the National Dialogue process in the late 1980s and the Second Encounter in 1991. These same visits revealed elite antipathy as well, as evidenced by threats and arrests.

In early 1992, the elite were gaining in their struggle with the popular sectors, as discussed earlier. The peace negotiations had been stalled, the government had overturned a law that provided compensation for fired workers, and the state had faced down a potential strike by its employees. The IMF had approved Guatemala's economic modernization plan, leading to a loan from the World Bank. As Menchú's nomination began to gain momentum, however, the government awarded its Order of the Quetzal, the nation's highest award, to a wealthy Caucasian woman known for her charitable work, Elisa Molina de Stahl. This was widely seen as part of a campaign to discredit Menchú, a campaign that squandered an excellent opportunity to build legitimacy for the government in the Mayan communities (MHerald 9/28/92: 12A).[47]

In October 1992, five hundred years after the Spanish Conquest began, the Nobel Committee awarded its Peace Prize to the Mayan leader Rigoberta Menchú, thereby taking sides in the Guatemalan struggle.[48] Reactions to Menchú's award are good symbolic indicators of the country's progress toward democracy. Serrano offered a "terse statement of congratulations," but Foreign Minister Gonzalo Menéndez Park decried the decision because of Menchú's alleged ties to subversive groups. The military reacted in similar fashion, saying she "has only defamed the fatherland" (NYTimes 10/17/92: 1). When Menchú was cheered by crowds in five cities, a new wave of assaults and threats against people associated with her began (*Excelsior* 10/21/92: 2A).[49] And in late 1992, the military increased its aerial bombardments of Mayan areas in the highlands (IPS 12/12/92).

The Peace Prize can and should be interpreted as another sign of international condemnation of the Guatemalan government. It indicates support for the popular sectors and their use of direct pressure and mass mobilization to achieve social progress and democratization. Moreover, the award is likely to help fuel the Mayan movement, engendered by Guatemala's tragic history and catalyzed by the quincentennial events.

Conclusion

The first two years of President Jorge Serrano's five-year term are noteworthy in their overall similarity to the patterns of the Cerezo administration that preceded it. Moderate successes occurred at the macroeconomic level, but massive social and economic upheavals disrupted the daily lives of the majority. From the perspective of social democracy, the nation made little if any progress during the biennium and wasted numerous opportunities—in the maquila and tax reform issues, for example—to enact policies that might have benefited the masses.

As far as procedural, liberal democracy is concerned, the key indicator during this period was the quality of the human rights climate. Signs of progress emerged, especially the outspoken efforts of the human rights ombudsman and some of the steps taken during the peace negotiations process. On the whole, however, political participation continues to be very problematic for most Guatemalans: human rights violations did not decline, and some statistics showed increases. Criminal investigations of violations, in spite of government rhetoric to the contrary, continued to be sporadic at best: violence to eliminate and intimidate other political participants essentially went unpunished.

Stagnation in human rights enforcement cannot be acceptable to democrats, because legitimacy can weaken over time if there is no progress, hence the conclusion that the Serrano period has been marked thus far by declines in the quality of democratic participation, in spite of popular pressures to improve the atmosphere.

Notes

1. "Guatemala holds one of the lowest positions in Latin America in terms of the quality of life," with 76 percent in poverty, 42.6 percent unemployed, 76 percent of the children malnourished and half of these acute, and 62 percent of the women without prenatal care. Almost half of the total earnings of society were earned by the upper 10 percent of the population (*Excelsior* 11/26/91: 2A).

2. Guatemala's tax revenue to gross domestic product ratio is 7.8 percent, second lowest in the hemisphere; only Haiti's is lower. By comparison, the ratio in the United States is 20 percent. The World Bank request was that the ratio reach at least 10 percent in Guatemala.

3. The Fiscal Modernization Program included:

1. The IVA rate stabilized at 7 percent, but all exempt goods and services eliminated. Originally created by the military government in 1983 with a tax rate of 10 percent, the IVA was reduced to 7 percent in 1984, but applied only to certain products;
2. Income tax; about 2 percent of Guatemalans had paid income tax before the reforms, and the goal was to increase this by changing the tax brackets and by tax simplification, as discussed in the text; and
3. Stamp taxes—taxes and fees on official transactions. The reform simplified the bureaucratic process by eliminating fees on most transactions, retaining them on major commercial contracts, and raising the rates (PCRP 7/92: 4–5).

4. Quoting an official of the USAID, Petersen further defines the strategy as "'the exportation of labor without sending workers abroad'" (Petersen: 5). The best source on the maquila sector in Guatemala is Petersen.

5. The labor code in 1992 provided twenty inspectors for 12,000 businesses in the capital and sixty others for 200,000 businesses in the rest of the country. Moreover, there were essentially no judicial sanctions against employers; only a court order could result from a formal complaint by a worker (IPS 10/22/92).

6. For details on the petition to the U.S. Trade Office, see ROG, and CSMonitor 7/7/92, from which many of the details in the following paragraphs are taken. A campaign also was organized to pressure Phillips–Van Heusen to permit the certification of unions in its Guatemalan maquila factories. For a good summary of the issues involved in attempting to unionize at Phillips–Van Heusen's two maquila factories in Guatemala, see ROG Wi/91: 8–9, and the various reports of the Phillips–Van Heusen campaign organized by the U.S./Guatemala Labor Education Project.

7. Business leaders in the apparel field claimed a U.S. investigation could mean the "initial loss of 200,000 jobs" (WPost 8/1/92: 18A).

8. For a similar argument, see Petersen: 175–176. Petersen adds that, moreover, even a humane maquila sector cannot solve the problems facing the country if it does not distribute land so that its people can begin to feed the nation and stop flocking to the cities.

9. The wage in late 1992 was $84 monthly; it was $2 a day in rural areas. The cost of a minimum rural existence was about $120 per month in rural areas and $160 per month in urban areas, according to the Guatemalan National Statistical Institute.

10. For additional details on the San Jorge la Laguna occupation and evictions, see *Excelsior* 4/7/92: 2A; CSMonitor 4/7/92: 4; and ROG Su/92: 8–9,14.

11. By comparison, Costa Rica has settled over $100 million of its debt in this way.

12. For details on many different types of development projects, some very labor-intensive, see CSMonitor 4/29/92: 10. One of the critical issues stressed here is time: the rainforest is being destroyed at an alarming rate.

13. For additional details on Serrano's recognition of Belize and the subsequent constitutional challenges to his action, see PCRP 11/91: 6–7, 3/92: 8, and 11/92: 2–3.

14. By comparison, the growth rate was 2.5 percent for the U.S. in the same period (ROG Wi/91: 10).

15. Exports were down 1.5 percent, from Q925 million to Q911, while imports were up 11 percent, from Q1.2 billion to Q1.3 billion (*Excelsior* 1/2/92: 2A).

16. UNICEF reported 6 million people, two-thirds of the total population of 9.2 million, with no access to health services and 3.6 million lacking potable water.

17. As of late 1991, thirty-five years of warfare in Guatemala had produced 150,000 dead, 50,000 detained or disappeared, 200,000 orphans, 100,000 widows, 100,000 peasants internally displaced in the mountains, at least 50,000 refugees in Mexican camps, and hundreds of political exiles (*Excelsior* 1/16/92: 2A).

18. For a good summary of changes in the ideological and political tendencies within the Army during this period, see ROG Fa/91: 13.

19. The round of talks that began after Serrano's election were called the second round of talks—the Oslo round (see Chapter 8) being the first round. For additional details on the trajectory of the negotiations through 1991 and 1992, see

monthly issues of PCRP, many of which include extensive sets of documents reflecting the positions of the participants and other organized sectors of Guatemalan society. For example, see "Guatemala: Proceso de Paz" (PCRP 7/92: Suplemento Especial); and the document section of PCRP 8/92. For an excellent, complete collection of documents on the peace negotiation processes in both Guatemala and El Salvador, see *Cronologías*.

20. For the full text of the document, see PCRP 8/91, Suplemento Especial: i–ii.

21. For a detailed look at the issues behind the negotiations impasse in late 1991 and early 1992, including good expositions of the participants' positions, see GMG 3/92: 2–4; and ROG Sp/92: 2–5, 14. For a view of the URNG positions on various issues, including ethnic questions affecting the popular movements at this time, see the interview with Pablo Monsanto, a leader of the URNG command, in ROG Fa/91: 2–3, 10.

22. Three municipalities had formally petitioned that the military leave their community and the PACs be disbanded. Santiago Atitlán was first, after the massacre there in late 1989, and Joyabaj in El Quiché requested this in February 1992. San Lucas Tolimán on Lake Atitlán became the third town to request military and police withdrawal after an incident involving violence against local citizens, but the town did ask for the police to return after several incidents of common crime occurred. Defense Minister García claimed these requests were a URNG ploy (CSMonitor 3/11/92: 3).

23. For details on how the military has forced civil patrols to murder sometimes innocent victims, especially in the early 1980s' counterinsurgency, see SFChronicle 11/12/91: 10A. Speaking against the PACs, the adjunct human rights ombudsman, César Alvarez Guadamuz, said "'the impunity continues, as does the violence.'" The military position on the question of human rights is that the PACs never violate human rights and that guerrillas are the ones responsible for the deaths that occur (MHerald 10/4/92: 35A).

24. On the issues of human rights immunity and past violations, see SFChronicle 12/16/91: 12A. On corruption, the issues included involvement in fraudulent deals to help the antigovernment contras in Nicaragua; see LATimes 9/19/91:22A. On drug trafficking, evidence showed major transshipments of cocaine through Guatemala, with its hundreds of rural airstrips and lack of aviation radar control. Given the military's capacities in rural areas, this implies that high-level officials are condoning the drug trade. See *Excelsior* 9/9/91: 3A; and NYTimes 12/16/91: 6A for more details.

25. As an ironic indicator of the military's attitude, on the same day that negotiators were agreeing in Mexico City to end forced military recruitment practices in Guatemala, the Army staged a recruitment raid in poor barrios near Guatemala City and kidnapped several dozen young men for military service. Whereas in the past this would probably have been met with public silence, in 1992 there were outcries from the church and popular organizations (ROG Sp/92: 14). For details of a forced recruitment experience from a victim's perspective, see ROG Su/92: 6–7,14.

26. For more details on the wave of violence in April and May and its rightwing genesis, see LAP 6/18/92: 6; *Excelsior* 5/11/92: 2A; and MHerald 5/21/92: 27A.

27. The narrow agenda was the URNG's insistence on its demands for dissolution of the PACs, international supervision of human rights, and a truth commission to determine responsibility for past human rights violations (WPost 5/26/92: 13A).

28. For details on these and other developments in late 1992, see *Excelsior* 1/2/93: 1 (Mundial section); GMG 10/92: 5–7; ROG Wi/92: 4–5, 13–14; NYTimes 1/15/93 and 1/28/93; and *Resumen Noticioso, 1992.*

29. Some thirteen hundred refugees were repatriated in 1991, and half that number in 1990, Cerezo's final year in office. For background on the refugee situation, including attempts to negotiate a return during the Cerezo administration, see WOLA 1989a. For a summary of the situation during the Serrano administration, see ROG Wi/91: 6–8. For an outstanding account of the reintegration process for earlier refugees and displaced rural groups, see *Dónde Está*, a project originally coordinated by Myrna Mack. It is generally agreed that Ms. Mack was assassinated because of her work on this study.

30. With the possible exception of a provision guaranteeing them access to land, the refugees' demands were so basic that a casual observer would be nonplussed at the need for such protracted negotiations to secure the government's reluctant agreement to these six provisions: (1) the return is voluntary; (2) refugees would have the right of free organization and association; (3) refugees would have the right of free mobility; (4) international witnesses would be present during the return and resettlement periods; (5) land would be made available in the refugees' original places of origin; and (6) "their lives [would] be respected" (*Excelsior* 9/27/92: 2A).

31. See NYTimes 1/15/93: A3 and 1/25/93: A6; and MHerald 1/21/93: 16A for descriptions of the first group's return in early 1993.

32. In one incident the military is alleged to have bombed two towns (Angeles and Pueblo Nuevo II) in the Ixil area, one supposedly inhabited by CPR people outside of military control. The Army denied bombing any towns, alleging there were no towns in the area. But a human rights lawyer working with the CPR groups claimed some twenty-four thousand people were living in these two towns and invited President Serrano to go with him to view the area (IPS 8/28/92).

33. For detailed and fairly well-balanced accounts of the human rights situation throughout this period, see the monthly issues of PCRP. For an excellent set of documents related to the human rights situation in 1991 and early 1992, including the text of a speech by President Serrano, UN observer Tomuschat's report, and the resolution of the UN's Human Rights Commission (Geneva), see PCRP 3/92: Dossier Especial.

34. The government claimed that the death squads were not connected to the Army or government and attributed violence to drug trafficking. In fact, some of the victims were repeat-offender criminals (*Excelsior* 8/5/91: 2A).

35. The Archbishop's office also condemned forced recruitment of children into the Army and asked the defense ministry to "respect the Constitution and stop the kidnapping of young men" (GMG 1/92: 7).

36. A key government negotiator, Manuel Conde, said: "When Guatemala no longer has an internal confrontation, the human rights situation will improve immediately" (MHerald 8/23/91: 12A). For an additional example of this position, see LATimes 9/19/91: 1A, which points out that one of the difficulties all sides face in ending the violence are the right-wing groups, even civil defense patrol leaders, with vested interests in keeping violence levels high so negotiations will fail.

37. The United States initially supported the move to put Guatemala on the item 12 list but compromised with Latin America: the U.S. dropped its Guatemalan effort in order to obtain Latin support for putting Cuba on the same list (IPS 3/29/92).

38. More typical, however, is President Serrano's response to accusations at a conference at Catholic University in Washington that torture continued to be used in Guatemala. Serrano in effect threatened the lives of conference participants Amílcar Méndez of CERJ and Ronald Ochoeta of the Archbishop of Guatemala's human rights office: "'We are going to begin putting a stop to these various accusations being made. The Army does not torture; the government does not torture'" said Serrano (*Excelsior* 11/13/92: 2A), but Ochoeta "'follows the insurgents' line'" (IPS 11/23/92).

39. This is a paraphrasing of Hermann and Brodhead's "Demonstration Elections," or elections held in a foreign land to assure U.S. patrons that democracy is functioning smoothly and that foreign assistance is thereby deserved.

40. In late 1992, Mack's sister, Helen Mack Chang, was awarded the Right Livelihood Prize ($185,000) by the Swedish Parliament. The prize, considered to be the alternative Nobel Prize, was given for her efforts to instigate an investigation into her sister's murder (*Tico Times* 11/13/92: 7).

41. Guatemalan Attorney General Acisclo Valladares publicly disagreed with the verdict on the officer, Captain Hugo Contreras (SFChronicle 9/30/92: 10). Providing a different twist to this case, and adding further evidence to the case against Captain Contreras, the Guatemalan daily *El Gráfico* reported that Devine had been selling weapons to the guerrillas, weapons he first bought from the Army, which would then report them as missing in action. The paper's own investigation clearly implicated the exonerated Hugo Contreras (*Excelsior* 10/5/92: 2A).

42. Ortiz had brought one of two lawsuits in U.S. courts against retired General Gramajo, suing him for violating her human rights during his tenure as defense minister. Refusing to respond to the charges or to subpoenas, Gramajo was found guilty by default in November 1991, and assessed $10 million in damages (WPost 1/6/92: 13A and 4/8/92: 16A).

43. For an excellent study of the historical relationship between the Maya and the state (and elites) in Guatemala, see Smith. For particularly poignant and distressing testimonies about recent experiences of Mayan individuals and communities, see Montejo and Akab'.

44. For additional details on the Encounter and on some of these questions, see ROG Wi/91: 2–5, 15; SFChronicle 4/13/92: 10A.

45. The Pro-Mayans referred to integrated groups as "certain interests who want us to be cannon fodder for their political fights, but we've already suffered that" (MHerald 10/16/91: 6A).

46. For details, see Menchú's autobiography, edited by Burgos-Debray.

47. This source reports that a Guatemalan political cartoon at the time of Molina de Stahl's award showed Menchú being asked her opinion of the event. She replies that the only order she had ever received from the Guatemalan government was "an arrest order."

48. This is not a new position for the committee, which in the past decade has awarded the Peace Prize to such gadflies as Martin Luther King, Jr., the Dalai Lama, Lech Walesa of Poland, Daw Aung San Suu Kyi of Myanmar (Burma), Bishop Desmond Tutu of South Africa, Mairead Maguire and Betty Williams of Northern Ireland, and Adolfo Pérez Esquivel of Argentina.

49. For more details on the reaction to the award, see ROG Wi/92: 2–3,14; *Special Service* 10/92; and Maurovich.

10

The Popular Struggle
for Democracy

> There is a way to peace. There is evidence of hope that Guatemala can
> be a country of plurality and richness, or re-encounters between our
> communities.
>
> —Rigoberta Menchú

The 1980s began with a tragedy, the massacre of thirty-nine people at the
Spanish embassy. In the aftermath Guatemala descended into its darkest
hour of violence and isolation. For the Guatemalan military the crisis of
the early 1980s showed the need, and provided the opportunity, to defeat
the guerrilla insurgency in a no-holds-barred war, to establish direct military control over new regions and resources, and to reenter the international community by proclaiming a return to civilian government and
democracy. The strategy succeeded: between 1982 and 1985, the guerrilla
insurgency was dramatically weakened, rural areas militarized and largely
pacified, and a new constitution written and elections held.

In this text a primary focus on either elections and political parties or
the military activities just summarized could have led to either of two dia-
metrically opposed, but equally erroneous, conclusions: first, that Guatemala has achieved democracy, especially since two presidential elections
have now been held; or, second, that the country experienced no movement toward democracy at all, its elections being a sham and its civilian
government a facade for the Army and its allies.

Instead, this study started from a third thesis, the possibility that
though elections themselves do not signify democracy, they occasion an
opportunity for democracy to be created. Loosely based on the transition-
to-democracy school, this thesis argues that attempting to understand
Guatemalan democracy by focusing on superficial formal-legal changes
alone, such as elections, is to miss important data. But dismissing these
events completely, because data suggest total military dominance, is also

187

problematic. This text has treated Guatemalan politics as an opportunity to create democracy.

What is more important here is the quality of political participation and the public-policy record. While recognizing that many key actors never intended to create anything other than superficially democratic arrangements, others did in fact try to move the nation toward genuine democratic procedures and social arrangements. The question is therefore not whether Guatemala is or is not a democracy, but to what extent it moved in democratic directions during the Cerezo administration and the first two years of the Serrano term.[1]

To understand the transition required several types of data. Formal constitutional and legal arrangements regulating the political participation of citizens are important data but not in a contextual vacuum. The context in which participation occurs is a critical component. Elections may or may not be democratizing events, depending on the content of campaigns and the general political atmosphere. In Guatemala, among the most important elements is the human rights atmosphere, that is, whether citizens can participate freely and openly.

In societies where daily living is precarious, where quality of life is very low and stable personal environments are rare for large segments of the populace, social conditions imply an additional test for democracy. An elected government must be able to implement public policies with positive socioeconomic results. Government must be not only "by the people," but "for the people" as well. Therefore, it is not enough that citizens be able to organize and participate, although that alone would be a major step in Guatemala, where political participation has not often taken place in a civil atmosphere. Public policy must also be responsive to the needs and demands of its citizens, and on the whole, the quality of life should improve for the masses. This chapter summarizes Guatemala's performance on these indicators and discusses the quality of democracy that has resulted from that performance.

Democratization: Cerezo and Serrano

Elections and Effective Participation

Historically, Guatemalan elections show a pattern of fraud, intimidation, self-censorship, and above all, little tangible impact on social justice issues. In fact, the electoral process sometimes has led to increased repression of popular leaders who emerged from electoral campaigns. Few observers disputed the procedural quality of the 1984 Constituent Assembly election, which led to a new constitution, the 1985 elections that gave Christian Democrats the presidency, or the 1990 elections that resulted in Serrano's victory.

The context in which these elections were held, however, included the intimidating presence of the military and the effects of years of state terror aimed at political dissidents. Little or no public debate addressed the serious economic and social issues during the campaigns, for example, and political parties largely ignored the needs of the masses. None of the parties participating in these elections challenged the military's dominant role in society. Reformist parties abandoned their ideologies in favor of personalistic, media-oriented campaigns. The combination of violence and campaigns with no progressive solutions to urgent social and economic problems produced widespread disgust with the traditional parties and even with electoral processes.

Nevertheless, a political opening did occur in Guatemala after 1985. The country's poorest citizens, with their pressing needs and long tradition of communal activism, moved into the new arena created by constitutional government to express their demands and to demand responses. Popular groups stepped up their activities, pressuring the government with various modes of direct political participation. Ironically, though election campaigns failed to include major issues on their agendas, participation by popular groups brought these issues into the public arena and forced the government to respond, making Guatemala a more democratic nation in the process. To the extent that these groups were able to participate more freely because of the opening created by recent elections, Guatemala has moved toward democracy.

Public Policy and Social Justice

Beyond elections and direct participation, the test of democracy lies in the nature of public policy and the socioeconomic results of policy. Social conditions have been abominable in Guatemala for centuries, with a declining quality of life, increasing social needs and demands, seemingly fewer resources, and an elite usually unwilling to respond to popular demands. On this dimension, the data show a mixed balance sheet for the Cerezo and Serrano governments.

Macroeconomic policy, aided by foreign assistance, spurred economic growth, and tourism increased. But for the majority of citizens, growth did not translate into social reform to any significant degree. Popular groups mobilized frequently during the period, but their efforts resulted in few significant policy programs, as the poverty indicators show. Environmental degradation is a key issue, as a symptom of both continuing poverty and of elite impunity. As no measurable movement occurred toward a more widespread distribution of stable personal environments among the general population, the general picture remains bleak.

Human Rights

The quality of human rights is an essential part of measuring democracy in a polity, because it is a central dimension of political participation. Guatemala's abhorrent human rights record since at least 1954 makes this a critical measure of the transition to democracy after 1985. Again, the data are mixed. The human rights situation improved legally in Guatemala after 1985. The Cerezo administration made strides toward increasing legal participation for many hitherto excluded sectors, including exiled opposition groups allowed to participate in the National Dialogue process.

But with each formal-legal advance, threats and repression followed when popular organizations availed themselves of the new legal opportunities. After about the midpoint of President Cerezo's term, incidents of human rights abuses increased steadily, to the extent that the period was beginning to be compared with the late 1970s in terms of repression aimed at leaders of popular-sector groups. Again, more than just the absence of progress, the country showed a marked decline in the quality of the human rights climate after 1988, although conditions were still better than they had been in the early 1980s.

The Armed Forces

The concentration of political power in any single sector of the political spectrum is an obstacle to democracy, whether that sector be a monopolistic political party, a mass movement organized by a revolutionary government, or a well-armed military institution. Guatemala's history shows a pattern of increasing consolidation of power in the armed forces. The pattern reveals itself in two arenas. The first, more obvious, includes counterinsurgency war and various other types of state terrorism and paramilitary death-squad activity, historically a fundamental characteristic of Guatemalan politics. The second involves the skillful use of civil political processes. Here, the goal is not to establish a totalitarian state or a responsive democratic system but rather to meld both facets into a state best described as authoritarian politics with electoral structures, including several functioning political parties.[2]

In the early 1980s, faced with a powerful insurgency, international isolation, and declining economic resources, the Army acknowledged that business as usual could not succeed without renewing active civilian participation in government, if only to secure again the international assistance needed to return to some semblance of economic normalcy. Elections in 1984, 1985, and 1990 were therefore an explicit part of a military plan. The crisis of the early 1980s led to a more, not less, intensive role for the Army in the process of civil rule.

The strategy has been successful, at least in the short run. Elections enhanced international legitimacy and resulted in increased resources for the state. The counterinsurgency plan was successful in demobilizing political parties as vehicles for social change, while retaining parties as functioning, cooperative components of a procedural democracy that posed little threat to the political and social dominance of the armed forces, even as both Cerezo and Serrano spoke of civilian ascendancy over the military.[3]

Most evidence suggests, however, that the military continues to dominate. The policy preferences of the armed forces remain central, not peripheral, to the public agenda. Attempted coups in 1988 and 1989 noticeably altered the political style of the civilian government, away from responsiveness to popular-sector groups and toward accommodation with elite concerns, especially antireformist ones. The human rights violations that developed after President Cerezo's inauguration, and intensified after 1988, contrast dramatically with the ideology and public pronouncements of both Cerezo and Serrano, suggesting the military is controlling the institutions of civil government, not the opposite.

As of 1993, continued impunity, slow negotiations with the insurgency, and hard-line military posturing over the return of refugees all suggest that very little progress has been achieved. The armed forces continue to believe they are the final arbiters of regime configuration.[4] A society governed by an "armed minority"[5] is hardly a democracy, even when that armed minority shows conspicuous support for electoral structures.

Movements and Groups

Political institutions may have been tamed by the military plan, but other elements were more resilient. As discussed earlier, opposition groups began to function in the new political opening after 1985. Some of these were profoundly antireformist, showing a conspicuous willingness to use violence against other citizens and even to try to overthrow state institutions when these began responding to popular demands. Although rightist extremists have lost power during the rise of the new militarized state, extremist solutions to social and political problems remain major components of the political process.

The "old right,"[6] which refuses even the slightest accommodation with popular organizations or the welfare state, remains vocal and aggressive. Although the extreme right has become increasingly impotent within the new formal political structures, it has not lost its capacity for direct and sometimes violent political action, as seen in attempted military coups and the return of death-squad violence in the late 1980s. There is no reason to assume that this sector of the political spectrum will soften its confrontational style in the near future.

The extreme right may weaken the Army's hold on the political process, but its impact has been reduced by international support for the military, based on the professed belief that democracy in Guatemala depends on support for the moderate right and the military faction supporting the new constitutional institutions. Military assistance, a threat to genuine democracy because it tends to concentrate power in one single institution, is thereby transformed into democratic assistance. If in decades past apologists described the armed forces as "modernizers," now the argument is the "military as democratizers." Thanks in part to this international pressure, the military has maintained the upper hand, even vis-à-vis the right, which includes factions of the military officer corps itself and is hardly democratic.

If the right is one problem for the Army, a second is the popular sectors. Guatemala has a long history of struggle around issues of social justice. Institutional changes after 1984 were welcomed by the nation's progressive sectors. Political parties had become merely electioneering organizations, unable or unwilling to lead society toward progressive policies, leaving that task to the popular organizations. As a result, the mobilization of the popular classes was led by organizations oriented toward direct and disruptive political action.

Largely because of this pressure, major social problems were placed on the public agenda during the period under study. The popular groups stimulated the moderate success of the National Dialogue process in 1990 and peace negotiations in 1992, for example, and have continually exposed antidemocratic social and economic conditions and human rights violations. Mobilization will continue, since the social inequities that stimulate popular organizing will continue to exist for the foreseeable future.

Elites may have intended new democratic forms to be symbolic. Nevertheless, these structures provided an opportunity for popular organizations to participate openly, to have their agendas become part of the public record, to gain international attention, and to use the media and official institutions to further their interests. Formal-legal political openings created as part of a counterinsurgency plan gave popular movements opportunity to mobilize. On the whole, the popular organizations were the only sector forcing any meaningful movement toward democracy, but this threatens the success of the counterinsurgency strategy.

Well-organized opposition is the historical bête noire for the military, thus it becomes rational for elites to seek to retain the structure while eliminating the opposition.[7] Since popular mobilization remains the key to democratization, it is logical to expect more repression and state terrorism in Guatemala in the 1990s.

Conclusion: The Popular Struggle for Democracy

Diagnosis

The political apertura of 1985 was not a reformist project threatened by the Army, although there were and are military factions opposing it. The project was protected by the Army from antireformist sectors of the extreme right in a sophisticated strategy replacing the "primitive anticommunism blindly pursued by the Right in Guatemala since 1954" (Figueroa Ibarra 1988: 10).[8] The strategy was designed to resist shifts in power, not grant them.

Nevertheless, the new political structures after 1984 are evidence of weakness in the ruling coalition, and they provide therefore an opportunity for democratic groups to begin to participate and influence public policy. A transition to democracy in Guatemala would then mean at least the beginning of a shift in political power toward the country's nonelite voters. This shift in power should be visible both in the quality of political participation and in resulting public policy, not merely in the scheduling of elections. On the whole, with the conspicuous exception of the work of activist popular groups, Guatemala did not move closer to democracy in the 1980s, in spite of the development of institutional characteristics of democratic government.

The armed forces and death squads continued to be a major impediment to a real transition to democracy. Impoverished and organized citizens have resisted continuing oppression and new disruptions. If institutions are formally democratic—and that is the claim made by elites and their apologists—repression is needed to keep the popular sectors out of power. The key to understanding recent Guatemalan politics is recognizing that elite violence and elections are a combined strategy geared to avoiding threats to dominance. The simultaneous practice of democratic elections and human rights violations is perfectly consistent under the circumstances, precisely because the popular groups tend to be the force behind democracy and social reform.

The period between 1982 and 1992 shows an attempt by elites to impose a narrow form of democracy from above. Though the nation returned to constitutional government in 1985, the social context shows the persistence, indeed worsening, of economic inequality and poverty. Social problems that lead to mobilization remain unsolved, and the new political institutions have not provided the policy needed for social reform. The strategy has produced neither social stability nor democracy.[9]

Prognosis

Guatemala's new democratic institutions have a dubious future, for democratic forms without social justice will not produce a stable society. The nation continues to have great potential for instability, with worsening levels of social and political injustice but fewer institutions to resolve the resulting tensions. Political parties, though participating at one level in an apparently pluralistic political process, have abdicated their potential leadership position in the more fundamental struggle for justice and democracy. By not playing a vigorous role in mobilizing public support for reform, the parties have abetted the civil side, as opposed to the military aspect, of the counterinsurgency process. They are accessories to the persistent dominance of the military.

Patterns of mobilization may be changing, however. New leadership is emerging in the Mayan communities, and future popular struggle may well reflect ethnic tensions more than political issues. Well-organized and experienced women's groups have emerged from the human rights struggles and are likely to increase pressure on the political system. With many of the global aspects of the Cold War no longer a distraction for international public opinion, more attention will be given to specific cases like Guatemala, with more scrutiny of, and perhaps pressure on, the government and military to deliver at least a minimum of what is consistent with prevailing Western values.

In the past elites have shown willingness to alter their public policies in favor of the nation's impoverished inhabitants only when pressured by the popular sectors. If Guatemala moves toward democracy in the 1990s, it will be because of popular organizations, not reformist elites, and their skill in mobilizing pressure on the policy process. The popular sectors have shown they can take advantage of opportunities to move the country closer to democracy, but violence has thwarted most of their efforts, at least in the short run. Clearly, international pressure in support of better human rights conditions is necessary for a transition to democracy in Guatemala. Elites did not move the nation closer to democracy in the 1980s and early 1990s, although they may have, perhaps unwittingly, provided an opportunity. Movement toward democracy came from the struggle of the people, not from agreements or pacts among moderate elites.

The country's elites will continue to try to use the formal structures of liberal democracy, not to mention violence, to avoid democratizing society. The problem for the future, then, is the antidemocratic elite sector, including "reformists" in the military, not the bulk of the populace. Unless the power of the vicious and parasitic military can be curtailed through dialogue, popular pressure, and/or international pressure, the prognosis for further movement toward democracy is poor, despite the courageous efforts of so many "ordinary" citizens. Though inspired by their efforts, any thoughtful student of Guatemala is hard-pressed to feel optimistic about the future.

Notes

1. For additional studies of the transition process in Guatemala, see Rosada Granados 1989 and 1990.

2. For a complementary analysis, see Jonas 1991: especially chapter 11. Jonas sees this process of establishing domination as a project of a broader elite, not merely a goal of the military. Basically, she is correct: underneath the competition among various military and nonmilitary factions over specific policies and/or personalities lies a substructure of consistent unity that aims to keep elites dominant. Given this "pan-elite" hypothesis, the phrase "counterinsurgency state," which connotes constant, active military operations, may be a less-than-adequate phrase for describing the Guatemalan process, for the civil activities of the state work toward the same, antidemocratic ends. See Anderson and Simon for an approach that does use the counterinsurgency state metaphor.

3. In response to the question of where real power lies in Guatemala, for example, Cerezo said:

> The Army has changed. It is in an important process of recognizing its specific, professional role of providing security, which constitutes an intimate part of the government. The one who makes the political decisions in Guatemala is the president of Guatemala. As any political leader, he does so with the discussion and participation of popular, economic, and political sectors and the state security forces, but the ultimate decision is made by the president and you can be sure of that (Cerezo 1988: 9).

4. For example, Colonel Francisco Luis Gordillo, a junta member in the Ríos Montt coup in 1982, founder of his own political party for the 1984 and 1985 elections (the Emergent Concordance Movement—MEC), and a member of the Guatemalan National Reconciliation Commission, states:

> I believe that an army should not rule; unfortunately if the civilians don't have the norms and values to rule well, sometimes the army has to do it. I am not justifying [military rule] . . . but sometimes it's the lesser evil (quoted in LASA: 16).

5. U.S. government officials often have used this phrase to characterize rebel insurgencies as a means of delegitimizing them.

6. The old right, reactionaries who might be described (using a phrase attributed to Franklin Roosevelt) as "somnambulists walking backwards," should be distinguished from the new right in Guatemala, who reflect a neoliberal economic model and a willingness to accommodate a strong military taking its share of

economic wealth. The new right is often willing to accommodate popular groups as well: if the old-right approach to labor organizing was to mobilize a death squad to eliminate organizers, the new-right approach might at least begin with forming a solidarist labor group (see Chapter 6). The new right often reflects evangelical Protestantism's views on self-initiative and respect for authority, among others. See Thomas for an example.

7. Schirmer describes it:

> Democracy, within this national security logic, is not a belief in a system of rights; it is an instrument for the military to proscribe oppositional politics in which democratic rights are, at best, conditional, and at worst, nonexistent (Schirmer 1989a: 13).

8. Figueroa's view is that

> in Guatemala democracy doesn't exist; what exists is a restricted political space which has been opened by popular and revolutionary struggle, with a high price in blood and suffering. . . . Democracy that comes from above—the kind Gramajo, Cerezo and their kind wish for—is in essence a small concession designed to avoid losing more. Democracy that comes from below . . . would imply concessions by all social sectors, especially from those who always have held more wealth and power (Figueroa Ibarra 1988: 7, 10).

9. But even without repression, the democratic state has little legitimacy, and its component institutions even less. These institutions cannot deliver the reforms the popular sectors need, and many formal leaders will not even attempt reform because of the perceived futility of doing so and the fear of repression. Cruz Salazar (1990) notes that in several elections in Central America in 1989 and 1990, governing parties lost every time, which he attributes to a similar set of domestic and institutional factors. For a brief comparative discussion of transitions to democracy in Central America that touches on many similar domestic questions, see Lindenberg. His essay, adapted from a forthcoming book edited by Jorge Domínguez and Lindenberg, scarcely mentions the military in the transition process; the twenty-third of twenty-four recommendations, in its entirety, is "strengthen civilian control of the military." This approach to a study of obstacles to transitions is not surprising, inasmuch as the chapter on Guatemala in the forthcoming volume is authored by General Héctor Gramajo, minister of defense during the military's reconstruction of "democratic" institutions during the Cerezo administration.

Bibliography

Most textual references to periodicals use abbreviations. The second part of this bibliography lists periodicals alphabetically by the abbreviations used in the text.

Books, Articles, and Manuscripts

Adams, Richard N. "The Structure of Participation: A Commentary," in Mitchell Seligson and John A. Booth, eds., *Political Participation in Latin America: Volume II—Politics and the Poor* (New York: Holmes and Meier, 1979).

Adams, Richard N. *Crucifixion By Power: Essays on Guatemalan National Social Structure, 1944–1966* (Austin: University of Texas Press, 1970).

Aguilera Peralta, Gabriel, et al. *Dialéctica del Terror en Guatemala* (San José, Costa Rica: Editorial Universitaria Centroamericana, 1981).

Aguilera Peralta, Gabriel. "La Tragicomedia Electoral de la Burguesía: Un Análisis Sociológico del Proceso Electoral del 5 de marzo de 1978," *Política y Sociedad* (Guatemala: Universidad Rafael Landívar), segunda época, No. 5 (January–June 1978): 159–171.

Alvarado, Luis. "El Desarrollo Capitalista de Guatemala y la Cuestión Urbana," *Cuadernos Universitarios* (Guatemala: University of San Carlos), No. 4 (September–October 1979): 136–149.

Americas Watch. *Guatemala: A Nation of Prisoners* (New York: Americas Watch Committee, 1983).

Americas Watch. *Persecuting Human Rights Monitors: The CERJ in Guatemala* (New York: Americas Watch Committee, 1989).

Amigo, Hugo. "Características de la alimentación y nutrición del guatemalteco," *Alero*, tercera época, No. 29 (March–April 1978): 124–126.

Amnesty International. *A Government Program of Political Murder* (London: Amnesty International Publications, 1981).

Amnesty International. *Massive Extrajudicial Executions in Rural Areas Under the Government of General Efraín Ríos Montt* (New York: Amnesty International, 1982); reprinted in U.S. Congress, House Committee on Banking, Finance and Urban Affairs, Subcommittee on International Development and Finance. *Inter-American Development Bank Loan to Guatemala* (Washington, D.C.: 97th Cong., 2d Sess., 1982): 46–76.

Anderson, Ken, and Jean-Marie Simon. "Permanent Counterinsurgency in Guatemala," *Telos* 73 (Fall 1987): 9–46.

Arias, Arturo. "Changing Indian Identity: Guatemala's Violent Transition to Modernity," in Carol A. Smith, ed. (with the assistance of Marilyn M. Moors) *Guatemalan Indians and the State: 1540 to 1988* (Austin: University of Texas Press, 1990).

Barry, Tom. *Guatemala: A Country Profile*, 2nd ed. (Albuquerque: Inter-Hemispheric Education Resource Center, 1990).

Behar, Moisés. "Food and Nutrition of the Maya Before the Conquest and at the Present Time," in *Biomedical Challenges Presented by the American Indian* (Washington, D.C.: Pan American Health Organization, 1968): 114–119.

Benton, Beth, with Betsy Cohn, Charles Roberts, and Nathan Dudley. *On the Road to Democracy? A Chronology of Human Rights and U.S.–Guatemalan Relations, January, 1978–April, 1985* (Washington, D.C.: Georgetown University Central American Historical Institute—CAHI—Intercultural Center, 1985).

Black, George, with Milton Jamail and Norma Stoltz Chinchilla. *Garrison Guatemala* (New York: Monthly Review Press, 1984).

Blasier, Cole. *The Hovering Giant: U.S. Responses to Revolutionary Change in Latin America* (Pittsburgh: University of Pittsburgh Press, 1976).

Booth, John A., and Mitchell A. Seligson, eds. *Elections and Democracy in Central America* (Chapel Hill: University of North Carolina Press, 1989).

Booth, John A., and Thomas Walker. *Understanding Central America* (Boulder: Westview Press, 1990).

Booth, John A., et al. *The 1985 Guatemalan Elections: Will the Military Relinquish Power?* (Washington, D.C.: International Human Rights Law Group and the Washington Office on Latin America, 1985).

Bowles, Samuel, and Herbert Gintis. *Democracy and Capitalism: Property, Community, and the Contradictions of Modern Social Thought* (New York: Basic Books, 1986).

Brockett, Charles D. (1984a). "Malnutrition, Public Policy, and Agrarian Change in Guatemala," *Journal of Inter-American Studies and World Affairs* 26 (November 1984): 477–497.

Brockett, Charles D. (1984b). "The Right to Food and United States Policy in Guatemala," *Human Rights Quarterly,* Vol. 6., No. 3: 366–380.

Bronk, William, *The New World* (New Rochelle, N.Y.: The Elizabeth Press, 1974).

Burgos-Debray, Elisabeth, ed. *I Rigoberta Menchú: An Indian Woman in Guatemala*, English ed. trans. by Ann Wright (London: Verso Editions, 1984).

Cabrera Hidalgo, Alfonso. "La nueva etapa histórica que vivimos impone un nuevo estilo de solidaridad." Speech delivered to the Seventeenth General Assembly of the Organization of American States, Washington, D.C., 11 November 1987; reprinted in *Panorama Centroamericana: Pensamiento y Acción* (Guatemala: INCEP), nueva época, Nos. 7–8 (July/December 1987): 58–63.

Cáceres, Carlos. "El gobierno duda, la ultraderecha actúa," *Otra Guatemala* (Mexico), Vol. 1, No. 2 (February 1988): 11–13.

Cambranes, Julio Castellanos. *Coffee and Peasants in Guatemala: The Origins of the Modern Plantation Economy in Guatemala, 1853–1897*, English ed. (South Woodstock, Vt.: CIRMA/Plumsock Mesoamerican Studies, 1985).

Cambranes, Julio Castellanos (1986a). *Agrarismo en Guatemala* (Guatemala/Madrid: Centro de Estudios Rurales Centroamericanos—CERCA, 1986).

Cambranes, Julio Castellanos (1986b). *Introducción a la Historia Agraria de Guatemala, 1500–1900*, 2nd ed. (Guatemala: Serviprensa Centroamericana, 1986).

Carmack, Robert M. "Social and Demographic Patterns in an Eighteenth-Century Census from Tecpanaco, Guatemala," in Robert M. Carmack, John Early, and Christopher Lutz, eds. *The Historical Demography of Highland Guatemala* (Albany, N.Y.: Institute for Mesoamerican Studies, State University of New York at Albany, Publication No. 6, 1982).

Carmack, Robert M., John Early, and Christopher Lutz, eds. *The Historical Demography of Highland Guatemala* (Albany, N.Y.: Institute for Mesoamerican Studies, State University of New York at Albany, Publication No. 6, 1982).

Caviedes, César N. *Elections in Chile: The Road Toward Redemocratization* (Boulder: Lynne Rienner, 1991).

"CEPAL: evaluación económica preliminar de Centro América, 1988," *Panorama Centroamericana—Temas y documentos de debate* (Guatemala: INCEP), Nos. 19–20 (April/June 1989): 213–214.

Cerezo, Vinicio. "Guatemala aspira contribuir a la paz del mundo." Speech delivered to the Forty-second General Assembly of the United Nations, New York, 23 September 1987; reprinted in *Panorama Centroamericana: Pensamiento y Acción* (Guatemala: INCEP), nueva época, Nos. 7–8 (July/December 1987): 49–57.

Cerezo, Vinicio. "The Army Is Not in Charge of Political Dialogue," *GSS* (Ceri-Gua News Agency) 2 (March/April 1988): 7–9.

Cockburn, Alexander. "After the Press Bus Left: The Case of Guatemala," *In These Times* (June 8–21, 1988); reprinted in *Update on Guatemala* (June 1988): 2–4.

Colina, Cino. "On Its Last Legs," *Granma Weekly Review* (Havana), Vol. 25, No. 52 (30 December 1990): 11.

Concerned Guatemala Scholars. *Guatemala: Dare To Struggle, Dare To Win* (Brooklyn, N.Y.: Concerned Guatemala Scholars, 1981).

"Contrainsurgencia y Régimen Constitucional," *Temas de la Realidad Guatemalteca* (Mexico: Centro de Estudios de la Realidad Guatemalteca), Vol. 1, No. 1 (October–November, 1985).

Cronologías de los Procesos de Paz: Guatemala y El Salvador (Guatemala: Instituto de Relaciones Internacionales y de Investigaciones para la Paz—IRIPAZ, 1991).

Cruz Salazar, José Luís. *El Carácter Revolucionario del Movimiento de Octubre de 1944* (Guatemala: Asociación de Investigación y Estudios Sociales—ASIES, 1987).

Cruz Salazar, Luis. *Centroamérica: Elecciones Generales 1989–1990, Retrospectiva (Factores Decisivos)* (Guatemala: Asociación de Investigaciones Económicas y Sociales—ASIES, 1990).

CSUCS (Programa Centroamericana de Ciencias Sociales). *Estructura Agraria, Dinámica de Población y Desarrollo Capitalista en Centroamérica* (San José, Costa Rica: Editorial Universitaria Centroamericana, 1978).

Dalton, Roque. *Miguel Marmol,* English ed. (Willimantic, Conn.: Curbstone Press, 1987).

Davis, Shelton H., and Julie Hodson. *Witnesses to Political Violence in Guatemala: The Suppression of a Rural Development Movement* (Boston: OXFAM-America, 1982).

"Derechos humanos y democratización en Guatemala y El Salvador: un reto para la democracia cristiana de cara a la década de los '90," *Panorama Centroamericana: Pensamiento y Acción,* Nos. 15–16 (July/December 1989): 61–68.

Diamond, Larry, Juan J. Linz, and Seymour Martin Lipset, eds. *Democracy in Developing Countries,* Vol. 4, *Latin America* (Boulder: Lynne Rienner, 1989).

Diamond, Larry. "Promoting Democracy," *Foreign Policy* 87 (Summer 1992): 25–46.

Dónde Está el Futuro? Proceso de Reintegración en Comunidades de Retornados (Guatemala City: Asociación para el Avance de las Ciencias Sociales en Guatemala—AVANCSO—Cuaderno de Investigación No. 8, 1992).

Drake, Paul W., and Eduardo Silva, eds. *Elections and Democratization in Latin America, 1980–1985* (San Diego: University of California at San Diego, Center for Iberian and Latin American Studies, 1986).

Drake, Paul W., and Iván Jaksic, eds. *The Struggle for Democracy in Chile, 1982–1990* (Lincoln: University of Nebraska Press, 1992).

Elections in Guatemala 1990–91: Political and Historical Context (Washington, D.C.: Network in Solidarity with the People of Guatemala—NISGUA, 1990).

Embassy of Guatemala. *General Elections in Guatemala* (Washington, D.C.: Embassy of Guatemala, 1985).

Esquít Choy, Albert, ed. *Foro del Pueblo Maya y los Candidatos a la Presidencia de la Guatemala* (Guatemala: Centro de Documentación e Investigación Maya, 1992).

Fauriol, Georges, and Eva Loser. *Guatemalan Election Study Reports,* No. 1 (Washington, D.C.: Georgetown University Center for Strategic and International Studies, 1985).

Fauriol, Georges, and Eva Loser. *Guatemala's Political Puzzle* (New Brunswick, N.J.: Transaction Books, 1988).

Figueroa Ibarra, Carlos. "Luchemos por la democracia," *Otra Guatemala* (Mexico), Vol. 1, No. 2 (February 1988): 7–10.

Figueroa Ibarra, Carlos. *El Recurso del Miedo: Ensayo sobre el Estado y el Terror en Guatemala* (San José, Costa Rica: Editorial Universitaria Centroamericana—EDUCA, 1991).

Fletcher, Lehman B., et al. *Guatemala's Economic Development: The Role of Agriculture* (Ames: Iowa State University Press, 1970).

Foweraker, Joe, and Ann L. Craig, eds. *Popular Movements and Political Change in Mexico* (Boulder: Lynne Rienner, 1990).

Frank, Luisa, and Philip Wheaton. *Indian Guatemala: Path to Liberation* (Washington, DC: EPICA Task Force, 1984).

Fried, Jonathan, et al. "Indian Rebellions, 1524–1944," in Jonathan Fried et al., eds. *Guatemala in Rebellion: Unfinished History* (New York: Grove Press, 1983).

Galeano, Eduardo. *Guatemala: Occupied Country* (New York: Monthly Review Press, 1969).

Gamer, Robert E. *The Developing Nations: A Comparative Perspective,* 2nd ed. (Boston: Allyn and Bacon, 1982).

García Bauer, Carlos. *Sistemas Políticos y Organización Social de las Antiguas Civilizaciones Indígenas Americanas: Mayas, Aztecas e Incas* (Guatemala: Universidad de San Carlos, Editorial Universitaria; Colección Monografías, No. 16, 1983).

Gershman, Carl. Speech delivered at the International Conference of the Latin American Studies Association—LASA, Boston, 24 October 1986.

Gleijeses, Piero. "The Guatemalan Silence," *The New Republic* (10 June 1985): 20–23.

Goepfert, Paul L. "'Democratic Opening,'" *The Progressive* 49 (November 1985): 36–39.

González, Luis E. *Political Structures and Democracy in Uruguay* (Notre Dame: University of Notre Dame Press, 1992).

Gordon, Max. "A Case History of U.S. Subversion: Guatemala, 1954," *Science and Society* 35 (Summer 1971); portions reprinted in Fried et al., eds. *Guatemala in Rebellion: Unfinished History* (New York: Grove Press, 1983).

Goudvis, Patricia, and Robert Richter. *Under the Gun: Democracy in Guatemala/ Transcript* (New York: Robert Richter Productions, 1987).

Graham, Carol. *Peru's APRA: Parties, Politics, and the Elusive Quest for Democracy* (Boulder: Lynne Rienner, 1992).

Greenberg, Edward S. *The American Political System: A Radical Approach*, 5th ed. (Glenview, Ill.: Scott, Foresman, 1989).

Gros Espiell, Héctor. "Estudio de la situación de los derechos humanos en Guatemala." Excerpts from the Report of the United Nations Special Observer to the United Nations Commission on Human Rights, 1990; reprinted in *Panorama Centroamericana: Reporte Político* 21 (February 1990): Documents section 8.

"Guatemala: Elecciones Generales, 1990," *Panorama Centroamericana: Reporte Político* 21, Special Issue (November 1990).

Guatemala Health Rights Support Project. Untitled pamphlet (Washington, D.C.: 1987).

Guatemala, Registro Electoral. *Resumen General y por Distritos Electorales y Departamentos de la República, de las Planillas Inscritas por las Diferentes Entidades Políticas y Comités Cívicos Postulantes* (Guatemala: Registro Electoral, 1980).

Guatemala: The People United (San Francisco: Solidarity Publication, 1982).

Guatemalan Bishops Conference (GBC). *The Clamor for Land* (Guatemala: February 1988); reprinted in translation in IGE (May 1988): 8–18.

Guatemalan Human Rights Commission. "Guatemalan Children Today," (September 1986), cited in IGE (May 1988): 5.

Handy, Jim. *Gift of the Devil: A History of Guatemala* (Boston: South End Press, 1984).

Herman, Edward S., and Frank Brodhead. *Demonstration Elections: U.S.-Staged Elections in the Dominican Republic, Vietnam, and El Salvador* (Boston: South End Press, 1984).

IADB (Inter-American Development Bank). *Nutrition and Socio-Economic Development of Latin America.* Proceedings of a symposium held in Washington, D.C., 28 June 1978 (Washington, D.C.: Inter-American Development Bank, 1979).

ICOPS. *Guatemala: Election Factbook* (Washington, D.C.: Institute for the Comparative Study of Political Systems, 1966).

IGE (Guatemalan Church in Exile). "Guatemala, 'A New Way of Life': The Development Poles," in *Guatemalan Church in Exile* (Special Edition), Vol. 4, No. 5 (September–October 1984).

IGE (Guatemalan Church in Exile). "Development: The New Face of War," in *Guatemalan Church in Exile* (Special Edition), Vol. 6, No. 1 (April 1986).

IGE (Guatemalan Church in Exile). *The Church of Guatemala: Lessons of History* (Managua: Guatemalan Church in Exile, 1987).

IGE (Guatemalan Church in Exile). *Reflections: The Clamor for Land* (Mexico City: Guatemalan Church in Exile, 1988).

Immerman, Richard H. *The CIA in Guatemala: The Foreign Policy of Intervention* (Austin: University of Texas Press, 1982).

Informe Económico (Guatemala: Banco de Guatemala, annual publication).

Inforpress. *Guatemala: Elections 1985* (Guatemala: Inforpress Centroamericana, 1985).

Ismaelillo. "A Guatemalan Indian Testimony, November, 1980," in Ismaelillo, and Robin Wright, eds. *Native Peoples in Struggle* (Bombay, N.Y.: Anthropology Resource Center and ERIN Publications, 1982).

Jensen, Daniel. "Fight for Land and Dignity," *Maryknoll,* Vol. 87, No. 2 (February 1993): 20–25.

Jonas, Susanne (1974a). "Guatemala: Land of Eternal Struggle," in Ronald G. Chilcote and Joel C. Edelstein, eds. *Latin America: The Struggle with Dependency and Beyond* (New York: Schenkman/John Wiley, 1974).

Jonas, Susanne (1974b). "The Democracy Which Gave Way: The Guatemalan Revolution of 1944–54," in Susanne Jonas and David Tobis, eds. *Guatemala* (New York: NACLA, 1974).

Jonas, Susanne (1974c). "The New Hard Line: U.S. Strategy for the 1970's," in Susanne Jonas and David Tobis, eds. *Guatemala* (New York: NACLA, 1974).

Jonas, Susanne (1974d). "Masterminding the Mini-Market: U.S. Aid to the Central American Common Market," in Susanne Jonas and David Tobis, eds. *Guatemala* (New York: NACLA, 1974).

Jonas, Susanne (1974e). "Showcase for Counterrevolution," in Susanne Jonas and David Tobis, eds. *Guatemala* (New York: NACLA, 1974).

Jonas, Susanne (1974f). "Anatomy of an Intervention: The U.S. 'Liberation' of Guatemala," in Susanne Jonas and David Tobis, eds. *Guatemala* (New York: NACLA, 1974).

Jonas, Susanne. "Archbishop Deplores Violence," *San Francisco Chronicle* (11 October 1989): 2.

Jonas, Susanne. *The Battle for Guatemala: Rebels, Death Squads, and U.S. Power* (Boulder: Westview Press, 1991).

Kariel, Henry S., ed. *Frontiers of Democratic Theory* (New York: Random House, 1970).

Karp, Russell, "Statement," in U.S. Congress, House of Representatives, *Hearing Before the Subcommittee on Western Hemisphere Affairs of the Committee on Foreign Affairs* (Washington, D.C.: 98th Con., 1st Sess., 9 March 1983).

Kinzer, Stephen. "Guatemala: What Has Democracy Wrought?" *New York Times Sunday Magazine* (26 March 1989).

Kirkpatrick, Jeane J. "Statement Before the Conference on Free Elections, November 4, 1982," in *Promoting Free Elections* (Washington, D.C.: U.S. Department of State, Bureau of Public Affairs, Current Policy, No. 433, November 1982): 2–3.

Krueger, Chris, and Kjell Enge. *Security and Development Conditions in the Guatemalan Highlands* (Washington, D.C.: Washington Office on Latin America, 1985).

"La victoria será del pueblo," *El Socialdemócrata* (Guatemala: Democratic Socialist Party—PSD) 1 (November 1990).

LaFeber, Walter. *Inevitable Revolutions: The United States in Central America* (New York: Norton, 1983).

LASA (Latin American Studies Association). "Final Report of the LASA Commission on Compliance with the Central America Peace Accord," *LASA Forum* 19 (Spring 1988): Appendix, 1–44.

Linares Morales, Aquiles. "La Constitución Guatemalteca de 1985," *Cuadernos* (Mexico: Ciencia y Tecnología para Guatemala—CITGUA) 2 (October 1985).

Lindenberg, Marc. *Democratic Transitions in Central America and Panama* (Boston: World Peace Foundation, 1993).

López Larrave, Mario. "La libertad sindical y sus garantías," *Universidad de San Carlos: Publicación Anual* (Guatemala: Universidad de San Carlos), segunda época, No. 5 (1974).

Lovell, W. George. "Collapse and Recovery: A Demographic Profile of the Cuchumatán Highlands of Guatemala (1520–1821)," in Robert M. Carmack, John Early, and Christopher Lutz, eds. *The Historical Demography of Highland Guatemala* (Albany, N.Y.: Institute for Mesoamerican Studies, State University of New York at Albany, Publication No. 6, 1982).

Lovell, W. George. "Resisting Change in Guatemala," *The Toronto Star* (24 April 1990): A19.

Maldonado Ruiz, Rodolfo. "La concertación en el mundo del trabajo," *Panorama Centroamericana: Pensamiento y Acción* (Guatemala: INCEP), nueva época, Nos. 7–8 (July/December 1987): 42–48.

Manz, Beatriz. "In Guatemala, No One Is Safe . . . ," *The New York Times* (27 October 1990): 23.

Martz, John D. *Central America: The Crisis and the Challenge* (Chapel Hill: University of North Carolina Press, 1959).

"Masacre en la Embajada de España," *Adelante* (Guatemala) 25 (January–February 1980): 2, 12.

Maslow, Jonathan Evan. *Bird of Life, Bird of Death: A Naturalist's Journey Through a Land of Political Turmoil* (New York: Simon and Schuster, 1986).

Maurovich, Frank. "Nobel Prize for Noble Lady," *Maryknoll* 87 (February 1993): 35–38.

McConahay, Mary Jo. "Death Back with a Vengeance in Guatemala," *National Catholic Reporter* (27 October 1989): 8.

McCreery, David. *Desarrollo Económico y Política Nacional: El Ministerio de Fomento de Guatemala, 1871–1885* (Antigua, Guatemala: Centro de Investigaciones Regionales de Mesoamérica—CIRMA, 1981).

Melville, Thomas, and Marjorie Melville. *Guatemala: The Politics of Land Ownership* (New York: The Free Press, 1971).

Millett, Richard. "Guatemala," *Latin American and Caribbean Contemporary Record* (1986–1987).

Monsanto, Pablo. "The Militarization of the Country Is the Major Obstacle to Democracy." Interview in *Ceri-Gua: Special Service* 2 (March/April 1988): 2–5.

Montejo, Victor, and Q'anil Akab', eds. *Brevísima Relación Testimonial de la Continúa Destrucción del Mayab' (Guatemala)* (Providence: Guatemala Scholars Network, 1992).

Moors, Marilyn M. "Indian Labor and the Guatemalan Crisis: Evidence from History and Anthropology," in Ralph Lee Woodward, Jr., ed. *Central America: Historical Perspective on the Current Crisis* (Greenwich: Greenwood Press, 1988).

Mörner, Magnus. "Evolución del trabajo en América Latina con anterioridad al Sindicalismo," *Política y Sociedad* (Guatemala: Universidad de San Carlos), tercera época, No. 18 (January–June 1986): 73–88.

Muñoz, Joaquin. *Guatemala: From Where the Rainbow Takes Its Colors* (Guatemala: Tipografía Nacional de Guatemala, 1940).

O'Donnell, Guillermo, and Phillipe Schmitter, eds. *Transitions from Authoritarian Rule* (Baltimore: Johns Hopkins University Press, 1980).

On Their Own: A Preliminary Study of Youth Gangs in Guatemala City (Guatemala: Asociación para el Avance de las Ciencias Sociales en Guatemala—AVANCSO, *Cuadernos de Investigación* No. 4 (1988).

Oramas León, Orlando. "We'll Go to the Constituent Assembly Armed," *Granma: International Weekly Review* (24 June 1990): 11.

Padilla, Luis Alberto. "Conflict Resolution Theory and Its Applicability to Guatemala's Socio-Political Context" (Guatemala: manuscript, 1990): 10.

Paige, Jeffery M. "Coffee and Politics in Central America," in Richard Tardanico, ed. *Crises in the Caribbean Basin,* Vol. 9, *Political Economy of the World-System Annuals* (Newberry Park, Calif.: Sage Publications, 1987).

"Partidos demócrata cristianos de Centro América: plataformas programáticas 1989," *Panorama Centroamericana: Temas y documentos de debate* 5–6 (September–December 1990): 9–38.

Paul, Benjamin D., and William J. Demarest. "The Operation of a Death Squad in San Pedro la Laguna," in Robert M. Carmack, ed. *Harvest of Violence: The Maya Indians and the Guatemalan Crisis* (Norman: University of Oklahoma Press, 1988).

Payeras, Mario, *Days of the Jungle: The Testimony of a Guatemalan Guerrillero, 1972–1976* (New York: Monthly Review Press, 1983).

Peeler, John A. *Latin American Democracies: Colombia, Costa Rica, Venezuela* (Chapel Hill: University of North Carolina Press, 1985).

Petersen, Kurt. *The Maquiladora Revolution in Guatemala* (New Haven: Schell Center for International Human Rights, Yale Law School, 1992).

Phillips–Van Heusen Campaign Update. (Chicago: U.S./Guatemala Labor Education Project, 1992).

Pinto Soria, Julio César. *Centroamérica, de la colonia al Estado nacional (1800–1840)* (Guatemala: Editorial Universitaria de Guatemala, 1986).

Pinzón, Lorenzo. "Guatemala 1982: Hacia una nueva farsa electoral," *ALAI* 5 (11 September 1981): 11–15.

Poe, Steven C. "Human Rights and Economic Aid Allocation Under Ronald Reagan and Jimmy Carter," *American Journal of Political Science* (February 1992): 147–167.

Poitevín, René. *El proceso de industrialización en Guatemala* (San José, Costa Rica: Editorial Universitaria Centroamericana, 1977).

Rabine, Mark. "Guatemala: 'Redemocratization' or Civilian Counterinsurgency?" *Contemporary Marxism* 14 (1986): 59–64.

Rarihokwats, ed. *Guatemala: The Horror and the Hope* (York, Penn.: Four Arrows Press, 1982).

Resumen Noticioso, 1992 (Guatemala: Prensa Libre, 30 December 1992).

Rodriguez, Javier. "Guatemala: Difficulties of Dialogue," *Granma: International Weekly Review* (11 November 1990): 10.

Rosada Granados, Hector. *Guatemala 1984: Elecciones para Asamblea Nacional Constituyente,* Cuadernos de CAPEL, No. 2 (San José, Costa Rica: Centro de Asesoría y Promoción Electoral—CAPEL, 1985).

Rosada Granados, Héctor. *Guatemala 1985: Elecciones Generales* (Guatemala: Asociación de Investigación y Estudios Sociales—ASIES, 1986).

Rosada Granados, Héctor. "Transición Política en Guatemala y sus Perspectivas," *USAC—Revista de la Universidad de San Carlos* 6 (June 1989): 57–65.

Rosada Granados, Héctor. "Los Problemas de la Transición," *Estudios Internacionales* (Guatemala: IRIPAZ) 1, no. 1 (January–June 1990): 92–94.

Ruiz de Barrios Klee, Elena. "La realidad del niño guatemalteco," *Revista Universidad de San Carlos* (Guatemala), segunda época, No. 10 (1979); reprinted in Serie Separatas Anuario, No. 20.

Sandoval V., Leopoldo. *Estructura Agraria y Nuevo Régimen Constitucional* (Guatemala: Asociación de Investigaciones y Estudios Sociales—ASIES, 1986).

Schirmer, Jennifer (1989a). "Interview with Guatemalan 'Golpistas,'" *Human Rights Internet Reporter* 13 (Spring 1989): 13–16.

Schirmer, Jennifer (1989b). "Waging War to Prevent War," *The Nation* (10 April 1989): 478–479.

Schlesinger, Stephen, and Stephen Kinzer. *Bitter Fruit: The Untold Story of the American Coup in Guatemala* (Garden City, N.Y.: Doubleday, 1982).

Seligson, Mitchell A., and John A. Booth. "Development, Political Participation, and the Poor in Latin America," in Mitchell A. Seligson and John A. Booth, eds. *Political Participation in Latin America: Volume II—Politics and the Poor* (New York: Holmes and Meier, 1979).

Seligson, Mitchell A. "Development, Democratization, and Decay: Central America at the Crossroads," in James M. Malloy and Mitchell A. Seligson, eds. *Authoritarians and Democrats: Regime Transition in Latin America* (Pittsburgh: University of Pittsburgh Press, 1987).

Sereseres, Caesar D. "Military Development and the United States Military Assistance Program for Latin America: the Case of Guatemala, 1961–1969." Ph.D. diss., University of California, Riverside, 1972.

Shapiro, Michael J. *The Politics of Representation: Writing Practices in Biography, Photography, and Policy Analysis* (Madison: University of Wisconsin Press, 1988).

Sharckman, Howard. "The Vietnamization of Guatemala: U.S. Counterinsurgency Programs," in Susanne Jonas and David Tobis, eds. *Guatemala* (New York: NACLA, 1974).

Silver, William (pseudonym). "Los Campesinos del Padre Girón," in Julio C. Cambranes. *Agrarismo en Guatemala* (Guatemala/Madrid: Centro de Estudios Rurales Centroamericanos—CERCA, 1986).

Simon, Jean-Marie. *Guatemala: Eternal Spring—Eternal Tyranny* (New York: Norton, 1987).

Smith, Carol, ed., with Marilyn M. Moors. *Guatemalan Indians and the State: 1540 to 1988* (Austin: University of Texas Press, 1990).

Soberanis Reyes, Catalina. "Democracia Cristiana, marxismo y liberalismo: una aproximación a sus diferencias," *Panorama Centroamericana: Pensamiento y Acción* (Guatemala: INCEP), nueva época, Nos. 7–8 (July/December 1987): 3–8, 48.

Solórzano Martínez, Mario. "El papel de la Democracia Cristiana en la actual coyuntura Centroamericana," *Nueva Sociedad* 48 (May–June 1980): 22–33.

Sommerfield, Raynard M. *Tax Reform and the Alliance for Progress* (Austin: University of Texas Press, 1966) (Latin American Monographs, No. 4, Institute of Latin American Studies, University of Texas, Austin).

Sosa López, Lizardo. "Guatemala ha entrado tardamente en la estrategia exportadora," *Seminario ACEN-SIAG* 104 (17 April 1989): 4–6.

Stix, Bob, et al. *Democracy or Deception? The Guatemalan Elections, 1985* (Washington, D.C.: NISGUA, 1985).

Tejada Valenzuela, Carlos. "Nutrición y prácticas alimentarias en Centroamérica: un estudio histórico de la población maya," *Universidad de San Carlos: Publicación Anual*, segunda época, No. 1 (1970): 103–108.

Tenneriello, Bonnie. "Abuse in Guatemala," *The Christian Science Monitor* (11 October 1989).

Tenneriello, Bonnie. "Confronting Guatemala's State Terror," *Boston Sunday Globe* (11 November 1990): 5.

"The Actors of Esquipulas II," *God, Christians and Peace in Central America* (Managua, Nicaragua: Guatemalan Church in Exile, 1988): 7–10.

The Trade Union Movement in Guatemala, 1986–1988 (Mexico City: Ciencia y Tecnología para Guatemala—CITGUA, 1990).

Thesing, Josef. "Elecciones y Cambio Político en Guatemala," *Política y Sociedad* (Guatemala: Universidad de San Carlos), segunda época, No. 2 (July–December, 1976): 5–33.

Thomas, Fritz. "Guatemalan Democracy Looks Better from the Inside," *The Wall Street Journal* (30 November 1990): A15.

Trudeau, Robert H. "Guatemalan Human Rights: The Current Situation," *LASA Newsletter,* Vol. 13, No. 3 (Fall 1982): 13–16.

Trudeau, Robert H. "Statement," in United States Congress, House of Representatives, *Hearing Before the Subcommittee on Western Hemisphere Affairs of the Committee on Foreign Affairs* (Washington, D.C.: 98th Cong., 1st Sess., 9 March 1983).

Trudeau, Robert H. "The Guatemalan Election of 1985: Prospects for Democracy," in John A. Booth and Mitchell A. Seligson, eds. *Elections and Democracy in Central America* (Chapel Hill: University of North Carolina Press, 1989): 93–125.

Trudeau, Robert H., and Lars Schoultz. "Guatemala," in Morris J. Blachman, William M. LeoGrande, and Kenneth E. Sharpe, eds. *Confronting Revolution: Security Through Diplomacy in Central America* (New York: Pantheon, 1986).

Tulchin, Joseph S., ed., with Gary Bland. *Is There a Transition to Democracy in El Salvador?* (Boulder: Lynne Rienner, 1992).

United Nations Development Program and UNICEF. "Plan of Action for Social Development." Report to the Guatemalan Legislative Assembly, January 1992.

URNG. "The Unity Statement of the Revolutionary Organization—EGP, ORPA, PGT—To The People of Guatemala," in *Guatemala: The People United* (San Francisco: Solidarity Publication, 1982).

USAID. *Report of the AID Field Mission in Guatemala* (Guatemala City: USAID, 1980); cited in WOLA, *Guatemala: The Roots of Revolution* (Washington, D.C.: Washington Office on Latin America, 1983): 6.

Veblen, Thomas T. "Native Population Decline in Totonicapán, Guatemala," in Robert M., Carmack, John Early, and Christopher Lutz, eds. *The Historical Demography of Highland Guatemala*, (Albany, N.Y.: Institute for Mesoamerican Studies, State University of New York at Albany, Publication No. 6, 1982): 81–102.

Villacorta Escobar, Manuel. *Recursos Económicos de Guatemala* (Guatemala: Editorial Universitaria, Colección "Aula," No. 19, 1979).

von Hoegen, Miguel. *La Concentración Geográfica del desarrollo en Guatemala* (Guatemala: Asociación de Investigación y Estudios Sociales—ASIES, 1988).

Walker, Jack L. "Normative Consequences of 'Democratic' Theory," in Henry S. Kariel, ed. *Frontiers of Democratic Theory* (New York: Random House, 1970).

Weaver, Jerry L. "Political Style of the Guatemalan Military Elite," *Studies In Comparative International Development* 5 (1969–1970): 62–81.

When The Mountains Tremble (video) (NewYork: Skylight Productions, 1983).

Who's Who in the Guatemalan Elections, 1990–91 (Washington, D.C.: Network in Solidarity with the People of Guatemala—NISGUA, 1990).

WOLA. *Guatemala: The Roots of Revolution* (Washington, D.C.: Washington Office on Latin America, 1983).

WOLA. *Who Pays the Price? The Cost of War in the Guatemalan Highlands* (Washington, D.C.: Washington Office on Latin America, 1988).

WOLA (1989a). *Uncertain Return: Refugees and Reconciliation in Guatemala* (Washington, D.C.: Washington Office on Latin America, 1989).

WOLA (1989b). *The Administration of Injustice: Military Accountability in Guatemala* (Washington, D.C.: Washington Office on Latin America, 1989).

WOLA. *The Administration of Injustice: Military Accountability in Guatemala* (Washington, D.C.: Washington Office on Latin America, 1990).

Woodward, Ralph Lee, Jr. "Economic Development and Dependency in Nineteenth-Century Guatemala," in Richard Tardanico, ed. *Crises in the Caribbean Basin,* Vol. 9, *Political Economy of the World-System Annuals* (Newberry Park, Calif.: Sage Publications, 1987).

World Bank. *Guatemala: Economic and Social Position and Prospects* (Washington, D.C.: World Bank, 1978); cited in Brockett, "Malnutrition, Public Policy, and Agrarian Change in Guatemala," *Journal of Inter-American Studies and World Affairs* 26 (November 1984).

Zagorski, Paul W. *Democracy vs. National Security: Civil-Military Relations in Latin America* (Boulder: Lynne Rienner, 1992).

Zinner, Josh. ". . . Not Even the Children," *New York Times* (27 October 90): 23.

Periodicals

AAS: *Austin* (Tex.) *American-Statesman.*

Boletín ACEN-SIAG (Mexico: Agencia Centroamericana de Noticias ACEN-SIAG).

CAR: *Central American Report.*

Centroamérica Hoy (San José, Costa Rica: Consejo Superior Universitario Centroamericano, Proyecto de Apoyo a la Paz—CSUCA-PAX).

CSMonitor: *Christian Science Monitor* (Boston).

El Gráfico (Guatemala City).

Enfoprensa, *Information on Guatemala* (Washington, D.C.: Enfoprensa USA).

Excelsior (Mexico City: daily newspaper).

GMG: *Guatemala: Monthly Glance* (Mexico: Ceri-Gua—Guatemala News Agency).

GNIB: *Guatemala: News in Brief* (New York: Americas Watch Committee).

Green Revolution (periodical).

GNN: *Guatemala Network News* (Washington, D.C.: NISGUA).

Guatemala! (Berkeley, Calif.: Guatemala News and Information Bureau).

Guatemala News (Guatemala: weekly English-language newspaper).

Guatenoticias (Guatemala: Lic. Mario A. Sandoval, biweekly).

Inforpress Centroamericana (Guatemala: Inforpress, periodical newsletter).

IPS: Internet Press Service.

La Epoca (Guatemala: weekly newspaper).

LAP: *Latin American Press.*

LATimes: *Los Angeles Times.*

LUOG: *Legislative Update on Guatemala* (Washington, D.C.).

MHerald: *Miami Herald.*

Momento (Guatemala: Asociación de Investigaciones y Estudios Sociales—ASIES).

N&A: *News and Analysis* (Washington, D.C.: Council on Hemispheric Affairs—COHA).

NFAW: *News from Americas Watch* (New York: Americas Watch).

NYTimes: *New York Times.*

Panorama Político (primera época) (Guatemala: Instituto Centroamericano de Estudios Políticos—INCEP) (publication interrupted in 1980).

PCRP: *Panorama Centroamericana: Reporte Político* (Guatemala: Instituto Centroamericano de Estudios Políticos—INCEP).

Prensa Libre (Guatemala City).

ROG: *Report on Guatemala* (Oakland, Calif.: Guatemala News and Information Bureau).
SFChronicle: *San Francisco Chronicle.*
Special Service (Mexico: Ceri-Gua News Agency).
Tico Times (San José, Costa Rica).
TOA: *Times of the Americas* (Miami).
UOG: *Update on Guatemala* (New York: Committee in Solidarity with the People of Guatemala).
VM: *Vistazo Mensual* (Mexico: Centro Exterior de Reportes Informativos sobre Guatemala—Ceri-Gua News Agency).
Weekly Briefs (Washington, D.C.: Council on Hemispheric Affairs).
WOLA: Update (Washington, D.C.: Washington Office on Latin America).
WPost: *Washington Post* (Washington, D.C.).
WRH: *Washington Report on the Hemisphere* (Washington, D.C.: Council on Hemispheric Affairs—COHA).

Index

Acevedo, Carlos, 149
AEU. *See* Asociación de Estudiantes
  Universitarios
AFL/CIO, funding from, 101, 110(n15)
Agrarian reform, 31(n20), 86, 109(n10),
  136; description of, 22, 23, 25; oppo-
  sition to, 98, 99; UNAGRO and, 97.
  See also Land reform
Agriculture, 88, 96; diversification of,
  24; inequities in, 32(n31); problems in,
  82–83; wages paid by, 32(n26), 96
AIFLD. *See* American Institute for Free
  Labor Development
Alliance for Progress, 21, 22, 26, 38, 59;
  Kennedy and, 24; social reform and, 57
Alvarez Ruíz, Donaldo, 44; Ríos Montt
  campaign and, 156(n35)
American Institute for Free Labor
  Development (AIFLD), 101, 110(n15)
ANACAFE. *See* National Association of
  Coffee Growers
ANC. *See* Asociación Nacional
  Campesina Pro-Tierra
Anticommunism, 26, 36, 40, 56, 57,
  132–133, 163, 193
Anzueto Vielman, Gustavo, 45, 46, 131
Arana, Francisco, 20, 21; assassination
  of, 56
Arana Osorio, Carlos, 45, 59; counter-
  insurgency and, 58
Arbenz Guzmán, Jacobo, 20, 21,
  31(n19), 57; assassination of, 56;
  economic modernization and, 23
Arbenz government, 25; economic
  development and, 22; opposition to,

31(n22); reforms of, 22, 24, 32(n25),
  91(n5)
Arévalo, Juan José, 55–57, 75(n5);
  reform by, 21; spiritual socialism and,
  20–21
Arias Peace Plan. *See* Central American
  Peace Accords
Armas, Carlos Castillo: counterrevolution
  by, 23, 56–57
Armed forces. *See* Military
Arzú, Alvaro, 145, 155(n30)
Asociación de Estudiantes Universitarios
  (AEU), 107
Asociación Nacional Campesina Pro-
  Tierra (ANC), 105, 109(nn6, 7);
  demands of, 98–99, 100; mobilization
  of, 96; opposition to, 98
Assassinations, 44, 60, 64, 110(n16),
  113, 114, 117, 119, 120, 122, 124,
  126(n4), 127(n12); controversy over,
  175; investigation of, 177; number
  of, 42
Ayau, Manuel, 149, 156(n43)

Baker, James A.: Antigua summit and,
  87
Barrera, Byron: attack on, 123
Bay of Pigs operation, 36, 58
Belize question, national protest over,
  165–166
Berger, Oscar, 147, 156(n41)
Blandón de Cerezo, Raquel, 97
Bolaños, Juan Léonel: National Dialogue
  and, 139, 140
Bombings, 119, 132, 171, 184(n32)

209

About the Book and Author

Guatemala, though unique in many respects, has been part of the recent movement toward constitutional regimes and democracy in Latin America. By 1986, a consitutional and an elected civilian government were in place; in 1990, a second round of elections culminated in the country's first transfer of the presidency from one elected civilian to another; and as of the end of 1992, many of the formal ingredients for a transition to democracy were in place.

But might this be a misleading picture? Trudeau expands the discussion of the formal transition to democracy in Guatemala to focus on popular political participation between elections and on the public policy of recent governments. He concludes that the new political space created by the constitutional regime has come about not as a result of government or elite-reformist efforts, but because of pressure from popular-sector organizations. Persistent social injustice and concentrated power—still in the hands of the military—provide both an explosive mixture and a constant threat to the democratic movement nurtured by the popular sector.

Robert H. Trudeau is professor and chair of the Department of Political Science and director of the Latin American Studies Program at Providence College. He has contributed to several major volumes on Central America, including *Confronting Revolution, Elections and Democracy in Central America* and *Handbook of Political Science Research on Latin America.*